BTEC national
2nd Edition

Travel & Tourism
Book 2

Gillian Dale

WITHDRAWN

www.harcourt.co.uk

✓ Free online support
✓ Useful weblinks
✓ 24 hour online ordering

01865 888118

Heinemann is an imprint of Harcourt Education Limited, a company incorporated in England and Wales, having its registered office: Halley Court, Jordan Hill, Oxford OX2 8EJ. Registered company number: 3099304

www.harcourt.co.uk

Heinemann is the registered trademark of Harcourt Education Limited

Text © Gillian Dale 2007

First published 2007

12 11 10 09 08 07
10 9 8 7 6 5 4 3 2 1

British Library Cataloguing in Publication Data is available from the British Library on request.

ISBN 978 0 435445 89 8

Typeset and illustrated by 7\ Tek-Art, Croydon, Surrey, UK
Original illustrations © Harcourt Education Limited 2007
Picture research by Sally Claxton
Cover photo © Getty Images/Aurora
Printed by Scotprint, Haddington, Scotland, UK

Websites
The websites used in this book were correct and up-to-date at the time of publication. It is essential for tutors to preview each website before using it in class so as to ensure that the URL is still accurate, relevant and appropriate. We suggest that tutors bookmark useful websites and consider enabling students to access them through the school/college intranet.

Contents

Acknowledgments

Gillian Dale gives grateful thanks to former students, friends and family who have shared their experiences and travel anecdotes, in particular Ann Lertora for her lost baggage tale.

Photographs
The author and publisher would like to thank the following individuals and organisations for permission to reproduce photographs:

Icons
Case study, Knowledge check, Theory into practice – Corbis
Consider this – Jupiter Images/Photos.com
End of unit assessment, Grading tips, Research tip – Getty Images/Photodisc
Thinking points – Creatas

Alamy/Profimedia International SRO – page 56
Alamy/Chris Fredriksson – page 207
Alamy/Ian Patrick – pages 36–7
Alamy/Dominic Burke – pages 194–5
Alamy/INSADCO Photography – page 224
Alamy/Peter Titmuss – page 127
Alamy/Skyscan Photo Library – page 235
Alamy/Steven May – page 206
Alamy/TNT MAGAZINE – page 76
BAA Photolibrary/InPress/Dave Poultney – page 201
Bedruthan Steps Hotel – page 177
Canvas Holidays – page 78
Corbis/Barry Lewis – page 13
Corbis/dpa/Horst Ossinger – pages 72–3
Corbis/Eurasia Press/Steven Vidler – page 172
Corbis/Jeff Turnau – page 238
Corbis/Leo Mason – page 106

Corbis/Morton Beebe – page 24
Corbis/Paul Harris – pages 136–7
Corbis/W.A. Sharman/Milepost 92 1/2 – page 145
Corbis/zefa/Rainer Holz – page 166–7
fotolia.com/Gilles Paire – page 59
Getty Images – page 174
Getty Images/Chris Jackson – page 75
Getty Images/Hulton Archive – page 5
Getty Images/Jamie McDonald – page 178
Getty Images/Photodisc – page 46
INTECH – page 147
istockphoto.com/Kevin Jarratt – page 152
istockphoto.com/Susanna Fieramosca Naranjo – page 28
Lowry Centre/Len Grant – page 141
Mountfitchet Castle – page 158
National Trust Picture Library/Ian Shaw – page 148
PA Photos – pages 109, 230–1
Princess Cruises – pages 2–3
Salcombe Donkey Sanctuary – page 144
Virgin Limobikes – page 199
Windjammer Barefoot Cruises – page 16
World Travel Market – pages 104–5

Artwork/text
The author and publisher would like to thank the following individuals and organisations for permission to reproduce copyright material:

ABTA – page 42
Adfero Ltd – page 212
BAA Limited – page 204
Bales Worldwide – page 27
Best Western – page 170
British Airways – pages 211, 215

Introduction

Welcome to this BTEC National Travel and Tourism course book, specifically designed to support students on the following programmes:

- BTEC National Certificate in Travel and Tourism
- BTEC National Diploma in Travel and Tourism.

This BTEC Travel and Tourism course book accompanies Book 1 and covers eight of the specialist units you will be taking if you are studying for a BTEC National Certificate or a BTEC National Diploma in Travel and Tourism. These are:

- Investigating the cruise sector
- Tour operations
- Roles and responsibilities of holiday respresentatives
- Events, conferences and exhibitions
- The appeal and importance of UK visitor attractions
- Hospitality operations in travel and tourism
- Handling air passengers
- Current issues in travel and tourism.

Like Book 1, this book follows the BTEC specification closely so that you can easily find information and see where you are up to in your studies.

You will have developed a sound knowledge of the travel and tourism industry by reading and working through Book 1. Now you should be ready to explore the different sectors in greater detail. Using Book 2 will help you to achieve your qualification and gain Merit or Distinction grades. Besides deepening your knowledge, you will gain a perspective on what its like to work in the different sectors and what opportunities there are for you. For example, you may be attracted by life on a cruise ship or you may want to work in the thriving air transport sector. Some of you may be attracted to a career in hospitality, perhaps in hotel management.

This book is full of new case studies and activities which will help you explore this exciting industry. The case studies have been carefully researched so that they reflect current practice and use the most up-to-date facts and statistics available at the time of writing. However, the travel and tourism industry changes daily. Everything in the book has references and website addresses so that you can go directly to the sources yourself and bring the information right up to date. Make sure that you read the trade press magazines or websites regularly as well so that you know what current developments are.

You will also find many opportunities to practise your research skills, particularly in a new unit about current issues in travel and tourism. Here, you are given ideas for research projects and guided step by step on how to tackle your research. This unit is assessed at Level 4, so it will challenge you and allow you to demonstrate your independent research skills. Completing this unit will provide you with ideal skills to use after you have achieved your qualification, either in the workplace or at university.

Guide to learning and assessment features

This book has a number of features to help you relate theory to practice and reinforce your learning. It also aims to help you gather evidence for assessment. You will find the features identified in the sample spread below in each unit.

Your teacher or tutor should check that you have completed enough activities to meet all the assessment criteria for the unit, whether from this book or from other tasks.

Teachers/tutors and students should refer to the BTEC standards for the qualification for the full BTEC grading criteria for each unit (www.edexcel.org.uk).

Assessment features

Activities and assessment practice

Activities are also provided throughout each unit. These are linked to real situations and case studies and they can be used for practice before tackling the preparation for assessment. Alternatively, some can contribute to your unit assessment if you choose to do these instead of the preparation for assessment at the end of each unit.

Grading icons

Throughout the book you will see the **P**, **M** and **D** icons. These show you where the tasks fit in with the grading criteria. If you do these tasks you will be building up your evidence to achieve your desired qualification. If you are aiming for a Merit, make sure you complete all the Pass **P** and Merit **M** tasks. If you are aiming for a Distinction, you will also need to complete all the Distinction **D** tasks. **P1** means the first of the Pass criteria listed in the specification, **M1** the first of the Merit criteria, **D1** the first of the Distinction criteria, and so on.

Preparation for assessment

Each unit concludes with a full unit assessment, which taken as a whole fulfils all the unit requirements from Pass to Distinction. Each task is matched to the relevant criteria in the specification.

Accommodation

There are many different types of accommodation available in the travel and tourism industry. We will look at the different types but remember that accommodation can be serviced which means that meals are on offer and your room will be cleaned for you, or it can be non-serviced where you look after yourself and do your own cleaning, shopping and cooking.

Hotels

Hotels may be independently owned or part of large chains. The chains tend to be more impersonal, but they do provide consistency of quality throughout the world. For example, if you were to stay in a Mercure hotel in London or in Paris, the room would offer exactly the same facilities, and even the layout is often the same.

Assessment practice

1 List the hotels in your town or local area. Find out which ones belong to which group. Are there any independent hotels?

2 Choose one of the hotels in your area. Describe how the hotel appeals to different tourists   **P1 M1**

Many hotels are owned by international groups who encompass several chains within them, aiming at different types of customers. An example is InterContinental Hotels Group, a large international group that has 3,500 hotels. They are not all owned outright – some are run on a franchise arrangement. This means that the owner pays for the right to use the hotel name, but in return must follow corporate policies.

Guest accommodation

This includes bed and breakfast accommodation, guesthouses and farmhouses. Homeowners who wish to capitalise on having extra space available often run this type of accommodation. Many tourists consider it charming and an opportunity to experience local culture. This type of accommodation is very popular in France, where gites are rented out for holidays.

Holiday parks and campsites

Holiday parks and campsites are popular with British tourists heading for France and Spain, although camping is probably less popular in the UK because of the unreliable weather. Holiday parks offer chalets and mobile homes so that tourists do not have to worry so much about the weather.

Self-catering

Self-catering accommodation may be in holiday parks or in rented apartments or houses. Cooking facilities will be provided.

Rail travel

Network Rail owns and operates the national rail network in the UK. Its role is to maintain the infrastructure and renew tracks as necessary.

The train-operating companies (TOCs) lease trains from rolling-stock companies. There are 25 TOCs in the UK, and they compete for franchises to run each service.

The Strategic Rail Authority issues these franchises. This body also monitors the train-operating companies to make sure the interests of rail passengers are protected; they can fine the TOCs if they fail to meet agreed standards. The TOCs are commercial companies and aim to make a profit, but they do receive government grants.

Examples of TOCs are Virgin Trains and Central Trains. The National Express Group, a British-owned transport group, owns Central Trains.

Other important aspects of the rail system are the London Underground, Docklands Light Railway and, of course, Eurostar. Eurostar is the passenger train service through the Channel Tunnel. It operates from London Waterloo and Ashford in Kent to Paris, Lille and Brussels. Eurostar is owned by London and Continental Railways, and run by a management company.

As always, I am grateful to the many travel and tourism industry colleagues and organisations who have lent their support to this book in the form of interviews, company information and material for case studies.

Travel and tourism is a challenging and exciting industry and provides a lot of career opportunities. I hope you discover these and that you enjoy your studies – and your travels.

Gillian Dale

Learning features

1.1

Case study

In summer 2004, an investigation was undertaken by the Rail Passenger Council, the watchdog for the rail sector. Passengers had complained that advance tickets, normally much cheaper, were not always available. For example, passengers travelling from London to Manchester should be able to buy tickets for £22. Instead they were forced to book later at higher prices – an open return from London to Manchester costs £182.

The problem occurs because Network Rail does not give the TOCs advance notice of engineering works, so timetables cannot be confirmed. Customers telephone to book advance tickets and are told they are not yet available as train times cannot be confirmed until engineering works are scheduled.

Sceptics have suggested that Network Rail is disregarding passenger interests and that the TOCs are profiting from the situation by receiving higher fares.

1 **Describe the roles and responsibilities of the organisations mentioned.**

2 **Describe how the problems outlined affect the travel and tourism industry.**

3 **What is your opinion of this situation? How can it be resolved? Recommend a course of action, with justifications. Discuss it with your group and write up the findings.**

Theory into practice

Visit your local Tourist Information Centre. Your tutor may wish to organise a group visit. Find out about the services it offers, and try to determine how many of its services generate revenue for the TIC. Discuss your findings with the group when you return.

Consider this

Sometimes trade associations have a code of ethics. These are not compulsory but members are asked to abide by them. Numbers employed in travel and tourism.

There are an estimated 1.4 million jobs in tourism in the UK, some 5% of all people in employment. Approximately 130,400 of these jobs are in self-employment.

	Total (millions)	Tourism-related (millions)
Total employment	28.4	1.42
Employee jobs	24.6	1.29
Self-employment	3.6	0.13

Table 1.4 Employment in tourism-related jobs

Theory into practice

These practical activities allow you to apply theoretical knowledge to travel and tourism tasks or research. Make sure you complete these activities as you work through each unit, to reinforce your learning.

Case studies

Interesting examples of real situations or companies are described in case studies that link theory to practice. They will show you how the topics you are studying affect real people and businesses.

Consider this

These are points for individual reflection or group discussion. They will widen your knowledge and help you reflect on issues that impact on travel and tourism.

Key term

Association of British Travel Agents – the body representing the sector. It also has tour operators as members. According to ABTA figures, in 2005 it had 866 tour operator members and 1468 travel agency members with 6164 travel agency offices.

Roles and responsibilities

We have looked at the roles and responsibilities of various organisations as we have discussed the various components of the travel and tourism industry. However there are some general points to be made about how roles and responsibilities may differ from sector to sector.

Knowledge check

1 How did the development of low-cost airlines impact on travel and tourism?

2 What is meant by deregulation?

3 What are the elements of a package holiday?

4 Give an example of legislation affecting tourism in the UK?

5 What are the problems affecting the UK railways?

6 Describe the different methods of distributing travel and tourism products to consumers.

Key terms

Issues and terms that you need to be aware of are summarised under these headings. They will help you check your knowledge as you learn, and will prove to be a useful quick-reference tool.

Knowledge check

At the end of each unit is a set of quick questions to test your knowledge of the information you have been studying. Use these to check your progress, and also as a revision tool.

Investigating the cruise sector

Introduction

This is a fascinating sector of travel and tourism to study as the market for cruises is growing as cruise operators respond to demand for different types of cruising across all market segments. In addition, there are lots of opportunities to work in the cruise sector and it is a popular choice for young people with no family commitments, as you can travel the world as you work.

In this unit you will find out about the cruise sector, its recent development and the variety of cruises on offer and their facilites. The appeal of different types of cruises to different customers will be examined. You will investigate the main cruise areas of the world and the impacts of cruising on these areas. You will find out about the types of work available in the cruise sector and what skills and qualities are needed to apply for jobs. You will explore the work environment on board ship and the roles and responsibilities of the staff.

It would be a good idea for you to collect a selection of cruise brochures to help you work through this unit. You will also be introduced to a number of websites which you should bookmark for future reference.

After completing this unit you should be able to achieve the following outcomes:

1   Understand the development and structure of the cruise sector
2   Know different types of cruises, ships and the facilities they offer
3   Be able to select cruises to meet specific customer needs
4   Know the impacts of cruising on the main cruise areas of the world
5   Know the employment opportunites within the cruise sector.

Talking points

The cruise industry is the world's fastest growing leisure sector, with expansion averaging 9 per cent per annum. The Passenger Shipping Association (PSA) reported that 1.2 million Britons took an ocean cruise in 2006 – 12 per cent more than the 1.07 million who cruised in 2005. The market has doubled in the last decade. This growth is expected to continue, with 1.5 million cruise passengers predicted for 2008.

There are some key differences in cruise holidays and other types of holidays. Cruise holidays are obviously not land based. Most are booked through travel agents, unlike other types of holidays where there is a trend towards direct or internet booking. Many training courses are available to help travel agents sell cruises. They are provided by the cruise lines themselves and through the PSA's training scheme, the Association of Cruise Experts (ACE).

Have you been on a cruise? Do you know someone who has? If so, ask them about their experiences.

Development

Origins

Routes, customers and facilities

Sea travel used to be of utmost importance for trade between countries. Today freight is often carried by air but before the development of aviation that was not an option. The first routes were trade routes. Transport by a fast regular steamship service was the key to a successful trade empire in Victorian Britain. The government sponsored routes and the building of ships, and the Royal Navy was responsible for protecting the routes and their supply bases.

In the nineteenth century, steamships regularly crossed the Atlantic. The first company to operate on the transatlantic shipping routes was the British and North American Royal Mail Steam Packet Company. This later became Cunard Steamships Limited, a famous cruise ship name. The company's first steamship was the *Britannia*, which sailed from Liverpool to Boston with a passenger and cargo service in 1840.

The famous engineer Isambard Kingdom Brunel was responsible for the design of the *Great Britain*, a ship built to provide transatlantic services. This 3270-ton ship set the standard for ocean liners for many years to come. It was equipped with cabins and staterooms for 360 passengers. By 1853, the *Great Britain* had been refitted to accommodate up to 630 passengers. It operated a London to Australia service and continued to do so for nearly twenty years.

Brunel was responsible for another ship, the *Great Eastern*. This could carry 4000 passengers and enough coal to get to Australia without refuelling on the way. It was the largest ship in the world until it was taken out of service and broken up in 1888.

Some ships were requisitioned for the Crimean War (1854–6) as troopships. This is a pattern that continued throughout the two World Wars and to the more recent Gulf War.

Many passengers on ships in those days were migrants going to new lands and new lives. There were few passengers travelling for pleasure, as journeys could take a long time.

In 1881, electricity was introduced onto a passenger ship for the first time. By 1911, a ship, the *Franconia*, had a gym and health centre on board. There were many other facilities of a luxurious standard for wealthy passengers. At the other end of the scale, those travelling in 'steerage' had basic facilities, that is, a bunk in a cabin and somewhere to eat.

Golden age

The period from the 1930s to the 1950s was known as the 'golden age' of cruising. Liners such as the *Queen Elizabeth* and the *Queen Mary* used to compete on transatlantic crossings for the famed 'Blue Riband': recognition of the fastest crossing. Cruising was a means of luxury travel and could only be afforded by the more affluent classes.

The *Queen Mary* was to make 1001 journeys across the Atlantic in her time of service. Queen Mary launched this liner in 1934 and it was the largest liner ever built at that time. The ship was in service until 1967.

The *Queen Elizabeth* was launched in 1938 by Queen Elizabeth, the Queen Mother. This liner did not enter commercial service until 1946 due to the Second World War.

1960s

In 1961, the 44,807-ton *Canberra* was launched. She was the largest post-war British passenger ship. Other ships at this time were about 20,000 tons. The ship was to serve as a long-distance liner on the route from Southampton to Australia. The name was in honour of the Australian capital. The ship was built by Harland & Wolff at a cost of £17 million and became known as the 'Great White Whale'. Her maiden voyage began on 2 June 1961.

Case study: the *Titanic*

I am sure you have seen the film *Titanic* but do you remember where the ship was going and what type of people it was carrying? The ship began her maiden voyage from Southampton to New York on 10 April 1912. On the night of 14 April, the ship struck an iceberg. The RMS *Titanic* was the largest passenger steamship in the world at the time of her launching and it was hoped that she would dominate the transatlantic ocean liner business. The owners were the White Star Line. The ship could hold up to 3300 passengers and had 899 crew. RMS stands for Royal Mail Steamer and meant that the ship carried mail. The ship was supposed to be at the forefront of technology and unsinkable. It was also extremely luxurious as shown clearly in the film.

On this maiden voyage there were 2208 passengers; 1496 of them died. There were not enough lifeboats on board to save all the passengers – the number of lifeboats needed was calculated on the ship's tonnage not on passenger numbers. After the sinking of the *Titanic*, changes were made in ship construction and in wireless telegraphy. There was also the first International Convention on the Safety of Life at Sea, held in London. This conference led to the formation of the International Ice Patrol, an organisation that monitors and reports on the location of icebergs in the North Atlantic which might threaten ships. Following the sinking, other important safety measures were introduced, including lifeboats for everyone on board, drills and radio communications operated 24 hours a day along with a secondary power supply, so as not to miss distress calls.

1. Summarise the impact of the sinking of the *Titanic* on the cruise ship industry at the time.

2. Find out about the International Ice Patrol today. Write a few sentences on its mission. You can find information at www.uscg.mil/lantarea/iip.

3. Choose a cruise ship that is currently operating. Find out what safety measures it has on board. Cruise brochures will help you with this.

Figure 10.1 RMS *Titanic* ▶

The *Canberra* carried out a large number of trips to Australia. Many of these trips were taking emigrants from the UK to Australia. These passengers were able to buy a one-way ticket for only £10 under the government's assisted-passage scheme. By the end of the decade there were not so many emigrants and so the *Canberra* became a full-time holiday cruise ship.

1970s, 1980s and fly-cruises

Once it was easy to cross the Atlantic by air the lucrative cruise transatlantic route went into decline. Cruise operators had to find new, alternative routes, such as Caribbean destinations. Also tour operators began to appreciate the demand for cruising, and began to create cruise packages. Some operators bought their own ships and introduced cruises at competitive prices. Cruise ships at this time were smaller than today, carrying about 600–800 passengers, and cruising was very much a luxury activity.

In the 1980s, 'straight-to-the-sun' fly-cruising took off, enabling people to take Caribbean and other far-away cruises without the long ship journey to reach the destination. This meant a cruise could be taken in a one- or two-week holiday.

Changing consumer demands and needs

Economic changes

Growth in cruising reflects the increase in disposable income for average British people. With more money to spend, people are able to take more holidays and look for different experiences. Another factor leading to growth in the market is that for the last few years prices of cruising have been heavily discounted as more competition enters the market. Lower prices have encouraged first-time cruisers and changed the profile of the market.

Fashion and areas of popularity

As cruising is growing in popularity it could be said that it is becoming more fashionable. It is true to say that as younger people and families try cruising and enjoy it, they tell their friends about their experiences and the idea becomes attractive a to a wider cross-section of society.

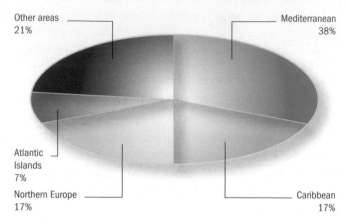

(Source: http://www.irn-research.com/downloads/CruiseCensusUK06.pdf)

▲ **Figure 10.2 UK cruises by destination 2006**

There are changes in which areas are most popular. For example, the Mediterranean has increased by 22 per cent to 38 per cent of the market, while the Caribbean has fallen in popularity. The Atlantic islands have also decreased in popularity.

Consider this

Why do you think the Mediterranean has increased in popularity? Do you know where the Atlantic islands are? Check on a map.

Cruises taken from a UK port (ex-UK cruises), also increased 12 per cent. Over 450,000 British, or four in ten British cruise travellers, chose to cruise from the UK. The most significant increase in carryings came with Fred Olsen Cruise Lines' Boudicca, Cunard Line and Travelscope. The PSA predicts that 2007 will see the ex-UK trend continue to grow. *Navigator of the Seas* is replacing *Legend of the Seas*, doubling the capacity of Royal Caribbean (RCI) on these itineraries. Other significant capacity increases from UK ports will come from MSC Cruises as it begins sailing from the UK for the first time. Princess Cruises is also adding to its capacity from Southampton, with more sailings with the *Sea Princess* and the *Grand Princess*.

Demographics

The average age of cruise passengers is slowly falling. In the early 1990s, it was 60. It is now about 52. This may seem high but remember it is an average and it has been brought down by the increased number of families with children who go on a cruise. Also it reflects an ageing UK population which will have 20 per cent more 40- to 60-year-olds and 23 per cent more of those who are 60-plus in 2010. Passengers under 35 represent 15 per cent of all passengers.

Trends

Currently, the cruise sector is popular with travel agents as it is one of the few sectors where high commissions are to be earned. Passengers are more likely to book with a travel agent than over the internet as they are spending a lot of money and are likely to need advice about the type of ship, cabins and facilities.

To cater for increased demand and to encourage growth in the market, the cruise lines are building new ships and providing a greater variety of types of cruises. Cruise ships are getting longer, wider and taller to accommodate more people and generate more revenue for cruise lines by achieving economies of scale. The average number of passengers aboard a modern cruise ship is approximately 1500, with some ships carrying as many as 3000 passengers. The average width of new ships is 90 feet, which is almost the maximum allowed for going through the Panama Canal.

New and better ships are being built to provide more cruise capacity. One example is the launch of the *Queen Mary 2* by Cunard in 2004. The *Queen Mary 2* is the world's largest, longest, tallest and most expensive passenger liner. The *Queen Mary 2* can take 2620 passengers and has 14 decks with 10 different restaurants.

Larger ships impact on ports, which have to be able to accommodate them and the large numbers of passengers and baggage that they carry. Berths have to be wider, and gangways and terminals have to be higher to meet the passenger disembarkation point.

Structure

Consider this

There are about 270 cruise ships in the world with a further 29 due for delivery before 2010.

Cruise operators

There are so many cruise operators that we cannot discuss them all here so we will look at some examples and you will find more examples as you work through the unit. Thirty-six cruise lines belong to the Passenger Ship Association and you can find details of these on the 'Discover Cruises' website at http://www.discover-cruises.co.uk/CruiseLines.aspx.

Well-established operators

■ Carnival Cruises

Carnival Cruise Lines is the giant of the sector and comprises 12 different brands accounting for nearly half of all UK cruise sales.

- Carnival Cruises
- Princess Cruises
- Holland America
- Windstar
- Seabourn
- P&O Cruises
- P&O Cruises (Australia)
- Cunard
- Ocean Village
- Swan Hellenic
- AIDA/A'ROSA
- Costa Cruises

Some of these brands arrived in 2003 when the company merged with P&O Princess.

The Carnival Corporation began as an independent company in 1972. It carries more than 2 million passengers a year and has its headquarters in Miami. The brands operate more than 77 ships totalling more than

128,000 lower berths. Twenty-two of these ships operate under the Carnival Cruise line. New ships are due from 2008 through to 2011. The largest are 130,000 tons each.

■ Royal Caribbean

Royal Caribbean Cruises Limited is a global cruise company that operates Royal Caribbean International and Celebrity Cruises, with a combined total of 29 ships in service and a passenger capacity of approximately 60,500. The world's largest cruise ship, the *Freedom of the Seas*, belongs to this group.

Consider this

Do you like rock climbing? Many Royal Caribbean ships feature a rock-climbing wall, while there are ice-skating rinks on their *Voyager of the Seas* class of ships and a surf park on the *Freedom of the Seas*. The ships operate worldwide with a selection of itineraries that call on approximately 160 destinations.

■ NCL/Star

Norwegian Cruise Line is owned by Star Cruises plc of Malaysia. This is the third-largest parent group, operating a combined fleet of 20 ships. Carnival has, however, acquired a 40 per cent stake in this group. It has three 150,000-ton ships on order, with the first arriving in 2009.

New companies

Tour operators have made forays into cruising over the last few years, wishing to take advantage of a growing market. The UK's major operators have cruising divisions. MyTravel incurred losses of £8 million on three of its four ships in the year to September 2003 and decided to get rid of them to reduce fixed costs. One of them, *Sunbird*, was bought by Thomson and was renamed *Thomson Destiny*. With this addition Thomson had a fleet of five ships. Its ships are old and chartered rather than new-build. Its latest ship, which was introduced in 2007, was built in 1968.

EasyCruise is one of the new entrants to the cruise market. It has a 170-passenger ship, *easyCruiseOne*, which cruises along the French and Italian rivieras during the summer and the Caribbean in the winter. There is also the 100-passenger river cruiser *easyCruiseTwo* which offers trips along the canals and rivers of Europe, visiting Amsterdam and other cities.

Links with other sectors

■ Transporters

Many cruises are fly-cruises. This means the passengers are flown to the departure port to start the cruise. As the new ships are so large, the cruise operators are able to charter planes to transport their passengers from their home country to the port. The cruise lines have special departments whose role is to organise the flights and liaise with suppliers and passengers.

Princess Cruises, for example, has arrangements with dedicated charters hired to serve its 'Golden Princess' cruises. In addition, cruise lines work with 'preferred partners'. Princess works with British Airways as a preferred partner – so when there is not a dedicated charter for a cruise, flights are provided with British Airways.

The cruise lines have links with other transporters, for example coach operators, to bring passengers to the ship when they are joining at a home port.

Key term

Preferred partner – an arrangement between companies where they promote each other's products or services.

A lucrative source of revenue for cruise lines is the provision of shore excursions. The liner makes advance arrangements with local coach or taxi operators to give tours. A full-day shore excursion will cost about £45 to £75 per person. It would usually be much cheaper for passengers to make their own plans but many prefer to have everything done for them. These tours can be booked before departure or in the tour office on board the ship.

Case study

Cruiselink

Eavesway Travel Ltd operates coach services from departure points across the UK direct to the cruise terminal and back for 2008 cruises.

Joining your fly-cruise

If you are flying from London Gatwick or Manchester and have a long journey to the airport, we can arrange an overnight hotel stay for the night before your flight, from £99 per room.

Details of airport parking facilities will be sent to you 2–3 weeks before travel.

Caribbean fly-cruises

For all the fly-cruises in this brochure, we'll arrange dedicated charter flights using aircraft of reputable carriers such as Thomas Cook Airlines, Thomsonfly and First Choice Airlines.

(Source: Cruise Holidays P&O Cruises brochure 2008)

1 This extract explains links with transporters and hotels. Can you identify them?

2 Why does P&O not prefer passengers to make their own arrangements to join the cruise?

■ Tour operators

Tour operators such as Thomson offer cruises by chartering ships and offering cruises under their own brand name. Island Cruises, a First Choice subsidiary, is a joint venture with Royal Caribbean Cruise Lines.

■ Travel agents

There are many dedicated websites and travel agents for selling cruises. This is not surprising as it is the sector of travel and tourism that pays the highest commission.

Some established travel agents have their own cruise division, for example, 1st4 cruising is operated by one of the UK's leading independent travel agents: Page & Moy. Agents who sell a large volume of cruise holidays earn cruise line membership of their prestigious agents' 'clubs', with higher commissions.

Integration

As in the rest of the travel and tourism industry, a few companies dominate the market. The cruise industry is a highly competitive industry, and is becoming more so each year. Carnival Cruise Lines has acquired many cruise lines to form a company that controls 33 per cent of the cruise market. This is a good example of horizontal integration as Carnival has reached this dominant position by taking over or merging with different companies but has often retained the original brand names in order to appeal to different market sectors. Royal Caribbean is also growing; it recently purchased the Celebrity cruise line and has invested $1500 in three 3000- to 4000-passenger ships.

Key term

Horizontal integration – two companies at the same level in the chain of distribution merge or one takes over the other.

Vertical integration – companies merge or one takes over the other at different levels in the chain of distribution, for example Carnival took over an airline.

There are benefits of integration for cruise operators:
- economies of scale
- control over the supply of berths on ships
- control over distribution
- larger market share
- less competition
- established reputation.

Regulatory bodies

■ Passenger Shipping Association (PSA)

This body is the main trade association serving the cruise sector. In fact, it represents all passenger shipping interests within the UK. The PSA membership is divided into two sections: cruise and ferry. There are regular meetings to discuss matters of interest to the members.

The main objectives are:
- the promotion of travel by sea by the public
- to encourage expansion in the volume of passenger travel, by sea and river
- to work towards the removal or prevention of the imposition of restrictions or taxes on passenger travel by sea
- to advise Member Lines to ensure that passengers travel in a safe, healthy and secure environment.

The PSA is also an important corporate contact for the media, seeking information on both cruising and ferry markets.

In addition, the organisation has the role of educating travel agents about the cruise sector through the ACE.

■ International Maritime Organisation

This organisation is based in the UK and has 300 international staff. It was established in 1948 but first met in 1959. Its aims are to develop and maintain a comprehensive regulatory framework for shipping and it establishes policy on:
- safety
- environmental concerns
- legal matters
- maritime security
- efficiency of shipping.

■ International Council of Cruise Lines (ICCL)

This is a US-based organisation but it is worth noting as all the large passenger cruise lines are members. The mission of the ICCL is 'to participate in the regulatory and policy development process and promote all measures that foster a safe, secure and healthy cruise ship environment'.

The ICCL actively monitors international shipping policy and develops recommendations to its membership on a wide variety of issues including:
- public health
- environmental responsibility
- security
- medical facilities
- passenger protection
- legislative activities.

In this section we are going to examine the different types of cruises and see how they differ in terms of facilities.

Types

The following types of cruises are currently available:

- fly-cruise
- round the world
- mini-cruise
- river cruise
- luxury cruise
- special interest cruise
- transatlantic cruise
- sail ship
- all-inclusive
- easyCruise.

Fly-cruise

All the major cruise lines offer fly-cruises. The prices quoted for fly-cruises include the flight and all the arrangements are made for the passenger. Flights may be charter, where the ship is large enough to warrant charters arriving from various departure airports, or they may be scheduled. The more expensive cruises often use scheduled flights because of the extra flexibility and the perception of luxury. Also included in the prices are the accommodation in cabins, all meals and usually room service, activities and entertainment on board. Advantages of fly-cruises are:

- passengers can be speedily delivered to the destination region
- baggage can be checked at the departure airport and taken straight to the cabin
- regional departures are possible
- there is a wide range of destinations and categories of ship available to choose from
- cruises can be from a few days to a few weeks.

Fly-cruises take the biggest market share for UK travellers, with 753,000 of all UK cruise passengers choosing a fly-cruise in 2006.

The nature of fly-cruises varies according to cost and the cruise line chosen. Some have extremely good service and are very luxurious, like Cunard cruises. Others are less formal and appeal to package holiday makers, like Thomson cruises or Carnival.

Assessment practice

The *Star Princess* and *Grand Princess* are two of the luxury superliners operated by Princess Cruises. You will find deck plans for these ships in the Princess Cruises Caribbean Cruises brochure. The extract below outlines the facilities on both ships.

Star Princess and *Grand Princess* 2600 passengers 109,000 tons

These innovative sister ships provide you with unparalleled onboard choice. Whether you're sailing on *Grand Princess* around the Mediterranean or *Star Princess* through the Baltic Sea, you'll be onboard a ship that is guaranteed to turn heads.

- 710 staterooms with private balconies
- 3 main dining rooms, 2 with 'anytime dining', 24-hour restaurant, Sabatini's Italian Trattoria, Sterling Steakhouse, pizzeria, patisserie and hamburger grill
- 4 glistening swimming pools, one with retractable magradome, 9 revitalising whirlpool spas and a children's splash pool
- 'Movies Under The Stars' (*Grand Princess* only)
- Wrap-around promenade deck
- 3 state-of-the art show lounges
- Lotus Spa health and beauty salon and ocean view gymnasium
- Wide variety of bars and lounges, including a wine and caviar bar
- 'Skywalkers' nightclub suspended 150 feet above the ocean
- Wedding chapel
- Writing room and Library
- Sport bar with live TV sports coverage

continued ▶

- 9-hole golf putting course, golf simulator and sports court
- 24-hour AOL, Internet Café and virtual reality centre
- Youth and teen centres
- Grand casino
- Shopping gallery
- Free 24-hour room service.

(Source: Princess Cruises Caribbean Cruises brochure 2007/2008)

Find details of another fly-cruise ship in a brochure or on the internet. Choose one of the less formal cruises like Carnival or Thomson. Describe the routes and the range of facilities on board and draw up a comparative chart, comparing with another type of cruise. Decide which cruise ship you would prefer and say why. Share your findings with your group. **P2** **M1**

The description and facilities should include:

- Size of vessel
- Deck plans
- Entertainment
- Accommodation
- Cabins
- Shops
- Payment methods
- Dining
- Sport facilities
- Creche
- Facilities to meet specific needs.

Round the world

This has to be the ultimate cruise experience. World cruises appeal to a lot of people but they cannot usually afford the time or the money to do them! Prices start at around £10,000 per person and can be two or three times that, depending on the choice of accommodation. Also it obviously takes some time to sail around the world so work commitments might get in the way. The customer profile tends to be older retired people – with plenty of money. The following are a couple of examples of world cruises extracted from the 'Discover Cruises' website. Have a look at the website if you would like to know more – or to plan your own world cruise.

Cunard Line

The world cruises of Cunard's flagship, *Queen Elizabeth 2*, continue a Cunard tradition that dates back to 1922 when the *Laconia* undertook the first ever world cruise. From New York to Southampton, the *QE2*'s 'Voyage of Great Discoveries' circles the world in 99 nights and calls at 27 ports, including cities such as Los Angeles, Auckland, Sydney, Hong Kong, Singapore and Bombay. A maiden call will be made at Phuket. Lead-in fares range from £10,449 for the *QE2*'s full 108-night Silver Jubilee World Cruise in 2007 or £9899 for the *Queen Mary 2*'s 75-night Maiden. Gratuities, normally added to the shipboard account, will also be included for those undertaking the complete world cruise.

(Source: http://www.discover-cruises.co.uk)

P&O Cruises

P&O Cruises programme includes the chance for passengers to circumnavigate the globe 'Jules Verne' style in an 80-day voyage on board the *Aurora*. The worldwide programme also includes a 100-day Grand Voyage, the longest journey ever taken by P&O Cruises. This takes place aboard the luxurious new ship *Adonia*, which joined the fleet in May 2003.

(Source: http://www.discover-cruises.co.uk)

Mini-cruise

Mini-cruises have been developed as a means of bringing more business to passenger ferries. These ships have improved in the last few years and offer a good range of facilities to passengers, including cabins, restaurants, shops and cinemas. The cruise may be for one or two nights and is sometimes combined with a city stay in the middle. They depart from many UK ports including Hull, Harwich and Newcastle. Cruises to Amsterdam from Newcastle are very popular with students, especially as the cost can be as low as £34.50!

The following mini-break is a cruise from Newcastle to Bergen. Note that very little time is spent in port.

Newcastle to Bergen

These Off-Peak short cruise breaks to Bergen, the 'Gateway of the Fjords' in Norway offer you an amazing insight into the country's beautiful west coast.

Sailing from Newcastle on Saturday evenings, you have a fun filled evening on board, where there are a whole host of things to do.

You can eat out, in one of our choice of 5 restaurants, from buffet-style to à la carte, to fun and dancing in our Columbus club, to catching the latest movies or having a flutter at the onboard casino, or just finding a quiet corner somewhere to unwind.

The next day you continue your leisurely cruise across the North sea to Norway en route for Bergen, and following brief stops at Stavanger and Haugesund you arrive in Bergen late on Sunday evening.

You get approximately 11 hours in port, with the opportunity to either briefly explore the city in the morning, or just relax over breakfast on board on Monday morning, before the ship sets sail for the UK on Monday morning, arriving back in Newcastle Tuesday lunchtime.

(Source: http://www.dfds.co.uk)

River cruise

Many destinations are popular for river cruising but the Nile is probably the best known. Figure 10.4 shows the relative popularity of river cruise areas.

▲ Figure 10.3 Fjords near Bergen, Norway

River cruising and ocean cruising are quite different experiences. On a river, passengers are close to shore and can see sights very clearly. Often shore excursions are included in the price. This is important because passengers are unlikely to want to spend all their time on the ship, since the facilities are not as varied as on an ocean-going liner due to restrictions on space. A river vessel may carry 100 or 200 passengers rather than thousands.

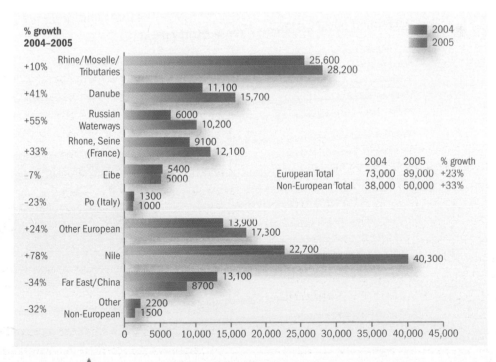

Figure 10.4 River cruise holidays ▲

(Source: Annual Cruise Review/PSA(ACE)-IRN Cruise statistics)

Case study:
river cruises

Look at Figure 10.5 from the Cadogan Holidays River Cruises brochure.

Describe the facilities available on the *Viking Century Sky* and *Viking Century Sun*. Who do you think would go on this type of ship? What clues are there in the extract from the brochure?

The description and facilities should include:

- Size of vessel
- Deck plans
- Entertainment
- Accommodation
- Cabins
- Shops
- Payment methods
- Dining
- Sport facilities
- Crèche
- Facilities to meet specific needs.

Figure 10.5
Viking Century Sky and
Viking Century Sun

VIKING CENTURY SKY & VIKING CENTURY SUN

Viking Century Sky and Viking Century Sun, identical 5-star sister ships, were built to accommodate discerning travellers and maximize the comfort of your journey. Custom built to Viking River Cruises specifications and designed by internationally acclaimed naval architects Yran & Storbraaten.

The 5-deck deluxe cruise ships are the newest and best ships sailing China's Yangtze River. On board you will find stylish comfort and beautiful Finnish design. Each of the 153 spacious outside cabins features a balcony, private bathroom with shower, hairdryer, hotel-style beds, individual climate control, telephone and television (with English programming including CNN Asia, BBC, China's CCTV and Hong Kong's Star TV, depending on satellite reception). At 221 square feet, the standard cabins are the largest among any ship in China. You will enjoy an array of fine amenities that you would expect from a 5-star hotel including two lifts, a gym, sauna, massage rooms, business centre, internet café and coffee bar as well as the services of a doctor and beauty salon.

All meals are served in the well-appointed gourmet dining room. The menus were designed to give you a wonderful combination of authentic Chinese cuisine and traditional Western favourites. Viking River Cruises was the first to introduce Western food aboard its ships and specifically designed its kitchens to accommodate the preparation of both styles of cooking.

With just 306 fellow passengers, the intimate and friendly atmosphere allows you to get to know your travelling companions. The on board Swiss hotel management and award-winning, gracious English-speaking staff are the best in China.

Observation bar

Cadogan River Cruises: 023 8028 2329 or visit your travel agent

(Source: Cadogan Holidays River Cruises Europe & China 2007 brochure)

Luxury cruise

Ultra-luxury cruise lines are defined by the PSA as ships with fewer than 1000 passengers, a staff to customer ratio of at least one to two and a space to passenger ratio of more than 40 square metres. The cost will be at least £500 per day.

There is an alliance called the Exclusive Collection for ultra-luxury cruise lines. Members include Crystal Cruises, Hebridean Island Cruises, Seabourn and Windstar.

Consider this

Royal Caribbean Cruises has introduced a luxury ship designed in conjunction with Finland's Kvaener Masa-Yards. It is large enough to carry 3600 passengers and weighs 160,000 gross tons. Known as the *Freedom of the Seas*, it is the largest cruise ship ever built. She is called an 'Ultra-*Voyager*' because she is an extension of the Royal Caribbean International *Voyager of the Seas* class. In 2008, another huge ship will be launched – the *Ventura*. She cost £300 million pounds to build and will carry 3600 passengers and 1200 crew.

Why do you think such 'super ships' are being built? What would it be like to holiday on a ship with so many passengers?

Special interest cruises

Most of the cruises we are studying are on the huge ocean-going liners. However, customers are always looking for something different and this sector of travel and tourism is no different. Special interest cruises offer a more unusual product, focusing on unusual destinations like Christmas shopping in Rio offered by Discovery World cruises or the Indian Ocean offered by African Safari Club.

Many of these special interest cruises cater for a younger clientele who are looking for more activity on their cruise and a little bit of adventure. Some Alaskan cruises offer excursions like dog sledding, whale watching and rock climbing.

Celebrity Cruises offer a trip to the Galapagos Islands with lots of exploration for adventurous types, including going ashore in inflatable landing crafts.

Transatlantic cruise

A transatlantic crossing is a legendary travel experience. It copies the journeys of early cruisers like those on the great liners including the *Titanic* mentioned earlier! It is still a fantastic way of travelling to America. The *Queen Mary 2* is one of the more famous ships making this crossing.

Consider this

The *QE2* allows dogs on her transatlantic runs; she has a kennel on board and even a lamp post to make dogs feel at home!

Case study: the *QE2*

The *QE2* undertook her maiden voyage on 2 May 1969 from Southampton to New York. She had cost her owners, Cunard, £2.5 million to build. The ship undertook her first world cruise in 1974. The trip generated over £1 million in profit. In 1982, the *QE2* was called into war service. The ship was requisitioned by the Government for service as troop transport. In Southampton, the ship was converted and had a communication system installed and helicopter flight decks added. The fifth infantry brigade, comprising the Scots and Welsh Guards and the Gurkhas, then boarded the ship and it set off for South Georgia on 12 May. After the Falklands War the ship was converted back to commercial service.

1 Where is the *QE2* now? Visit the website www.queenelizabeth2.fsnet.co.uk to find out.

2 Who owns the *QE2*?

Figure 10.6 Tall ship

An alternative to 'lazy days' is to sail the ship yourself. Such holidays are very adventurous and are offered on tall ships. A small crew sails the ship under the expertise of a permanent skipper and mate. The holiday is hard work but fun. Accommodation is hardly luxurious but very informal.

Assessment practice

Choose and research two different special interest cruises from different types of ship. Describe the facilities available on each.

Compare and contrast the routes and ship facilities available.

The description and facilities should include:

- Size of vessel
- Deck plans
- Entertainment
- Accommodation
- Cabins
- Shops
- Payment methods
- Dining
- Sport facilities
- Crèche
- Facilities to meet specific needs.

Sail ship

An exciting way to cruise the Caribbean is to take a tall sail ship cruise. This very informal type of cruising on a 'Windjammer' ship is described below.

Lazy days at sea – I spend hours reading the latest bestsellers and watching the sails in the breeze. Luckily no seasickness for me, though some of my friends are not so lucky. It's great to get away from city life – we don't have to dress up – in fact I only packed shorts, sandals and swimsuits. Some days I haven't even bothered to put shoes on. I'm slapping moisturiser on every five minutes but haven't used make-up.

The food on board is simple but tasty and we all sit round one huge table sipping rum punch along with our meal. You can have wine if you want it – but it costs extra. Coke flows freely for the kids and iced water is always available.

When we reach the shore life is equally laid back. We transfer to a launch boat and go to the beach. There we can swim, sunbathe or snorkel to our heart's content.

Key term

All-inclusive – this term is used throughout the holiday industry but is particularly applicable in the cruise sector as it means that everything apart from excursions and tips is included: accommodation, food and drink and entertainment. This is the norm for most cruises but budget cruises like easyCruise are the exception.

Passenger space ratio – the gross registered tonnage divided by the number of passengers. The higher the figure the more space available for each person.

EasyCruise

Case study: easyCruise

I am sure you are familiar with easyJet. Now there is easyCruise, and this is probably the cheapest cruise ever. EasyCruise follows the trend set by Ocean Village in ditching formality on cruises. This product is aimed at 20-, 30- and 40-year-olds.

As you might expect there are no frills but prices are cheap with cabins from £29 per night. The first ship launched in May 2005. It is not a new ship but has been refitted and can carry 180 people. The ship cruises in the Mediterranean and then in the Caribbean. Passengers make their own arrangements to reach the ship and book nights on board as you would a hotel. Passengers are encouraged to book over the internet, with early bookings attaining cheaper prices. Food and drinks are available but passengers have to pay for them – just like on an easyJet flight.

You can take a virtual tour of an easyCruise at www.easycruise.com.

Write a description of an easyCruise. Include as many as you can of the following.

- Size of vessel
- Deck plans
- Entertainment
- Accommodation
- Cabins
- Shops
- Payment methods
- Dining
- Sport facilities
- Crèche
- Facilities to meet specific needs.

Compare the routes and facilities with those of a cruise on a luxury liner.

10.3 Be able to select cruises to meet specific customer needs

Types of customers and appeal

There are cruises to suit all ages, tastes and budgets. Some cruise lines aim their product squarely at a traditional market while others aim at younger and more adventurous customers.

Customers can be targeted by age, lifestyle, income and special interest.

Whatever the type of customer, their choice of cruise will be affected by different appeal factors. Some of these factors have led to a growth in cruise taking. What influences a customer to take one cruise rather than another?

The itinerary: Does the cruise visit the ports we would like to see? Some cruises pack as many ports as possible into the itinerary, others are more leisurely. Is it in an area we want to visit? How long is it?

Etiquette: How formal is the cruise? Do we have to dress up?

Board: Is everything included? Do we have to tip? How much?

Social factors: Is there enough to do? What entertainment is there? Families will not be attracted to a cruise unless there are facilities and activities for the children.

Climate: What will the weather be like?

Cost: How much is it? Some ships are more expensive than others and more luxurious. Cost is also affected by cabin choice.

Convenience: Where do we join it? Should we embark on a cruise that goes from a UK port or fly?

Novelty: Do we want a cruise that offers something adventurous or allows us to pursue a special interest?

On-board facilities: What exactly is available on board? The longer the cruise the more important this might be. Keeping in touch by e-mail or having a lot of things to keep you occupied on board are more important if you are on the ship for months.

Passenger crew ratio (PCR): How good will the service be?

Passenger space ratio (PSR): Will we a have lot of room or will we be cramped?

We will look at some examples of cruises and how they meet needs and then you can try selecting some cruises for customers yourself.

By age and lifestyle – for 'people who don't do cruises'

Ocean Village is an example of a company that targets a younger age group than the average for cruising. This brand of cruising was introduced in 2003 by P&O Princess Cruises, now Carnival UK. The brand firmly targets British first-time cruisers, specifically in the 30- to 50-something age group. Now you might think that's old! However, cruises have a reputation for attracting much older people and for being very 'fuddy duddy'. Ocean Village tried to get right away from this image and appeal to someone like the person described below:

You like doing your own thing and you'd rather dress down than up when you go away. You're adventurous, a bit of a thrill seeker – not the usual cruise holiday type. Relax. Ocean Village is no ordinary cruise. Informal and easy-going, it's for thirty to fifty-somethings who want to explore new places without the formality of traditional cruises.

(Source: http://www.oceanvillageholidays.co.uk/)

This is clever marketing, as who doesn't want to be adventurous and a thrill seeker?

The cruises are based in the Mediterranean and in the Caribbean and offer many ports of call with action activities on shore, for example river rafting and mountain biking. A new ship was introduced in 2007. The PSR is 2.75:1.

By age

Saga cruises are exclusively for over-50s. There are two ships to choose from, the *Saga Rose* and the *Saga Ruby*. It is possible to go a round-the-world trip on one of these ships but there are also Baltic, Mediterranean and Caribbean cruises.

By lifestyle

The proportion of children going on cruises has increased in the last decade. By 2005, 10 per cent of UK cruisers were under 26. Many of these were children going on family cruises. This is one of the major gowth areas in cruising. Most cruise lines now offer family-friendly facilities. Carnival claims to carry 500,000 children per year.

The following extract shows what this cruise line offers for families.

All Aboard
Camp Carnival (kids 2–15, in 4 age groups), offers activities like face painting and treasure hunts, with PS2's and video games for juniors and a dance club and soft drinks bar for teens. On deck is a children's pool and an amazing 200 ft spiral waterslide.

After Hours
Evening babysitting is available at a nominal fee of $6 per hour from 10pm to 3am in the playroom in a 'pyjama party' atmosphere! Babysitting is also available in the playroom for some mornings in port.

Kids' Meals

Family favourites include fish and chips, pizza, tacos and healthy snacks served in our informal restaurants while purchase of a 'Fountain Fun Card' means unlimited soft drinks throughout the cruise.

Shore Excursions

Special kids shore excursions include the opportunity to crew a genuine America's Cup racing yacht in St Maarten, swimming with dolphins or horseback riding through a jungle in Belize, as well as other watersport and land based activities.

Family Accommodation

Family accommodation ranges from value inside facing 3- and 4-berth cabins to spacious staterooms with interconnecting doors and floor to ceiling picture windows. Cribs and pushchairs can be requested in advance.

(Source: http://www.carnivalcruise.co.uk)

Other ships boast of not having children at all and catering for an adults only lifestyle.

Take Kids out of the Equation.
Adults only + Thomson Spirit = a great cruise

14 August 2006 – Thomson

Following the sell out of the adults cruises last year and the success of 2 adult only cruises in June this year, Thomson Cruises is now set to offer four adult only cruises throughout September on the Thomson Spirit. With the kids back in school, September is the perfect time for parents, couples or single adults to get away. Adult only cruising could mean a break from the kids, a romantic getaway or just the chance to experience the freedom of cruising without children onboard.

As an added bonus, Linda Barker, celebrity interior designer has personally designed the suites on the Thomson Spirit. These can now be booked for up to 50% off the normal price of a cabin upgrade.

(Source: Thomson Cruises)

There are several budget cruises available. EasyCruise offers seven-night cruises from £75 per person per night. The First Choice and Royal Caribbean Island Cruise brand is aimed at a budget market. The *Thomson Spirit* mentioned above has prices starting from £679 per person for a week. This means that people who previously thought cruising was too expensive for them are able to try it.

The difference between this type of cruising and the more traditional luxury type is that the experience concentrates on visiting lots of places in the time available rather than focusing on the actual experience aboard ship.

For those who want to take a budget cruise with fewer facilities there is the option of travelling on a working vessel such as the St Helena. This ship provides a year-round service to the tropical South Atlantic island of St Helena. The ship holds only 128 passengers and the route takes in the South African coastline.

At the other end of the scale the cruise ship MS *Deutschland* has art nouveau styling and crystal chandeliers. It has an indoor spa and also offers kidney dialysis stations so that kidney patients can join the cruise. It is not cheap – prices start at £2350 for a 12-night cruise.

Some examples of special interest cruises were mentioned earlier. Special interests can also be catered for by themed cruises. If you are a 'Strictly Come Dancing' fan you can take a cruise with Carnival where celebrities from the show will dance with passengers. Holland America run a culinary theme cruise with Michelin star chef on hand to run workshops.

Study the customer profiles given below and then find a suitable cruise for each of them. Describe the cruise chosen for each customer and say why it would appeal to them.   **P3**

Explain how the selected cruises appeal to different customers.   **M2**

Profiles

1   Graham Cutter is 75 years old and he is an experienced cruiser. He has been on 16 cruises. He always travels with his friend, Gordon. All the cruises they have been on have been luxury cruises and now they would like a world cruise – money is no object.

2   Sanjit is a first-time cruiser and is choosing a cruise for his honeymoon. He wants to try scuba diving so he thinks the Caribbean is a good idea. He wants a romantic cruise and he doesn't want to be on a ship with hundreds or even thousands of people. He thinks a sail ship might be a good plan. He wants a personal ambience.

3   Rodney Burrows is taking 11 friends with him on holiday. Some of them have a limited budget so they don't want a very expensive cruise and they don't want a long flight either. They only want to go for a week and they want to have lots of things to do. They are all keen on adventure. They want entertainment in the evening too.

4   James and Jessie Stavros want a family cruise with their four-year-old son. They have never been on a cruise before. They don't want a long flight with a child. They hope that there will be other children so that their child will make friends and that there will be children's clubs and activities.

10.4 Know the impacts of cruising on the main cruise areas of the world

Cruise areas

In this section we will investigate the different cruise areas available to UK cruise passengers.

We will look at some examples of cruises in these popular areas to see what they have to offer to travellers and what kind of people they appeal to. We will investigate the impact of cruising on these areas.

Table 10.1 shows the increase in cruising in different areas. This massive growth has had an impact. We will consider this impact and study some of the most popular areas.

We will investigate:

● the Mediterranean
● Asia/Far East
● the Caribbean/Americas
● Scandinavia
● Antarctica
● the Nile (a river cruise).

Some cruise areas are subject to specific impacts but most can be investigated in general terms.

Impacts of cruising

Economic impact

The economic benefits of cruise activity and development are as follows:

● jobs in servicing the port and the ship
● jobs in construction – particularly in ship-building and in ports and shopping areas
● increased spending by visitors boosts the economy
● increased prosperity for residents.

The economic value of the cruise sector has been recognised by VisitBritain, which has set up a new initiative named Cruise UK to develop cruise business

Area	1997	1998*	1999	2000	2001	2002	2003	2004	2005	2006
UK – Port Cruises										
– Mediterranean	43	60	38	45	52	71	75	100	107	130
– UK – Western Europe	9	20	13	25	27	29	53	56	67	88
– Norway	20	21	22	27	31	30	38	37	57	59
– Baltic	15	16	23	19	25	26	36	48	51	54
– Atlantic Islands	23	22	28	37	43	36	44	45	50	51
– Caribbean	4	6	6	9	7	9	9	7	14	15
– Other areas (Greenland, Iceland, Artic, USA+)	5	13	3	4	1	3	3	9	28	26
– Line voyages	13	13	13	16	15	19	9	9	18	18
– Charter	8	8	10	11	16	9	14	5	9	10
Total UK – UK port cruises	**140**	**179**	**156**	**193**	**217**	**232**	**281**	**316**	**403**	**451**
Fly Cruises										
– Mediterranean/Black Sea	156	163	241	187	218	230	305	288	247	308
– Mediterranean/Ex-Cyprus	45	63	91	102	64	53	31	23	16	14
– Caribbean/Bahamas/Bermuda	116	160	143	141	139	162	179	228	208	195
– Indian Ocean, Red Sea, Persian Gulf	<	<	<	<	<	<	<	<	<	40
– Atlantic Islands	<	19	39	26	34	37	41	44	46	35
– W. Coast/Mexico/Hawaii/Panama Canal	9	8	12	10	11	19	23	24	34	35
– Alaska	12	14	15	18	16	17	13	22	26	29
– Scandinavia/Baltic	9	8	9	14	15	14		20	14	7
– Transatlantic – repositioning	<	<	<	8	9	10	15	16	18	25
– Far East/Australia	9	21	14	15	17	15	18	7	15	15
– Round the World fly sectors and Round the World	8	9	8	10	12	9	9	13	10	13
– South America	<	<	<	5	6	6	15	12	7	14
– Other areas (South Pacific, Antarctica etc.)	13	11	12	13	13	13	17	13	29	20
– Charter	7	7	4	12	6	4	2	4	3	3
Total Fly Cruises	**382**	**484**	**590**	**561**	**559**	**590**	**683**	**713**	**669**	**753**
TOTAL	**522**	**663**	**746**	**754**	**776**	**822**	**964**	**1,029**	**1,071**	**1,204**

* Passenger figures from Paradise Cruises and Salamis Cruises (Cyprus) included for the first time from 1998.

< Included in other areas.

(Source: Compiled for the Passenger Shipping Association by IRN Research (www.irn-research.com))

▲ Table 10.1 Open sea cruise passengers (000s) by main area, 1997–2006

in the UK. Cruise UK encompasses all cruise-related organisations in the UK. It aims to increase the number of visitors taking a cruise to the UK and acts as the first point of contact for developing the cruise industry to the UK's ports. Its first task was to get representatives from different parts of the cruise sector to participate. It set up an advisory board with members from tourist boards, ports, tour operators, airlines and airports. The next step was to set up regional partnerships combining the interests of the different groups.

According to Cruise UK, the economic value of cruise ships to the UK is worth about £17.5 million to ports of call. Add to this the value of ships using UK ports for embarkation, and the value soars to about £35 million.

The main economic benefits of cruising are achieved by ports. Building, decking out and furnishing these liners is a business in itself. Cruise ships generate local employment in the ports where they berth and their passengers and crews are potential spenders.

Case study: waive the port fees, says Carnival boss

Cruise lines that bring valued income into destinations should have port charges waived – or even be paid to visit.

Philip Naylor, Carnival UK's fleet operations general manager, claimed existing port charges did not reflect the economic benefits that cruise lines could bring to destinations.

'We sometimes feel like we are providing a free source of tourists to these destinations,' he said.

'It might make economic sense to exempt cruise lines from some or all costs, or perhaps cruise ships could even be paid for port calls.'

Naylor criticised many ports for poor planning and failing to give a clear indication of berth availability.

But his view was countered by Albert Poggio, director of the Gibraltar Port Authority and senior vice-president of MedCruise, which represents cruise ports in the Mediterranean. He said cruise lines tended to overestimate the benefits they provide to ports of call.

'Talking to the chambers of commerce, they feel they do not get a fair slice of the cake on a cruise call,' he said.

'They feel most passengers go on a tour that the cruise lines benefit from and which leaves them very little time to spread the wealth in the rest of the community.'

Per Schmidt, vice-chairman of northern Europe port association Cruise Europe, added that it would be difficult to give cruise lines preferential treatment to cargo firms.

'Ships need ports and ports need ships, but you also have to recognise that most Cruise Europe ports are mainly cargo ports,' he said. 'Only 10% of earnings derive from the cruise industry.'

Poggio argued that investment in destinations needed to come from ports, cruise lines and the destinations themselves.

'You can't leave the job of marketing to the ports,' he said. 'The tourist boards need to take a more hands-on responsibility.'

(Source: *Travel Trade Gazette* 16 February 2007)

1   **Summarise the arguments for and against waiving port fees for cruise ships.**

2   **Assess the economic impact of cruise ships on ports and make notes for discussion.**   **P5**

Key term

Ports of call – ports that the ship visits and the passengers can take a shore excursion if they wish. They have to get back on before the ship sails again! Hybrid ports are a mixture of all the others. When ports provide a major link to other countries or access to destinations within a country for trade or passengers, they are described as gateway ports.

Environmental impact

The following extract from Responsible Travel.com summarises the adverse environmental impacts of cruise ships.

*According to Climate Care, a cruise liner such as Queen Mary 2 emits **0.43 kg** of CO_2 per passenger mile, compared with **0.257 kg** for a long-haul flight (even allowing for the further damage of emissions being produced in the upper atmosphere). That means it is far greener to fly than cruise ...*

*According to a report by **The International Council on Clean Transportation** (ICCT), worldwide, oceangoing vessels produced at least 17% of total emissions of nitrogen oxide and contributed more than a quarter of total emissions of nitrogen oxide in port cities and coastal areas. The report also points out that carbon-dioxide emissions from the international shipping sector as a whole exceed annual total greenhouse gas emissions from most of the developed nations listed in the Kyoto Protocol.*

'International ships are one of the world's largest, virtually uncontrolled sources of air pollution … air pollution from international ships is rising virtually unchecked,' said ICCT president Alan Lloyd.

On a typical one-week voyage a cruise ship generates more than 50 tonnes of garbage and a million tonnes of grey (waste) water, 210,000 gallons of sewage and 35,000 gallons of oil-contaminated water. On average, passengers on a cruise ship each account for 3.5 kilograms of rubbish daily – compared with the 0.8 kilograms each generated by local people on shore.

(Source: http://www.responsibletravel.com/Copy/Copy100858.htm)

Growing awareness of these issues has led to cruise companies being subject to basic environmental standards imposed by the International Maritime Organisation. Also the International Convention for the Prevention of Pollution from Ships gives guidelines on how to dispose of rubbish, waste and sewage.

Some ships are trying to reduce the waste produced by cutting down the use of disposable items. Recycling is possible, with Carnival, for example, achieving a 65 per cent recycling rate.

Another problem is that new development inevitably takes up land or sea and may result in the loss of a historic landscape. For example, all nature groups in and around Southampton are protesting about the port development at Dibden Bay which impinges on the New Forest National Park. This is a container port not a passenger port but will destroy salt meadows

and the habitat of rare birds and plants. Residents will experience an increase in heavy traffic to the port. The regional authorities argue that developing sea trade is vital to the region's economy.

Consider this

Think about the increase in pollution from many ships in port. What can be done to minimise this impact?

Social/cultural impact

Where new facilities are provided, such as shops and restaurants, they can provide a social benefit to local people – if they can afford to use them. However, many cruise shopping centres are closed to local residents and are built purely for the use of cruise passengers. With some types of tourism, local residents benefit from interaction with different cultures and from the provision of goods and services. Although we have noted that cruise passengers do increase spending in the ports of call, this type of tourism has severe drawbacks for locals. Passengers get all their meals on board so they do not need to eat in port. They do not stay in hotels so they spend less than those tourists who stay for one or two weeks. They are unlikely to interact with local people on a fleeting day visit.

Consider this

What could passengers do to try to bring positive social impacts to a destination port? **P4**

Case study: San Francisco cruise industry

The cruise industry in San Francisco is seasonal, lasting from May to October. This is because many cruises to Alaska start from San Francisco and these only take place in the summer. San Francisco is also a home port, as many Americans drive to the port to embark on their cruise and disembark at the end.

'Repositioning' also occurs in San Francisco. This means that ships which have been cruising in the Caribbean, for example, come to San Francisco at the end of the season in order to begin the Alaskan season. This happens in reverse at the end of the summer. San Francisco is also a port of call for round-the-world cruises.

As a port of embarkation it is vital that the city has access to a major international airport so that passengers can be flown in to join their cruise.

How can San Francisco alleviate the problems of seasonal activity at its ports?

Key term

Repositioning – cruise lines have to move ships at the end of a season to get them to the right place to start the next season. If they can they will sell these cruises to passengers. The cruises have a different itinerary from those advertised, with less time in ports, but they represent good value for money.

Let us look at some of the cruising areas in more detail. Make sure you are able to locate each area on a map.

The Mediterranean

The Mediterranean is the most popular destination for British travellers, whether sailing from home ports or by fly-cruise. Some of the increase in fly-cruises to the Mediterranean was accounted for by the new brand, Ocean Village. This is a P&O subsidiary and targets younger, first-time cruisers in the UK. The advantage of a fly-cruise to the Mediterranean is that the flight is very short and passengers reach the sun quickly. Another reason for the increase in trips to the Mediterranean is the greater range of UK departure ports for cruises, especially in the south of England. Using these ports allows passengers to take a western European cruise for a week or two without having to fly.

Cyprus used to be a popular departure port for cruises but it has slumped in popularity as it is so close to the Iraq conflict zone.

More than 20 cruise companies operate in the Mediterranean. It is split into four seas: the Adriatic, the Aegean, the Ionian and the Tyrrhenian, and cruises take varied routes around these.

Asia/Far East

Assessment practice

The following is an example of a cruise in Thailand offered by Kuoni.

> Voyage through Thailand's Andaman Sea on board the romantic tall ship, *Star Flyer* (Jan–Mar), and *Star Clipper* (Nov–Dec). Cruise around Phuket and Southern Asia seeing beautiful islands, beaches and cities.
>
> **Travelling on:** *Star Flyer* or *Star Clipper*
>
> **Our opinion**
> *Star Clipper*, a fully restored clipper ship with billowing sails, provides a fantastic cruising experience. A unique opportunity to combine traditional sailing with pampered relaxation and romance, whilst visiting hidden corners of the Orient.
>
> **Escorted**
> Local assistance given
>
> **Itinerary**
> Bangkok: 3 nights
> Cruise (South): 7 nights
> Visiting: Batong Group, Penang, Ko Lipe, Ko Khai Nok, Phong Nga, Ko Hong and Similan Islands
> Phuket: 4 nights
>
> (Source: http://www.kuoni.co.uk/cruise/Far_East/Thailand/tt88082007.html)

Find a map of these islands and sketch the itinerary. Identify the ports of call and the gateway port. Do some research on this area and its islands. Assess the impact of cruising on this area. **M3**

The Caribbean/Americas

This is the second most popular cruise area for UK cruisers. Almost all of these cruises are fly-cruises. The appeal lies in being able to take a one- or two-week cruise in the hot sun of the Caribbean without having to sail there first. It enables passengers to fit a cruise into their annual holiday period. The Caribbean is a popular cruising area for North American passengers because of its proximity to home. The Caribbean is also suitable for year-round cruising, whereas the Mediterranean has far fewer cruises in winter. This means that there are a lot of ships operating in the Caribbean and therefore a lot of capacity available.

The advantage of going on a cruise to the Caribbean is that the passengers get to see many of the islands, visiting a different one each day. The disadvantage is that they don't get to know any of the islands very well and don't have an opportunity to meet local people. There are many islands to visit, all with different characters. French islands are Guadeloupe, Martinique, St Barthelemy and St Martin. There are the Dutch Antilles islands, the US Virgin Islands and Spanish-speaking islands of Cuba, Dominican Republic, Cayman Islands and Puerto Rico. Former British islands are, among others, Barbados, Jamaica and St Lucia.

An important environmental problem in the Caribbean is that affecting coral reefs. Coral reefs are an essential part of marine ecosystems. They are home to many marine fish species and thousands of other species. The reefs are also a source of income for fishermen and as a source of pharmaceutical compounds. They are also an attraction to cruise passengers. Cruise ships have to take responsibility for protecting the reefs and they can do this by careful anchoring so that they do not damage the reef and by not discharging wastewater near the reef.

The majority of ports in the Caribbean are ports of call. Many of them are isolated and have little infrastructure and few facilities. When ships call at ports without terminal facilities, they anchor out to sea and take passengers in by tender. Local people are aware of cruise ship arrival times and will flock to the port to sell local produce or offer taxi services to the passengers. This brings economic benefit to the community.

Assessment practice

Below is the itinerary for a cruise offered by Princess Cruises in the Caribbean.

(Source: Princess Cruises Caribbean Cruises brochure 2007/2008)

▲ **Figure 10.8 Map of Caribbean**

1   Using a blank map of the Caribbean plot the route of this itinerary.

2   Choose two of the islands to be visited and describe what there is for cruise passengers to do in a day's visit.

3   Describe the impacts of cruising on the Caribbean area and on the ports in the area. Make detailed notes on your findings.   **M3** **P5**

4   Make realistic recommendations about how to maximise positive and negative impacts of cruising in this area.   **D2**

Day	Port	Arrive	Depart
1	**FLY UK/BARBADOS**		
	Transfer and embark *Sea Princess*		11.00pm
2	**ST. LUCIA**	8.00am	6.00pm
3	**ANTIGUA**	8.00am	6.00pm
4	**ST. MAARTEN**	7.00am	5.00pm
5	**ST. THOMAS** (US Virgin Islands)	7.00am	4.00pm
6	**GRAND TURK** (Turks and Caicos Islands)	1.00pm	6.00pm
7	At sea		
8	**MONTEGO BAY** (Jamaica)	7.00am	10.00pm
9	**GRAND CAYMAN** (Cayman Islands) ⚓	10.00am	5.00pm
10	At sea		
11	**ARUBA**	9.00am	6.00pm
12	**BONAIRE**	8.00am	5.00pm
13	**CARACAS** (Venezuela) from La Guaira	8.00am	5.00pm
14	**GRENADA** ⚓	12 noon	6.00pm
15	**BARBADOS**	7.00am	
	Disembark *Sea Princess* and transfer to the airport for your overnight flight to the UK.		
16	**ARRIVE UK**		

(Source: Princess Cruises Caribbean Cruises brochure 2007/2008)

▲ **Figure 10.9 Itinerary for Barbados**

Scandinavia

The Baltic region of northern Europe has been growing in popularity for a decade. The region includes the countries of Scandinavia and Russia and Estonia. People who choose Baltic cruises are more likely to be interested in seeing the culture of historic cities like St Petersburg and beautiful scenery than beaches. Good weather is not guaranteed although the summer months can be good and it is possible to see the midnight sun in Norway.

The following extract from Costa Cruises brochure gives a flavour of what is on offer in the Baltic.

> *Set sail for Northern Europe and prepare to be spellbound by a land of mesmerising scenery and natural splendour – waterfalls, islands, lakes, streams and rivers, not to mention green or snow-topped mountains! Quaint little villages, some dating back to mediaeval times and lively modern cities which all add up to create a place where beauty and wonder combine in perfect harmony, where the magnificence of the midnight sun will inspire you and the culture and traditions of the northern capitals will captivate you …*

(Source: Costa Cruising Summer 2007 brochure)

The economic impact of cruises to Oslo has been documented. Passengers spend 76 million Norwegian krone per year on excursions, shopping, restaurants and visits to attractions. This is replicated in all ports but as the weather is not so favourable in northern Europe spending is likely to be greater as passengers look for alternative activities.

Arctic

Cruise ships only visit this area in the summer months as some parts become unnavigable in the winter. UK passengers fly from home to join their ships in North America, often in Vancouver or Seattle. Visitors experience wonderful scenery at close hand on these voyages. They can see fjords, waterfalls and mountains.

Many trips include the cities and towns of Ketchikan and Juneau. Some of the ships pass along 'The Inside

Passage'. This is a narrow pass, shaped by the force of massive glaciers, through a chain of islands surrounded by mountains and forests. The islands separate the Inside Passage from the Pacific Ocean.

It is possible to take a route that goes from Vancouver to Anchorage and includes glaciers such as Hubbard Glacier in Yakutat Bay and Columbia Glacier in College Fjord.

In this area the shores are very delicate and vulnerable and subject to environmental danger.

Another problem in this area is that small communities of only a few hundred may be visited by a few ships at one time and be completely overwhelmed.

Antarctica

A really adventurous cruise crosses the Antarctic Circle, reaching an extreme latitude at the very bottom of the world. The most popular time is January and February, taking advantage of the long days at this time of year in the area. Passengers go to explore wildlife and can expect to see colonies of penguins, great whales and hundreds of seals. They will also see thousands of floating icebergs, glaciers and dramatic cliff views. On land, passengers may see leopard seals, elephant seals and Antarctic fur seals.

These cruises have to operate under high environmental safety standards to ensure the protection of the wildlife. The International Association of Antarctic Tour Operators sets guidelines on protection.

Nile

Some cruises take place on rivers and this type of cruising is also growing in popularity.

We will look particularly at the Nile as a destination. It is traditionally the most popular river cruise area but has fallen in popularity due to terrorist activity in Egypt against tourists and problems with food hygiene on river boats.

Holidays on the Nile are primarily intended for those who want to sightsee. This includes highlights such as visits to the temples of Karnak and Luxor, and the magnificent Valley of the Kings. At certain times of

the year, particularly in the winter months, there can be low water levels on the Nile and the itinerary then has to change. The river is very busy with cruise ships – some might find it overcrowded – and when boats are moored for the night all the passengers can see is the next boat.

Below is an example of a typical Nile itinerary.

DAY 1

In the afternoon visit the well-preserved XVIIIth Dynasty Temple of Luxor and the enormous Temple of Karnak, whose construction took more than 1000 years.

DAY 2

Early in the morning cross to the West Bank of the Nile to explore the tombs of the Pharaohs in the Valley of the Kings. We also see the Valley of the Queens, the elegant mortuary temple of Queen Hatshepsut at Deir el-Bahri and the Colossi of Memnon. Sail in the afternoon to Esna.

DAY 3

Sail to Edfu where a visit is made to the monumental Temple of Horus. Continue sailing to Kom Ombo.

DAY 4

At Kom Ombo visit the Ptolemaic temple dedicated to the two gods Sobek and Haroeris, from where there is also a fine view over the Nile. Sail to Aswan, where afternoon sightseeing includes the High Dam, the ancient Granite Quarries and the beautiful Temple of Isis at Philae.

DAY 5

Optional excursion to Abu Simbel.

(Source: Adapted from 'Treasures of the Nile' cruise from Bales Worldwide brochure)

Figure 10.10 A cruise ship on the Nile

Assessment practice

Choose four of the cruise areas described in this section.

1 Describe each area. **P4**

2 Describe the impact of cruising on each area, including the gateway ports and the ports of call. **P5**

3 Choose one of the areas and assess the impact of cruising. **M3**

10.5 Know the employment opportunities in the cruise sector

When we talk about working in the cruise sector, remember that not all jobs are on board ship. There are many opportunities at corporate headquarters and at terminals. However, it is likely that if you are attracted to this sector then you are thinking about travelling the world as you work!

Consider this

Do you get seasick? It is worth thinking about this because you will not be able to work on a ship if you do!

On-board job opportunities

Theory into practice

Spend a few minutes with your group discussing what types of jobs are available on cruise ships. Make a list.

There are probably more than 150 different jobs available on a ship so we will not attempt to cover them all.

You should have thought about jobs in the following different departments:

- retail
- entertainment
- engineering
- bars and restaurants
- fitness
- shore excursions
- reception
- beauty and hairdressing
- decks
- housekeeping
- tours
- medical
- casino.

There may also be openings for photographers, lecturers and florists.

Sometimes departments are contracted out and that means if you want to apply for a position you have to apply to the contracted company not to the ship. Beauty salon positions are often assigned in this way. Steiner is a salon that has many cruise ship contracts.

You need to match your qualifications and jobs to specific skills. It is likely that, as you are reading this book, you are a travel and tourism student and therefore interested in the types of positions that such a course could lead to. Of course, if you have a fitness training qualification, have done bar work before or worked in a shop, you have more areas open to you. Our examples will be those most closely related to travel and tourism.

Whatever job you are interested in, you will have to speak English fluently, and many jobs require one or two further languages, so sign up for those language classes now!

Activity

Below are three examples of cruise ship jobs for which travel and tourism students could apply. One requires a degree so we are thinking ahead in this case. For each example note the role and responsibilities and the entry requirements.

Job title: Assistant purser
Department: Reception
Responsibilities:
- gives general information
- deals with accommodation problems
- deals with complaints
- carries out shipboard announcements

Person specification:
Must have customer service experience. Must have excellent administration background. Good social and communication skills needed. Must be fluent English speaker. Second language preferred.
Location: Caribbean
Salary: £1600–1800 per month

Job title: Tour Assistant
Department: Tours
Responsibilities:
- gives passengers information about excursions
- takes bookings for shore excursions
- arranges disembarkation
- accompanies tours.

Person specification:
Must have customer service experience. Must have travel related or cruise ship experience – one year minimum. Good social and communication skills needed. Must be fluent English speaker. Second language preferred.
Location: Alaska cruises
Salary: US $2300 per month plus percentage of sales revenue.

Job title: Customer Service Director
Department: Administration
Responsibilities:
- achieves service goals through co-ordinating hospitality activities
- ensures that all guest requests, enquiries and complaints are responded to promptly
- arranges necessary maintenance and repairs

Person specification:
- good team-working skills
- professional appearance and excellent social skills
- degree in Hospitality Management or Tourism Management
- cruise ship experience desirable
- fluent English, additional languages preferred
- computer knowledge: Word and Excel.

Consider this

There are a lot of websites which will try to sell you books about opportunities on cruise ships. Don't buy them. If you want a book go to your college or school library. Cruise lines all advertise their positions on their websites so you can easily see what is available by going directly to the cruise-line websites.

Key term

OTE or on target earnings – often seen in advertisements for jobs, this means that you can expect to earn the stated figure if you meet the set targets. The basic salary may be only half this amount.

Landside job opportunities

The opportunities with cruise lines on land are similar to those of any tour operator. Some of the cruise lines are based in the USA and therefore it would be unlikely that British students would be able to get jobs with them. Some cruise lines have offices in Europe, for example Royal Caribbean has an office in Weybridge, Surrey.

The jobs you would expect to find would be in:

- marketing
- finance
- human resources
- customer service
- reservations.

Below is an example of a position in telesales.

**TELESALES – CRUISE COMPANY
OTE 16K BASIC TO 25K**

Responsibilities:

- to make outbound and receive inbound sales calls to sell cruises

- to maximise revenue by offering alternative dates, routes, classes, upgrades and other services to customers

- to participate in promotional campaigns.

The applicant must have at least 18-months' sales experience, preferably within a call centre. Must be a team player and must be able to meet performance targets.

Some homeworkers in travel sales prefer to specialise in selling cruises. They can earn higher commissions than from other sales and it is a growing market so there are many customers to target. Homeworkers are sometimes called 'travel counsellors' and may be affiliated to a large network. You cannot set up as a homeworker without a lot of experience in a travel agency.

Some landside job opportunities are available in port. The jobs available in a port are similar to those in an airport. Customers have to be checked in, their baggage has to be transferred to the ship and in addition staff are needed to run all the facilities at the terminal, such as restaurants and shops. These jobs do not require many qualifications or experience unless you are applying for supervisory or management level positions. As many of the jobs are customer facing, experience of customer service is useful.

Working environment

Shift work

You will work long hours – it is not a nine-to-five type of job. You might have to work seven days a week as well. You won't really be off duty because when you are not working you are still on the ship and you have to be pleasant to the passengers. You cannot escape from the work environment or your colleagues and that can be a cause of stress.

Accommodation

As a worker you will not get the 'royal suite' kind of accommodation! You will get the most basic cabin on the lowest deck and you will have to share. However, as ships become more and more luxurious it is true to say that the staff accommodation also improves. Also, the more senior your position the better your accommodation. There is no journey to work and even if you don't get paid much you will have food and accommodation provided. You will be able to save most of your earnings.

It will be your responsibility to make sure that your passport, visas and vaccinations are up to date, although you will be told what is required.

Holidays

Working on a cruise ship is a bit like a holiday. You will have the chance to see the world. There are opportunities to visit ports of call and the ship will revisit the same places regularly so you will get to know them quite well. Your contract will be for a few months and you will not be paid in the off-contract time. If you leave during the contract you will have to pay your fare home.

Consider this

What can employees expect from Carnival? Slightly lowered salaries and somewhat lower standards when selecting candidates compared to most of the other major cruise lines. Carnival crew members are like their clientele, they like to party and most of them believe that the more 'loose' atmosphere and the presence of younger passengers makes up for the slightly lower salaries.

If you are very interested in working for a cruise line take a look at www.cruiseplacement.com. It gives brief profiles of cruise lines and what to expect from working for them. There are also details of current vacancies.

Case study: matching profiles to jobs

1   Considering what you have read about the working environment on board ship and the examples of jobs available, study the three profiles of travel and tourism students below and say which ones are suitable for employment on a cruise ship. Explain why and say what kind of job they could do.

2   Now draw up a similar profile about yourself. Exchange this with a colleague and consider who is suitable for work on cruise ships. Decide what steps you might have to take to prepare for work on a cruise ship and produce a plan of action. **P6**

Student profile 1

Malika has completed a BTEC National Certificate in Travel and Tourism. She is 27 and wants to see the world. Before she returned to college to take her BTEC she worked in a bank for 6 years, so she has a lot of customer service experience. She also has several bookkeeping and banking qualifications which she achieved at the bank. Malika was born in Morocco although she does have a British passport now. She speaks fluent French, Arabic and English. While studying for her BTEC qualification she worked at the airport on check-in. She is sociable, charming and of smart appearance.

Student profile 2

Greg has completed a BTEC National Certificate and wants to see the world. He has found all the details of cruise lines and recruitment on websites already as he is very good at using the internet. Greg is a fairly quiet person. He doesn't contribute much in class as he is never sure that he has the right answers. His written work is poorly produced and without depth although he did do enough to pass the course. The other students never wanted to work with him as he has little to contribute to group work. His hobby is train-spotting and he has a part-time job in a cafe. He went to Majorca on holiday with two friends last year and enjoyed it. There was a residential study trip to Barcelona on his course but he didn't go as he didn't want to take the time off work.

Student profile 3

Charlotte is 19 and has also completed a BTEC qualification, the National Diploma in Travel and Tourism. She has travelled quite a lot on holidays with her family and twice with friends. She is a very loyal person and conscientious and has a lot of respect from others in her group. She is very well presented and works in a hairdressing salon in her spare time. She wants to work on a cruise ship but doesn't know how easy it will be to get a job at 19. She hasn't worked in travel and tourism apart from work placements as she has had the job in the salon for 3 years. The manager of the salon wants her to work full time and complete the NVQ in hairdressing.

Knowledge check

1 Describe the 'golden age' of cruising.

2 What is a fly-cruise?

3 What are the benefits of integration?

4 What does the Passenger Shipping Association do?

5 What is the appeal of the Mediterranean as a cruise area?

6 Describe the different kinds of ports.

7 What is the environmental impact of port development?

8 What is a repositioning cruise?

9 What is new about the Ocean Village cruising concept?

10 What is new about easyCruise?

11 Why is there an increase in cruising among UK tourists?

12 What are the pluses and minuses of working on a cruise ship?

13 Why are languages useful to work on a ship?

14 What kinds of jobs are available on land?

Preparation for assessment

You have managed to get a work placement on a travel and tourism trade magazine. This is a very prestigious placement and you are delighted. You are spending four weeks at the magazine. The first week was an introduction to the work and meeting all the staff. Now, your line manager wants you to take on your own project. The magazine produces a specialist supplement every three months and one of them is to be about cruising. The content has already been decided and your job is to do the research and put all the information together. You can include suggested text, illustrations, photos, maps and charts but the printing and publication will be done professionally later.

When you are doing your research and putting your information together remember that the supplement is not aimed at the general public but at the travel and tourism trade.

1 Explain the development and structure of the cruise sector. Consider:
   - Origins
   - Changing consumer demands and needs
   - Cruise operators
   - Links with other sectors
   - Integration
   - Regulatory bodies.   **P1**

Analyse opportunities for future growth witin the current cruise sector.   **D1**

Grading tip

To achieve distinction you must give at least two examples of possibilities for growth with your reasons.

2 Describe the facilities and cruises available from different types of ships.   **P2**

Grading tip

Do lots of research for this task and give specific examples.

Choose two different types of cruises and compare and contrast their facilities and routes.   **M1**

3 Select appropriate cruises that would appeal to the following customers.
   - A group of friends in their early thirties who have never cruised before. They do not want to spend more than £1000 each on a 7–10 night cruise. They can go anytime in the summer. They want to visit a lot of different places and they want plenty of activities on board. They are not interested in 'dressing up'.
   - Sheila and Brian are in their fifties. Their children are grown and independent. Sheila and Brian enjoy cruising and like luxury. They always have an outside cabin with a balcony. This time they want an adults-only cruise with a theme. The theme could be related to one of their interests such as cooking or dancing. They are prepared to pay a lot and they will expect high service and excellent food.   **P3**

Explain how the cruises you have selected appeal to these customers.   **M2**

4 Describe four cruise areas of the world. Include maps with the areas marked. **P4**

Grading tip

The regions should be described in terms of itineraries, ports of call, gateways, examples of excursions and types of ships.

5 Describe the positive and negative impacts of cruising on cruise areas, gateway ports and ports of call. **P5**

Choose one cruise area and assess the impact of cruising on that area. **M3**

Make realistic recommendations about how to maximise positive and minimise negative impacts of cruising in that area. **D2**

6 Describe the employment opportunities available in the cruise sector. **P6**

Grading tip

Include at least three different jobs from different areas or at different levels. Describe the job role and responsibilities and the entry requirements.

Grading criteria

To achieve a pass grade the evidence must show that the learner is able to:	To achieve a merit grade the evidence must show that, in addition to the pass criteria, the learner is able to:	To achieve a distinction grade the evidence must show that, in addition to the pass and merit criteria, the learner is able to:
P1 explain the development and structure of the cruise sector **Assessment practice page 10**	**M1** compare and contrast the routes and ship facilities of two different types of cruises **Assessment practice pages 11–12**	**D1** analyse opportunities for future growth within the current cruise sector **Assessment practice page 10**
P2 describe the facilities and cruises available from different types of ships **Assessment practice pages 11–12**	**M2** explain how the selected cruises appeal to the customer **Assessment practice page 20**	**D2** make realistic recommendations about how to maximise positive and minimise negative impacts of cruising **Assessment practice page 26**
P3 select appropriate cruises that would appeal to two different types of customers **Assessment practice page 20**	**M3** explain the impacts of cruising on a selected cruise area **Assessment practice page 25**	
P4 describe four cruise areas of the world **Consider this page 23**		
P5 describe the impacts of cruising on one cruise area, its gateway ports and ports of call **Consider this page 22**		
P6 describe three different employment opportunities available in the cruise sector **Consider this page 31**		

12 Tour operations

Introduction

Tour operators have been very important in the development of the travel and tourism industry, from the first Thomas Cook package to today's vast tour-operating industry.

In this unit you will find out what tour operators do and how they link with other organisations in the travel and tourism industry.

You will learn about different types of tour operators and examine their ranges of products and services and how they cater for different customer needs. Travel and tourism is a dynamic industry and tour operators have to respond to changes within it. We will examine their particular challenges and responses.

We will examine the ways in which the business of tour operating is carried out, including the planning, developing, selling and operating of package-holiday programmes, both in the UK and overseas.

You will undertake some practical activities in planning and costing a package for a tour operator.

After completing this unit you should be able to achieve the following outcomes:

1   Understand the tour operations environment
2   Know the range of products and services offered by tour operators for different target markets
3   Know how tour operators plan, sell, administer and operate a package holiday programme
4   Be able to plan and cost a package holiday.

Thinking points

A tour operator designs and puts together package holidays and tours for sale to customers. These products and services are sold through travel agencies or directly to the customer through call centres, websites and television channels. To put the package together, the tour operator must contract the services of airlines, hotels and transport organisations.

The number of visits abroad made by UK residents has more than tripled since 1985, to a record 66.4 million visits in 2005. Two-thirds of these visits abroad were holidays, just under half of which were package holidays. Although the number of holidays overall has continued to increase year-on-year, there has been a fall in the number of package holidays in the last five years.

(Source: Travel Trends 2006 (International Passenger Survey); http://www.statistics.gov.uk/CCI/nugget.asp?ID=178&Pos=2&ColR ank=2&Rank=224)

There are some important points to note from this extract from Travel Trends.

- UK residents are making more visits abroad than ever before.
- Nearly half of holidays taken abroad are package holidays.
- There has been a decline in the number of package holidays over the last five years.

In this unit we will find out what the impact of these facts is for tour operators.

Links with other sectors

Links with travel agents

Tour operators traditionally sell their products through travel agents. They pay agents commission – this is variable, but can be in the region of 10 per cent. They also provide travel agents with a range of support services to help them sell. These include training packages, special incentives and educational trips. They provide promotional material including brochures and posters.

The current situation is difficult, as tour operators try to balance their relationship with travel agents alongside offering customers direct booking and internet services. Even where operations are vertically integrated, tour operators are looking closely at the role of the travel agent and deciding whether to maintain so many branches or switch to other types of distribution.

Links with transport providers

■ Airlines

Tour operators use charter flights to provide transport to holiday destinations as part of the package. Some tour operators have their own airlines but still have to charter them within the group as they are run as separate companies.

If the own-brand airline cannot provide enough capacity, the tour operator will charter outside the group. Similarly, if the own-brand airline has excess capacity, planes can be offered for charter to another tour operator.

Charter airlines supply planes and staff to tour operators according to their specified needs. For example, a tour operator may ask for a plane and crew for a once-a-week service from Luton to Ibiza, from May until September. The tour operator orders planes for the routes and the length of time it needs. It has a contract with the charter airline and then sells the holidays itself. Many tour operators sell seat-only flights to fill spare capacity.

Key terms

Charter flight – a flight rented by a tour operator to fly for short seasons to holiday destinations. Small operators can group together to charter a flight.

Scheduled flight – a flight which runs to a set timetable throughout the year. Timetables are adjusted for winter and summer seasons.

Tour operators also offer scheduled airline seats on more 'upmarket' packages. They may buy a block of seats and then incorporate them into a package, or they may request seats from the airline as customers book the package. Such seats often involve a supplement to the passenger as they are more complicated to arrange and perceived as better service.

■ Rail and bus companies

Tour operators often provide transport other than flights as part of a package holiday. They may be organising a coach tour, in which case a coach must be chartered. Trains must be booked for rail tours. The tour operator will get favourable rates for tickets depending on the quantity booked.

Tour operators need fleets of coaches to transfer holidaymakers from airports to their destination in resort and to run their programmes of excursions.

■ Ferries and cruise ships

Camping tour operators in particular have traditionally arranged ferry crossings for customers who prefer to drive to their holiday destination. Some tour operators specialise in cruises and may book a number of places on ships or even own their own cruise ship.

Links with accommodation providers

Tour operators' links with hotels can be very complex. Large tour operators may have global deals organised centrally. There may be multi-property relationships when dealing with a chain of hotels or there may be an individual relationship between a tour operator and one hotel. The tour operator has to contract accommodation – beds, rooms or tents – before the season. The number of units booked is known as the allocation.

Accommodation is central to a package. Both parties must agree what is included and what the terms are. The allocation period must also be agreed. When bookings are taken, they are reserved from the allocation of accommodation units; any further capacity required is 'on request' from the accommodation provider.

Links with providers of ancillary products and services

Selling extra services brings more revenue to the tour operator just as it does to a travel agent or airline. A customer may be confused in trying to decide whether to buy car hire, insurance or add-on products from the travel agent, tour operator or airline. They are all in competition for the same business. The tour operator makes deals with car-hire companies and finance companies to sell their products.

Horizontal and vertical integration

Major integrated travel and tourism companies dominate the market. In 2007, First Choice Holidays plc merged with TUI UK and MyTravel Group plc merged with Thomas Cook UK Ltd. These companies are not only tour operators but own different brands of retail travel agents and airline operators.

See Table 12.1 for who owns whom. Distribution on the internet has not been included. Ownership is correct at the time of writing, but quickly changes as companies buy and sell subsidiaries – you should check for the latest information.

You are already aware of the concepts of vertical and horizontal integration, and Table 12.1 clearly illustrates the extent of integration in the largest UK tour-operating groups. You can see how it is possible for the groups to vertically control all of the chain of distribution, from creating the package to selling it via their own travel agents. Horizontal distribution is also apparent, especially in tour operating, where the groups have several subsidiaries.

Case study: Jet2 Holidays

Low-cost airline Jet2.com has joined forces with the On Holiday Group to offer real-time, dynamically packaged holidays and claims the new venture will 'attack the heart of traditional tour operating'.

It will launch Jet2holidays.com later this month, backed by a multi-million pound advertising campaign.

Jet2holidays.com is also currently in discussion with a major retail chain about selling the product within its network of shops.

Holidays will be dynamically packaged from three-, four- and five-star hotel stock and paired with Jet2.com flights, so customers are not constrained by weekly departure dates.

Packages will include taxi transfers and on-demand holiday reps.

Jet2holidays.com boss Philip Meeson said: 'Our business model is based on a relatively straightforward principle of matching low-cost flights with high quality hotel stock – but until new technology was developed, it had remained an untapped market.'

He said agents can add service charges if they wish, and there will be no brochures.

Instead, Jet2holidays.com will offer a website which allows agents to book the holiday their customers want at the click of a mouse, with no hidden extras or costs passed on from such wasteful practices as brochure production.

(Source: http://www.travelmole.com/stories/1115529.php?news_cat–10)

1 **Explain how Jet2 Holidays links with other sectors in the travel and tourism industry.**

2 **How will the Jet2 operation impact on other tour operators?**

There are benefits to integration:
- economies of scale as the company grows
- control over the supply of accommodation and flights
- control over distribution
- larger market share
- less competition
- established reputations.

A few years ago the large tour operators were in control of the holiday market and were acquiring everything they could, from hotels to cruise ships. Although these companies are still vast, they are now consolidating their operations, merging similar subsidiaries and concentrating more on specialist operations in the face of a changing market, where customers are no longer seeking mass-market products and are happy to travel independently.

You can expect to see further changes in these large groups over the next few years. To remain competitive, they will have to get rid of companies which are outside their core business of holidays, and they will have to change the nature of their products, concentrating on more specialist holidays. In addition, distribution is changing and all the tour operators have direct selling and online booking, although they have not abandoned the traditional travel agency route.

Case study

15 January 2007

Virgin enters First Choice mainstream bidding?

Virgin has emerged as a surprise new bidder for the mainstream business of First Choice.

MyTravel has already expressed an interest in the package holiday arm of First Choice while Thomas Cook is also seen as a likely candidate.

However, a Virgin spokesman was quoted in the *Daily Telegraph* as saying 'we're looking at it'.

Speculation centres on Virgin Holidays teaming up with a private equity firm to make an offer.

The First Choice mainstream holiday arm is expected to be worth more than £500 million.

(Source: http://www.travelmole.com/stories/1115167.php)

1 **Why do you think First Choice was planning to sell the mainstream part of its business?**

2 **Would Virgin be integrating horizontally or vertically with this acquisition?**

3 **Why would Virgin be interested in acquiring this company?**   **P1**

4 **What was the outcome of Virgin's interest?**

Consider this

Why do these large tour operating groups have so many brands? Should they make it obvious to the customer that they all belong to a particular group?

Theory into practice

Choose one of the large tour operating groups. Find out how it came to acquire so many tour-operating companies. For example, First Choice has a history page on its website (www.firstchoiceholidaysplc.com). Has the pattern of acquisition changed? Have any subsidiaries been sold? Make notes and compare them with your group.

Parent company	UK company	Tour operations (UK)	Retail travel (UK)	Airlines (UK)	Others
Thomas Cook AG	Thomas Cook	Club 18–30 Flexible trips JMC Latitude Neilson Style Sunset Sunworld Ireland Thomas Cook Thomas Cook Signature	Thomas Cook	Thomas Cook Airlines	Parent company has many other interests including hotels
First Choice plc	First Choice	Citalia Crown Blue Line Exodus Flexiski Flexi Conference and Incentive Falcon First Choice Hayes and Jarvis Island Cruises JWT Meon Villas Platinum Sovereign Sunquest Sunsail Sunstart 2wentys thevillapool Unijet	First Choice Travel Holiday Hypermarkets Hayes Travel	First Choice Airways	Also has Suncars (hire car) and First4extras
MyTravel Group	MyTravel UK and Ireland	Airtours Aspro Belgium Travel Services Bridge Cresta Direct Holidays Escapades Manos Paris Travel Services Panorama Swiss Travel Tradewinds	Going Places	MyTravel Airways	Global interests including hotels, e.g. Aquasun Also White Horse Insurance
TUI AG	TUI UK	American Holidays Club Freestyle Crystal International Holidays Headwater Jetsave and Jersey Travel Just Magic Travel Group OSL the Villa People Portland Direct Simply Travel Skytours Something Special Thomson brands Tropical Places	Thomson Team Lincoln	Thomsonfly	Parent company has several divisions including large hotel groups Thomson has five cruise ships

Table 12.1 Companies owned by the large tour operating groups before the merger in 2007

Links with trade and regulatory bodies

There are several associations and regulatory bodies which impact on tour operation. These include:

- Association of British Travel Agents (ABTA)
- Federation of Tour Operators (FTO)
- Association of Independent Tour Operators (AITO)
- European Tour Operators Association (ETOA)
- UKinbound
- Civil Aviation Authority (CAA).

ABTA

You were introduced to ABTA in Unit 1. Many tour operators join ABTA for the same benefits as travel agents. There are 808 tour operator members, and 85 per cent of the UK's package holidays are sold through ABTA members. The bonding requirements apply to tour operators as well as travel agents, and ABTA holds bonds of about £306 million for tour operators.

FTO

The role of the FTO is to act as a point of contact between outbound tour operators and government bodies in the UK, in the EU and in destinations served, on matters relating to tour operation. It represents its members' interests with other trade associations, and co-ordinates members' activities with regard to operational matters, for example on health and safety. It also represents its members at the International Federation of Tour Operators. A full list of its activities can be found on the FTO website (www.fto.co.uk) along with a list of members.

AITO

The AITO represents about 160 of the UK's specialist tour operators. All the members are independent companies, and often they are owner managed. The companies which join AITO agree to adhere to its Quality Charter, which has three key principles of choice, quality and service. Full details of the charter and

a list of members can be found on the AITO website, www.aito.co.uk. Like the other associations, AITO insists that its members are bonded and expects to see details of bonding arrangements before membership.

ETOA

The ETOA was founded in 1989 and has about 110 tour-operator members. The association was founded to ensure that tour operators were fully aware of the implications of the Package Holiday Directive. ETOA has established a track record of influencing travel and tourism legislation at both national and European levels. It provides individual companies with representation at European level, ensuring that members' needs and concerns are understood by EU institutions.

UKinbound

UKinbound is the official trade body representing UK inbound tourism. The association represents over 290 major companies and organisations in all sectors of the industry, operating over 4000 outlets in the UK.

The primary aim of the association is to help our members manage successful, profitable businesses that are part of a vibrant and sustainable inbound tourism industry.

Objectives

Advocacy – *To champion the interests of our members with Government to ensure we have a legislative and fiscal framework that allows their businesses to grow and prosper.*

Professionalism – *To promote 'Best Practice' and encourage lifelong learning. To facilitate the provision of vocational and management training that will improve quality, encourage staff development and provide the prospect of a fulfilling and rewarding career path.*

Networking – *To provide the opportunities for our members to develop relationships with suppliers, buyers and partners both abroad and in the UK through a programme of business and social events.*

(Source: http://www.ukinbound.org/content.php?page=conduct)

Case study: UKinbound

In 2007, UKinbound celebrated its 30th anniversary. It was decided to have a 30th Anniversary Convention & Workshop at British Tourism Week. The aim was to recognise the progress made by the inbound tourism industry over the past 30 years whilst looking forward to the future development required to succeed in an increasingly competitive environment. The convention gave opportunities to network and some training workshops as well as a themed seventies party in the evening.

1　Why would UKinbound wish to be represented at British Tourism Week?

2　Explain the links UKinbound has with tour operators and with other component areas of travel and tourism.

3　Discuss the particular challenges facing inbound tour operators.　**P1** **M1**

CAA

The CAA has a role to play in providing tour operators with Air Travel Organisers' Licensing (ATOL). All tour operators selling packages must be bonded or protect the prepayments they hold. That means if they become bankrupt before travel, customers should get a refund, or, if they are already abroad, they will be able to return home without any extra payment.

Package holidays that include flights must be protected by ATOL. ATOL is a statutory scheme managed by the CAA to protect the public from losing money or being stranded abroad because of the failure of air travel firms.

All tour operators selling flights and air holidays are required to hold a licence from the CAA. In order to obtain a licence the company must provide proof of a bond, that is, a financial guarantee provided by a bank or insurance company. If the company fails, the CAA calls in the bond and uses the money to pay for people

abroad to continue their holidays, and to make refunds to those who have paid but not travelled.

It is the largest travel protection scheme in the UK, covering 28 million people, and the only one for flights and air holidays sold by tour operators. Unfortunately, companies frequently collapse so the scheme is much needed.

A year-long legal case ending in appeal in 2006 decided that anyone selling a package holiday must be protected by an ATOL. ABTA had tried to remove the need for agents to hold ATOLs. The judgement clarified that even dynamic packages (those tailor-made for customers) needed an ATOL.

Legal framework

Tour operators must adhere to relevant consumer legislation. Consumer protection laws affecting tour operators include the following.

EU Package Travel Regulations 1992

As a result of a European Directive, since 1993 all UK tour operators offering package holidays have been subject to the Package Travel Regulations. The regulations set out the tour operators' responsibilities to their customers and what customers can do if the regulations are breached. If there is a breach, the customer has a case against the tour operator, not each individual supplier.

The two principal sections of the regulations provide financial protection for prepayments and require tour operators to provide what is promised.

The main provisions are:

- tour operators are responsible for the safety of their customers in the accommodation, on the flight and so on, and must provide assistance in the resort
- tour operators must not give inaccurate brochure descriptions
- last-minute surcharges cannot be imposed
- if the operator becomes bankrupt there must be a guaranteed refund.

There are also regulations about the information that should be provided to the customer, and what happens if the contract is altered in any way.

There are requirements for the customer too. If customers have complaints they should report them in the resort so that the representative has an opportunity to resolve them. If they need to write to the tour operator to complain, this should be done within a reasonable period (usually 28 days).

Compensation and legal redress are available for customers through the UK courts when there is a breach of regulations. Booking conditions are issued by tour operators and explain all the requirements for both parties.

The Department of Trade and Industry provides a free booklet, *Looking into the Package Travel Regulations*, which fully explains the regulations.

Trade Descriptions Act 1968

Descriptions given must be truthful and accurate. This Act primarily affects tour operators, as they have to be careful that brochure descriptions adhere to the rules.

Supply of Goods and Services Act 1982 (amended 1994)

This Act says that the tour operator and the travel agent should ensure that the booking is carried out correctly, and the contract for the holiday should also be carried out using 'reasonable skill and care'. The holiday should comply with any descriptions and be of a satisfactory standard.

Consumer Protection Act 1987

It is Part 3 of the Act that is of interest to tour operators as it states that 'All compulsory charges should be included in the headline price and accurate. Any additional charges should be clearly displayed and quantified when advertised.' This means that tour operators have to be very clear what is included in their prices and make sure they state what is not included.

Disability Discrimination Act 1995

A person with a disability is anyone who has a physical or mental impairment which has a substantial or long-term adverse effect on their ability to carry out normal day-to-day activities.

This Act makes discrimination against people with disabilities unlawful in respect of employment, education and access to goods, facilities, services and premises.

Tour operators, like any other organisations, are required to make reasonable adjustments to accommodate people with disabilities. Examples include facilitating wheelchair access and relocating people with limited mobility to the ground floor, either for employment or for accommodation and access.

Contract law

If consumers think that the contract with a tour operator is unfair, they may have a case under the Unfair Terms in Consumer Contracts Regulations of 1999. The Office of Fair Trading gives examples of the kinds of terms which might be unfair. These include contracts where customers are not allowed to change holiday arrangements when they are unable to travel, even when they give reasonable notice, and where tour operators seek to put false limits on compensation for problems.

Key term

Contract – a legally binding exchange of promises or agreement between parties that the law will enforce.

Responsible companies lay out conditions in a Fair Trading Charter, together with their booking conditions. These form the basis of a legally binding contract between the two parties.

There are many sources of help when customers want to make complaints. They can approach their local Trading Standards Office; ABTA has an arbitration scheme; and there are consumer groups who will help holidaymakers register a complaint. Unfortunately, many people complain because they have not enjoyed the holiday and not read the booking conditions. The regulations therefore help both parties.

Licensing

We have already discussed the ATOL provided by the CAA. Remember too that many tour operators choose to belong to ABTA and take advantage of its bonding scheme. This is explained in Unit 9 in Book 1.

Theory into practice

Find a holiday complaint in a newspaper or on a website (search for 'holiday complaints'). Decide whether you think the complaint is valid and, if so, which legislation would apply. Swap your holiday complaint story with those of other group members.

External influences on the tour operations environment

Environmental factors

Environmental factors can adversely affect a holiday and the whole travel market. Examples include a series of hurricanes in 2004 and the outbreak of diseases such as bird flu. Other possible problems include floods, avalanches and oil spillages.

Obviously it is difficult to plan for natural disasters, but companies should have contingency plans in place to cover all eventualities.

Political factors

Sometimes, tour operators have to pull out of destinations completely because of political factors such as war or terrorism. The British Foreign Office gives up-to-date information on its website (www.fco.gov.uk) about the safety of destinations.

It is important for tour operators to conduct risk assessments and have contingency plans in place for when things go wrong. Staff should be trained in crisis response. They should also have a plan for dealing with media enquiries if a disaster happens.

Case study: hurricane to hit Florida

Tour operators and airlines are currently working on contingency plans for Florida as Hurricane Matilda – a force 4–5 hurricane – is expected to hit the east coast of Florida and Orlando on Saturday. This will have a dramatic impact as airports will have to close and many flights leaving for the UK will be cancelled.

Both tour operatos and airlines will be affected. They must primarily consider the safety of their customers. They must keep in touch with what is happening in resort and take necessary actions including evacuation if necessary.

1   **What do you think tour operators should do in this situation to ensure the safety of their customers and carry on their business?**

2   **Present your ideas to your group, and discuss the implications of these measures for the tour operators.**

Case study: white water rafting holidays

Whether you are looking for a gentle introduction to rafting for the whole family, or a hair-raising white water descent over fearsome rapids, the Alps have something to offer you.

Your rafting experience will begin with a safety briefing, after which you will join your fellow rafters and head off down the river. There are usually 6–8 people per raft, however, some resorts offer 2- or 4-man rafts, doubling the excitement! Hold tight and paddle hard!

Please note that water levels and subsequently the grade of the river are dependent on prevailing weather conditions and snowfalls from the previous winter. Consequently, rafting conditions may vary throughout the season.

(Source: http://www.crystalactive.co.uk/activities/salesgrouping/white_water_rafting.html)

▲ Figure 12.1 White water rafting

Think about the problems that offering this type of package holiday presents.

Case study: dealing with strike action

Union members of British Airways cabin crew have voted overwhelmingly for strike action.

More than 98% of those polled – or 8132 staff – backed industrial action after a 'serious breakdown' in industrial relations, according to the Transport and General Workers Union.

The union said the cabin crew's concerns include issues over the implementation of sickness absence policies as well as pay grading and on-board staffing and responsibility levels.

'BA cabin crew have voted to say the airline has gone too far. BA must rebuild the trust of its cabin crew by negotiating rather than imposing change and by listening to its staff rather than riding roughshod over their concerns,' it said.

A BA statement said: 'We have arranged to meet T&G officials this week and we very much hope they will enter into meaningful discussion with us on the issues the union has raised.

'The union says that one of its key concerns is pensions – yet we have just concluded 16 months of talks by accepting a proposal put forward by the T&G and our other unions.

'On all the other issues the union has raised, we have suggested ways of meeting the union's concerns – but up to now it has either refused to discuss our proposals or rejected them out of hand.

'The leaders of the T&G cabin crew branch have created a worrying time for our customers and our staff. We hope they will grasp the opportunity to put aside threats of disruption and resolve their concerns through proper negotiation.'

(Source: http://www.travelmole.com)

This is a situation that occurs quite regularly in UK airports. Explain how BA and tour operators using the BA flights could deal with this problem.

Taking it further

Look back in news archives and find out what happened about this strike in 2007.

Economic factors

■ Currency fluctuations

Many of the costs paid by tour operators are in foreign currencies, usually euros or dollars. Such costs include accommodation, airport charges and transport. When the exchange rate varies, tour operators may have to pay more or less than they had originally calculated. This could cause problems if the rate change is not in their favour.

Operators are legally prevented from passing on the first 2 per cent of an increase in costs to customers. Of course, tour operators are aware of this and 'hedge' funds. This means sufficient funds are exchanged in advance of need, or contracted to be exchanged at a fixed rate. The bank charges for this service, but it is invaluable to the tour operator.

■ Price of oil

The cost of air travel is dependent on fuel prices and tour operators often charge a supplement for fuel to cover price rises. There is controversy, however, when fuel prices fall and tour operators continue to charge supplements. Oil prices fell in 2006 from about $75 a barrel to $59. Airtours brought their supplement for winter 2007–8 down to £25 rather than £40. Others continued to charge their original supplements.

Social factors

■ UK demographics

Tour operators need to be aware of the demographics of the UK to determine what products are needed for which demographic groups. For example, research has shown that younger travellers are more likely to book a package holiday. This is in spite of their familiarity with internet use, and is because lack of experience of travel leads to a desire for the reassurance of having everything organised.

The largest demographic group in the UK in terms of age is the 45–54 group. Experienced travellers and quite affluent, they are most likely to use tour operators to book long haul, less familiar destinations.

■ Exploitation in host country

Tour operators must also recognise the social and economic situation at the destination and how tourism can impact on issues such as unemployment and poverty.

A group of tour operators from different parts of the world have joined together to create the Tour Operators' Initiative for Sustainable Tourism Development. It is open to all tour operators regardless of their size and geographical location. The aim is to encourage tour operators to accept their ethical responsibilities and adopt practices that promote local economic development and reduce the adverse environmental impacts of tourism. Many tour operators are often criticised for paying lip-service to sustainable tourism, so these initiatives help promote truly sustainable travel policies.

Technological factors

The use of computerised reservation systems has been explored in Unit 9 Book 1. Tour operators use reservation systems to interface with travel agents to allow them to make bookings for their programmes.

Websites are an essential feature of the tour operator's service and will require the professional services of website designers. The sites must be easy to negotiate and present clear information. There may be areas dedicated to travel agents. A good website provides a permanent advertisement for a company's services, worldwide.

Challenges

The holiday market has become very competitive in the past few years. These are some of the challenges which tour operators face.

Dynamic packaging

There has been a trend towards the introduction of niche or specialist packages from tour operators. Such packages can be tailor-made or 'dynamically packaged' to meet customers' personal needs. They can be marketed through call centres or through the internet. Tour operators are less likely to use travel agents for such services as it reduces the personalisation, and travel agents may be in competition with tour operators in these markets.

Key term

Dynamic packaging – accommodation, travel and other services are separately researched and put together in a package for the customer.

Distribution channels

The challenge for distribution is to ensure that products and services are available where customers expect to find them and making sure that your tour operation is using the same channels as the competition.

The case study below illustrates how tour operators use new channels to respond to market changes.

Integration

The industry is constantly changing as one company takes over another or sells part of its operation, as we saw in the First Choice case study. Tour operators may find themselves subject to takeover bids themselves or face increased competition from merged companies. There were two examples of this in 2007 with the merger of First Choice and TUI and the merger of MyTravel and Thomas Cook.

Budget (low-cost) airlines

These are another factor leading to the increasing trend of passengers booking independently, as the low-cost airlines rarely link with tour operators and encourage internet direct bookings.

Maintaining market share

There are many new entrants into travel and tourism as e-commerce operations and exploiting online booking – such as Expedia. In addition, profit margins are low and there is a great deal of price competition. Tour operators have to try and maintain their market share in the face of a changing market. There are a number of strategies that can be taken to increase competitive advantage and maintain or even increase market share.

Assessment practice

More operators are likely to follow TUI's lead to reach customers in all channels and reduce their dependence on the package market in 2007, according to FTO director-general Andy Cooper.

Cooper assessed the issues the industry had faced during the past year in a report to members. He said factors such as terror alerts, the World Cup and bird flu had added to ongoing pressure on tradiitional operators from no-frills airlines and dynamic packagers.

He said some FTO members realised they had been 'slower than they would have liked' to compete in new channels, but many now understood the competititve importance of offering package components separately.

He cited Cosmos's shift to sales via Monarch Scheduled and somewhere2stay.com, and Kuoni's development of its fully functional bookable website, as examples of operators already branching out. Thomas Cook has also made no secret of its desire to drive more sales direct as it pushes online sales.

(Source: *Travel Trade Gazette* 6 October 1006, page 8)

1. Summarise and explain the pressures faced by tour operators referred to in the extract. **M1**

2. What actions did these challenges lead to? How effective were the actions of the tour operators in responding to these pressures? **D1**

3. How would use of 'new' channels reduce the tour operator's dependence on traditional packages? **D1**

Examples include:

- introducing new products and services
- improved distribution
- marketing
- discounted pricing
- using new technology.

Most of these are explored later in this unit.

Trend towards independent travel

Independent booking, especially on the internet, has intensified; even though packages are often cheaper than independently booked holidays, there is still a change in customer behaviour in favour of independent booking as access to the internet increases and people have more experience and confidence in using it.

Travellers may think that they can save money by booking themselves. However, tour operators are often able to command favourable rates with airlines and hotels. Even where there are cost savings to be made by independent booking, there are advantages to using a tour operator:

- good ones have specialist knowledge
- they do all the administration for the customer
- they make all the reservations
- they should be bonded – protecting the booking
- there is only one invoice to pay.

Consider this

Figures from Continental Research recently found that 17 million Britons will buy part of their main holiday online, with 21 million using the internet for research (source: http://www.travelmole.com/stories/1115168.php?mpnlog=1).

12.2 Know the range of products and services offered by tour operators for different target markets

Categories of tour operator

Outbound

Outbound tour operators are the ones you will be most familiar with. They package holidays for tourists who are travelling from the UK to European and worldwide destinations. They may be mass-market or independent operators. Mass-market operators carry high volumes of passengers and operate on low margins and low prices. They offer a product that in theory appeals to most people. Mass-market packages are typified by beach holidays on Spain's Costa Blanca, with high-rise hotels in resorts offering British food and pubs. Such mass-market products are becoming less common as the population becomes more sophisticated about travel, and more discerning. These operators can order from suppliers in bulk and command cheaper prices because of the size of their operations.

Inbound

Inbound tour operators direct their marketing towards tourists overseas who want to visit the UK. You may not be familiar with these as their advertising and promotional material are targeted at other countries.

Domestic

Domestic tour operators operate within the UK, persuading us to take holidays in our own country.

These are the most difficult packages to sell, as it is relatively easy for us to book and travel independently within the UK.

Independent

There are hundreds of independent tour operators who offer individual products and services. They are usually small to medium-sized organisations. They carry relatively small volumes of passengers compared with the large tour operators. They may carry 10,000 passengers a year, or up to 100,000. In order to compete with the large integrated companies, independents are more likely to concentrate on niche products and to establish long-term relationships with suppliers. They are more flexible in terms of the product they offer, allowing greater choice to customers.

Specialist

Specialists are likely to be independent operators. Specialist operators are growing in numbers as they respond to the public's desire for personal service and a specialist, tailor-made product. However, the integrated companies are also focusing on more specialised products in reaction to market trends.

Case study: Kirker Holidays

Upmarket short-break specialist Kirker Holidays was established in 1986 and now has 33 staff. It features more than 50 European cities in its programmes as well as many rural hotels.

Why Kirker?

Over the last five years the world of travel has changed dramatically, yet, in spite of the influence of the internet, our clients continue to rely on our service and advice to ensure that they get the best out of their holiday. If you delight in spending time surfing the worldwide web to secure the cheapest 'no frills' flights, and if you are confident in booking hotels on the strength of a tempting website photograph, then Kirker is perhaps not (yet!) for you. However, if you need **flexibility**, and would like the reassurance of speaking to a human being, then please do call us! Within our team we have over 150 years of experience and we willingly take responsibility for every aspect of your trip to ensure that we turn your short break into a really exceptional holiday.

Flexible and personal service

We aim to offer outstanding service from start to finish; whether you would like us to recommend and book a restaurant for a special celebration dinner, arrange private guided tours, organise opera or concert tickets, wine tasting, cookery courses or even a wedding in Venice or on the Amalfi Coast – we take full responsibility for the smooth running of every aspect of your holiday, so that you can relax and enjoy every minute.

(Source: http://www.kirkerholidays.com/aboutus.aspx)

1 **What type of tour operator is Kirker?**

2 **Describe the products and services provided by Kirker.**

3 **Identify Kirker's target markets.**

4 **How does Kirker's portfolio of products and services meet the needs of its target markets?**

Taking it further

Recommend, with justifications, how Kirker could expand its range of products and services for its current target markets. **D2**

Assessment practice

Carry out some research and find an example of each type of tour operator in the following list:

- inbound
- outbound
- domestic
- independent
- specialist.

Note that a tour operator may be in more than one category – for example, independent and specialist.

1 Describe each tour operator and say what its products and services are and what target markets they serve. **P2**

2 State which associations each tour operator belongs to and why. **P1**

You could present your work as a table, as in the example below. Add explanatory notes as needed.

Category	Tour operator	Products and services	Associations	Benefits
Inbound	British Tours	Personalised day tours in the UK for overseas customers, particularly from the USA	American Society of Travel Agents (ASTA)	ASTA: To gain representation in the US market
			UKinbound	UKinbound: To get support and representation in the UK
			London Tourist Board	London Tourist Board: To gain referrals
Outbound				
Domestic				
Independent				
Specialist				

Products range

Components of a standard package holiday

Key term

Package holiday – a holiday including at least two elements of transport, accommodation and other services, for example the services of an overseas representative.

This is the definition of a package holiday under the Package Travel Regulations. It must:

- be sold or offered for sale
- be sold at an inclusive price
- be pre-arranged
- include a minimum of two of the three elements of transport, accommodation and other tourist services.

Most package holidays are pre-arranged and presented in brochures by the tour operators. Customers visit travel agents and collect brochures on destinations of interest to them, or order brochures directly from the tour operator.

The brochure is an important sales tool for the package holiday. Because of the intense competition in the holiday industry, tour operators constantly review their products and introduce new packages.

Tailor-made package

A tailor-made package is dynamically packaged. That is, as we learnt earlier, the different elements of the package are specifically selected to meet the needs of a particular customer. Tour operators are offering tailor-made services much more frequently, as holidaymakers are often experienced travellers and do not appreciate the mass-marketing approach any longer. People have higher expectations in terms of product and customer service.

Range of destinations

Finding new destinations is part of product development for a tour operator. As people take more frequent holidays and become experienced travellers there is an increasing demand to visit new places. These may be far flung and exotic or may be countries that are opening up to tourism like those in eastern Europe.

Accommodation choices

Offering different types of accommodation is another means of offering a differentiated product to customers. Tourists expect to choose between different types of accommodation such as villas, hotels and camping. They are also used to choosing board packages such as bed and breakfast or all inclusive. Tour operators will also offer unprecedented luxury such as beach bungalows in Thailand or deluxe resorts. An example of a tour operator selling basic accommodation is 'Just' (part of the Thomson Group) whereas OSL (also Thomson) specialises in villas.

LINDIANVILLAGE

www.lindianvillage.gr

Lindian Village
Tel: +30 22 4403 5900
Fax: +30 22 4404 7360

A PREVAILING AEGEAN ENVIRONMENT IN RODOS ISLAND, Greece invites you to experience an atmosphere beyond your expectations. If you want to settle amid a lush garden of tropical flowers and trees, walk by a river, lie by a natural lake, smell the colourful bougainvilleas, view the sparkling sea, in a deluxe resort designed as a small village in classical island-style architecture, Lindian Village is the idyllic venue.

Guests can choose to dine from the five different restaurants.

Accommodation – 152 rooms
Luxury guestrooms. Mediterranean classic double rooms built in Aegean style architecture, all equipped with superb terraces amid fragrant flowers. Room amenities include voicemail, internet access, radio and cable/satellite TV, safe deposit boxes, air-conditioning, hairdryer, bath robes, bath toiletries, fresh beach towels daily, mini bar and 24-hour room service.

Hibiscus junior suites. Set amid abundant hibiscus trees, the junior suites open up to lovely private terraces with open air hot tubs.

Suite with private pool. Dressed in deep blues and stunning whites, these suites are set amid their own lush garden with private swimming pool and sun deck. They guarantee seclusion wrapped in total luxury.

Facilities include:
- Lindian Village Spa.
- Fully-equipped gym.
- Turkish bath.
- Tennis court.
- Pool complex.
- Children's area.
- Conference halls.
- The Lobby Bar.
- Deli Bar.
- Disco Bar.
- The Beach Bar.
- Small chapel.
- Shopping arcade.
- Watersports.

40   TTGexpert Luxury 2006

Figure 12.2 ▶
Luxury accommodation

(Source: *Travel Trade Gazette* Luxury 2006, page 40)

Transport options

Once again, this is a means of offering options that suit whatever the customer desires. Examples include adventurous train journeys and first class travel. On their own airlines, the big four tour operators have introduced a whole range of optional extras – which are chargeable.

Ancillary products and services

The marketing activities of tour operators have become very sophisticated in that they offer a vast range of extras that the tourist can add to a holiday – at an extra charge, of course!

The advantage for customers is that all their needs are catered for through one contact. The disadvantage is that all these extras cost money, and in some cases they are services that used to be included in a package, for example a meal on a flight. Here is a list of extras available on a typical First Choice package:

- holiday insurance
- foreign exchange
- airport car parking
- airport hotel
- airport lounge
- taxis
- car hire
- late check-out from the hotel
- upgrades to rooms
- kids' clubs
- tickets for attraction/events.

And on the flight:

- champagne
- chocolates
- meal in flight
- extra leg-room
- seats together
- day-before check-in.

Consider this

If you were going on holiday, which of these extras would you be prepared to pay for? You could get these extras from the tour operator, the travel agent or arrange them yourself. Which is best?

Target market

Tour operators plan their products with specific target markets in mind. Specialist operators aim for a niche market whilst the large companies offer a range of products, each aimed at a different group.

Products may be aimed at families, couples, solo travellers , specific age groups, special interests or people with specific needs.

Theory into practice

Match up the products with the target markets.

Families	We specialise in holidays that take account of local culture and the environment
Couples	If you are passionate about diving we have over a hundred dive sites to choose from
Solo travellers	This resort is offered without single supplements at certain times of the season
Over fifties	We offer free child places, interconnecting rooms, kids' club, early meals and babysitting
People interested in the environment	Relaxing spa holidays in luxury resorts for adults only
People wanting an activity holiday	An Amazon cruise – chattering, brightly coloured birds, dense jungle and shrub reaching down the banks to the edge of the river
Special interest travellers	An operator that has been arranging painting holidays for over 50 years and has wide experience in matching destinations and themes to the expectations of amateur artists

Case study: Thomson tips next big destinations

Charters to Cape Verde and Marrakesh will bring both destinations into the mainstream next year, Thomson predicts.

The operator named the two places, together with the west coast of Canada and Cape Town, as 2007's boom destinations.

Cape Verde, off the coast of Senegal, is a six-hour flight from the UK and is tipped to be the next big winter-sun hotspot.

Thomsonfly will start its own charter next year.

Astraeus already flies to Cape Verde for independent operators.

Thomson has brought forward the launch of its weekly Gatwick–Cape Verde flight from May to February because of strong demand. Next winter it will fly twice a week from Gatwick and weekly from Manchester.

Marrakesh is also set to receive a huge influx of UK visitors this winter on the back of deals between the Moroccan government and no-frills airlines.

Thomson started operating flights four times a week each from Luton and Manchester last month, and could expand to the regions next year.

A Thomson spokeswoman said western Canada was increasingly popular for family activity holidays, and predicted that the growth is set to continue.

She added that Cape Town was becoming a short-break destination despite the 12-hour flight.

(Source: *Travel Trade Gazette* 1 December 2006)

Read the article about new destinations. Make sure you can locate Cape Verde, Marrakesh and Cape Town on a map.

1 **Explain the possible reasons for increase in demand to these destinations.**

2 **Identify the target markets for these destinations.**

3 **Analyse how Thomson meets the needs of its target markets by offering these new destinations.**

M2

12.3 Know how tour operators plan, sell, administer and operate a package holiday programme

Activity: role and responsibilities of a tour operator

Imagine you are going on holiday and you have booked directly with a tour operator. Note all the things that a tour operator is responsible for in order to provide you with your holiday.

Responsibility	When?
Example: Contracting hotels, contracting flights, putting a brochure together	Pre-booking
	During booking
	After booking and pre-holiday
	During holiday
	Post-holiday

Discuss your ideas with your group and your teacher or tutor.

Planning

Planning includes the stages of:

- research
- product development
- methods of contracting
- costing the package
- data input.

Consider this

Think of at least three destinations tour operators cannot offer at present. Why is this?

Research and product development

Research has to take place on a continuous basis. Research informs product development. Tour operators are constantly monitoring their sales, the competition and the market, so that they can make decisions about capacity to be offered in existing destinations, new destinations to adopt and old destinations to drop.

They use many sources of data and trends to inform this process.

- Sales figures – when figures go down, perhaps it is time to leave the destination; when figures go up, it may be worth investing in more capacity.
- Communication with salespeople in reservations and with travel agents – they can report on customer demand. Internal communication should be efficient – marketing staff should work in conjunction with operations staff.
- Research findings, for example, Travel Trends, Mintel reports and Star UK reports.
- Travel and tourism conferences.
- PEST analysis – analysing political, economic, social and technological factors.

An organisation that is aware of and using all this information will make informed decisions about which destinations to include in a package-holiday programme. In spite of this, there will be occasions when an operator has to pull out of a destination because of factors which could not be foreseen, for example a terrorist attack. Product development does not just include destinations. It may mean changing the range of excursions offered in resorts, the services offered during the flight or holiday or the means of booking the holiday.

Methods of contracting

Contracts are typically fixed about 12 months ahead of the holiday season. This means that the tour operator needs to make an estimation of capacity in order to agree contracts with hotels and airlines. There will be some adjustments later, but it is difficult to make major changes as prices have been agreed and brochures have gone to print.

It is difficult to contract too far in advance, as tour operators have to make decisions, based on sales and other research, about what to include in their programme. Different types of contract that might be organised for accommodation include:

- a fixed contract
- an allocation contract
- a sale only contract.

The fixed contract is more advantageous to the supplier as it means that if the accommodation is not sold they will still be paid. Obviously this is not so practical for the tour operator.

Allocation contracts are also popular with hoteliers. To ensure that all their beds are sold, they contract with tour operators for more beds than they have available. The tour operator has to confirm, by an agreed date, how many beds it will actually take. This gives the hotel time to sell remaining beds at a competitive price.

Allocation contracts also apply to flights. A smaller tour operator cannot fill a whole charter aircraft, so it buys an allocation of seats on a flight. Once the allocation is sold, it requests seats for any extra bookings or looks for seats on an alternative flight. The customer may have to pay a supplement for these seats as they will not be acquired at the preferential rate of the original allocation. If the allocation is not sold, unsold seats can be returned to the airline, but the deadline for this is six to eight weeks before departure date.

A sale-only contract means that the tour operator estimates the amount of accommodation needed and then pays only for what is actually sold. This can leave hotels with unsold rooms which they have to sell at the last minute. They could do this through an agent such as lastminute.com or Expedia.

Fixed contracts are less common than they used to be as tour operators look for greater flexibility and control over costs. However, the type of contract also depends on who is the more powerful negotiator.

Theory into practice

Bella Vista is a glamorous new hotel overlooking a bay in Lanzarote. All the major tour operators want to feature it in their winter programmes. Damson, an independent tour operator, is in competition with the big four to secure 50 rooms for the season. Who has more power in this relationship? What kind of contract do you think will be issued? Check with your tutor to see whether you are right.

Flights are often contracted more than a season in advance, and again the tour operators have to predict how many people will be prepared to book a particular holiday from a particular airport. If predictions are wrong they will have to make adjustments – but sometimes this is not possible. They may be able to contract extra aircraft if available but it is difficult to cancel one without incurring costs.

Where there is no possibility of achieving the required load factor on a flight, a tour operator may decide to consolidate two flights. This simply means that one will be cancelled and the passengers will be transferred to the other flight. This action causes customer dissatisfaction as departure times and even airports will change. However, sometimes this can work in a customer's favour, as they may be given an extra couple of days' holiday to fit in with the new flight.

Costing the package

Margins on package holidays are extremely low at around 2–3 per cent. This means that costings have to be done extremely carefully with accurate forecasting. This is difficult as costings are done about 18 months in advance of sales and many of the costs are subject to fluctuation. Fuel costs may rise, exchange rates may adversely affect costs. Another complication is that under the Package Travel Regulations late surcharges are not allowed to be added to the holiday price.

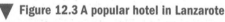 Figure 12.3 A popular hotel in Lanzarote

Selling

Brochure production

Holiday brochures are printed a long time in advance of the holiday season. The brochures include prices, and obviously it is difficult to determine prices a long time in advance.

Tour operators produce several versions of a brochure in order to update prices. But this practice is confusing for customers and travel agents, and also wasteful. A solution would be to print brochures without prices and to confirm the price at the time of booking, but this is illegal in the UK – a price must be set for the package.

It has been suggested by Trading Standards officers that a maximum brochure price is set which cannot be exceeded, but which can be discounted. This suggestion has not yet been adopted.

The brochure is an important sales tool and traditionally the main source of information for the customer. Unless the business is new or a new venture for an existing operator, the brochure will be largely based on the previous year's version. This means it is unnecessary to photograph every hotel every year and rewrite all the copy (text). In spite of this, it still takes a lot of time to produce. Time is needed to:

- design the brochure
- take photos
- write copy
- determine prices.

The brochure must appear in good time to allow sales to take place. A brochure for the summer season will be published in September or October of the previous year.

Brochures are costly to produce, with each costing between 75p and £1.20. This takes up a large part of the marketing budget. One operator estimates that 25 per cent of its marketing spend goes on brochures.

Many of the brochures never reach a customer; as second and third editions appear, travel agents have to discard the earlier editions. An agent reported spending £500 on getting rid of these – this amounted to more than three skips of brochures. Travel agents also have to devote a lot of valuable storage space to brochures.

Consider this

Since travel agents are throwing away so many brochures, why don't you ask an agent if you can have some copies for your school or college? They will help you with your research.

There is a solution to the brochure problem. Technology allows for printed brochures to be abandoned in favour of e-brochures.

Key term

E-brochure – an electronic version of tour operator information of the type that traditionally appears in print.

There are advantages to these – e-brochures do not waste paper, ink, space or money. They can also be more precisely targeted, as a travel agent or other intermediary can download information that is of interest to a specific customer.

However, an e-brochures system is not as simple as transferring the brochure to the internet. It requires investment in a content management system by the tour operator in order to be done properly.

The main question is whether customers will accept e-brochures in place of brochures they can browse through at home. Also, it is likely that small operators will be deterred by the investment required.

Theory into practice

Find a tour operator's e-brochure online. You could look at www.kuoni.co.uk. Compare the experience of using the e-brochure with a traditional brochure. Make a comparative table.

A number of pricing strategies are commonly used by tour operators. These include the following.

▲ Figure 12.4 Pricing strategies

■ Fluid pricing

The brochure is issued a long time before the season and is printed with prices. The price at this stage may not be a true reflection of the price that the customer will ultimately pay. Operators may raise prices if costs increase, or if there is a surge in demand. Also, many tour operators may use the same hotel but arrive at different prices for the package.

Theory into practice

Gather a selection of summer sun brochures. Choose a mainstream summer sun holiday in Spain. Find the same holiday (same resort, same hotel, same dates) in three package-holiday brochures. Compare the prices charged by the different operators for a one-week holiday, for half-board, for a couple. Put your results in a table and comment on your findings.

■ Discount pricing

Prices may be discounted if holidays remain unsold. By fixing contracts and therefore prices a long time ahead of the season, tour operators purchase their supplies (flights and rooms) at the cheapest prices. In order to ensure that holidays are not left unsold and that cash flow is good, tour operators must encourage early bookings. When early bookings are high, the tour operator knows whether there will be any excess capacity in holidays – hopefully none – and takes a substantial deposit per person. Tour operators are able to use or invest this money as they do not need to pay their suppliers until the holidays are taken.

When there is excess capacity, tour operators are forced to discount holidays at the last minute. Tour operators aim to sell 95 per cent of holidays available in order to maintain profitability. This means it is important to try to match supply and demand very closely.

Large tour operators achieve very small margins of profit. They may make only 5 per cent of the price of the holiday as profit. The CAA states that some margins are as low as 3 per cent. If the holiday is discounted, they may not make any profit. In that case the aim is to cover the costs.

You can see why the selling of ancillary products is so vital – this is where the profits are to be made. Tactics employed by tour operators with discounted holidays include charging for the transfer, charging a late booking fee and for a meal on the plane.

Table 12.3 provides an example of a cost breakdown for a holiday.

Flight	£214.55
Accommodation and transfer	£149.70
Marketing	£14.97
Distribution	£74.85
Overheads (salaries, offices, administration, etc.)	£19.96
Total	£474.03

Table 12.2 Holiday cost breakdown

■ Seasonal pricing

Tour operators divide the year into different seasons. First, there is a broad division into winter and summer season. In summer there are more beach holidays, and in winter ski programmes are running. A summer brochure will typically cover the period May to November, and a winter one will run from November to April. Within these periods there are peak seasons, shoulder seasons and off-peak seasons.

Tour operators vary their capacity during the season but must fill the planes they have contracted. This can result in discounted prices at shoulder season. At peak season – the school holiday period of July and August in summer, and the Christmas holidays in winter – demand and therefore prices are at their highest. Tour operators have been heavily criticised for charging their highest prices in school holiday times, but they have to make their profit when they can.

Key terms

Peak season – the busiest times, coinciding with school holidays.

Shoulder season – the slightly less busy times either side of the peak season.

Off-peak season – the least busy times.

Case study: mobile home holiday in France

holiday commencing	12 nights	+/– nights
28 April – 11 May	294	12
12 May – 18 May	294	14
19 May – 24 May	564	22
25 May – 01 Jun	650	30
02 Jun – 08 Jun	594	27
09 Jun – 22 Jun	614	32
23 Jun – 29 Jun	774	37
30 Jun – 06 Jul	1026	58
07 Jul – 13 Jul	1088	59
14 Jul – 20 Jul	1190	65
21 Jul – 27 Jul	1288	74
28 Jul – 10 Aug	1328	74
11 Aug – 14 Aug	1298	71
15 Aug – 17 Aug	1278	71
18 Aug – 20 Aug	1124	62
21 Aug – 24 Aug	1012	56
25 Aug – 27 Aug	631	33
28 Aug – 31 Aug	585	28
01 Sep – 07 Sep	401	18

Your price includes

- 12-night accommodation for 2 adults – all children under 18 years FREE of charge
- Return midweek Dover–Calais–Dover ferry crossing for a standard car and up to 5 passengers with P&O Ferries

(Source: Siblu brochure, 2007; © Siblu)

1 **Give reasons for the variations in price shown in the table from the Siblu brochure.**

2 **When are the peak season and the shoulder season?**

3 **What else do you think a family would have to pay for on this holiday?**

Make notes for discussion with your group.

▲ Figure 12.5 A family holiday home in France

■ Competitive pricing

Mass-market operators are very keen to remain competitive on price; they will often match prices offered by the competition. Sometimes more upmarket operators will do this as well, so it is worth customers asking them.

■ Promotional pricing

Tour operators have tried various promotions linked to price over recent years, including a two-for-one offer. This was not very successful as many customers believed that the original prices had been raised to cover the offer. Early booking promotions with price discounts are more credible.

Distribution

Tour operators must determine how best to distribute their products and services in order to maximise sales. Traditionally, distribution is via travel agents who stock tour operators' brochures and sell on their behalf on commission. Although this method is still common, it is now used in conjunction with internet distribution where customers can find information and even book via the tour operators' own websites or via a travel agent's website. When products and services are sold via the tour operator's website or by telephone, this is known as direct sell. Some tour operators, for example Portland, only use direct methods. Most tour operators use a combination of distribution methods.

Promotion

Promotion is the work of marketing personnel, as you saw in Unit 5. The nature of promotion depends on the budget available, and ranges from television advertising campaigns to press releases about new products and destinations. You can find examples of the use of press releases in travel trade magazines. Promotion may be aimed at the final consumer or to the trade. Trade promotion can be just as important as consumer promotion as travel professionals can bring preferred products to the attention of their customers. Examples of trade promotions include educational trips for agents to resorts, competitions and sales incentives.

Reservations

Most tour operators use computerised reservation systems. Reservations staff are salespeople so they have to be well informed about the products they sell. This is easier for tour operators than for travel agencies, as the salesperson needs to know about only one company's products and will have received intensive training.

Reservations staff may be at a call centre, in which case they have targets to meet in terms of calls answered and sales made. Others take bookings over the computerised reservation system from travel agents, or over the internet. They will need to contact customers only if there is a query about a booking or availability. Once a booking is made, a reference code is assigned to it alongside the customer details, so that the booking can always be traced through the system.

Theory into practice

Choose a well-known tour operator. Find out how its products are distributed. To do this you will need to vist a travel agent, look on the internet and see if its products are listed on teletext or available by telephone.

Theory into practice

Role-play the part of a reservations clerk in a call centre, with a colleague acting as a customer. Prepare by choosing some holiday brochures to work with. Make a list of the information you will need from the customer in order to take a booking. Be prepared to answer the customer's questions about the resort, accommodation, etc. If you can, record the role-play so that you can evaluate it to see whether you missed any important information.

Commission

Commission is traditionally paid to travel agents who book holidays for customers on behalf of tour operators. If you book your holiday direct the tour operator saves this commission so you might negotiate a cheaper price. Reservations staff are sometimes paid a commission on sales as an incentive to sell.

Late sales

If you look at at a travel agent's window or a tour operator's website you will find late sales advertised. Tour operators do their best to avoid late sales and encourage customers to book holidays in advance. This gives the tour operator the benefits of adjusting contracts to meet demand, making a better margin on sales and enjoying good cash flow. Late sales harm cash flow and are usually discounted so less profit is made.

Administration

Confirmations and itineraries

Once reservations are made, further administration is dealt with by another team. They issue booking confirmations and invoices after booking and send out reminders for payment. They issue any tickets, itineraries and other documentation; this can be quite complex. Camping operators send out guides to the campsite, a guide to the local area, car stickers and maps as well as the booking details.

Passenger manifests and rooming lists

The administration department has to make sure that suppliers are informed of bookings. Passenger lists and details of forthcoming bookings are sent to airlines and hotels. If cancellations are made these too must be dealt with by the administrative team and suppliers notified.

Key term

Passenger manifest – this is a list or record of passengers.

Errata

This is a term used in publishing and refers to corrections made after a publication, in this case a brochure, has gone to press. Rather than republish the whole brochure at great cost, a list of corrections is sent out to be read alongside the brochure.

Cancellations and amendments

Any cancellations or amendments made by the tour operator must adhere to the Package Travel Regulations. A customer will be able to read policies on cancellation or amendment in the tour operator's terms and conditions when they book their holiday. If the tour operator has to cancel a holiday they will offer a full refund or an alternative holiday.

Alteration or cancellation of booking by us

(a) Although we make every reasonable effort to avoid doing so, occasionally we may have to alter your holiday arrangements and we reserve the right to do so at any time. If we have to make a significant alteration, we will inform you as soon as reasonably possible, and we will give you the choice of accepting the altered arrangements with any consequential price adjustments, or having a full refund of your money. Examples of 'significant alterations' include changes to your UK or end destination airport, your resort area or having to offer accommodation of a lower official classification. Examples of 'minor' changes are changes to aircraft type or the operating airline, changes to routes (via points), time changes of less than 12 hours and changes of accommodation to another of the same standard and such changes are not deemed to be significant.

(b) If an alteration is forced on us by force majeure (which is explained in Condition 11) no compensation is payable. In other cases, if we make a significant alteration for any other reason we will offer you compensation in accordance with the table below.

No. of days before departure	Compensation per person
More than 56 days	nil
43 – 56 days	£10
29 – 42 days	£20
15 – 28 days	£30
0 – 14 days	£40

(c) In exceptional cases, we may have to cancel your holiday. If so, we will inform you as soon as we can, and we will offer you (if possible) an alternative holiday with any consequential price adjustments or a full refund of your money. This does not apply if the holiday is cancelled through your own fault.

(d) If the cancellation is forced on us by force majeure, no compensation is payable. If we cancel your holiday for any other reason (not your fault), we will pay you compensation in accordance with the table above.

(Source: Premier Holidays World Choice brochure, July 2006–December 2007)

Operations

Consolidations

Consolidations occur when insufficient bookings mean there is spare capacity of air seats or hotel rooms. Rather than leave these flight seats or rooms empty and yet paid for, capacity is cut and flights and rooms cancelled (where contracts allow). People with bookings for these cancelled flights or rooms are transferred to other flights which have seats available or different accommodation.

Transport operations

This refers to organisation of charter flights and in-resort transfers. Transfers are usually included in the package. The transfer from the airport to the hotel is usually by coach. On many late bookings, tour operators now charge extra for the transfer to compensate for discounting the holiday. Representatives take it in turns to be on airport duty – normally one day a week. These representatives meet the plane and accompany the coach loads of passengers to their accommodation.

The tour operator may use other forms of transport and will have a close working relationship with whichever suppliers it uses. In the case study on the mobile home holiday we saw that P&O ferries were included in the holiday price. This is a cost that the tour operator incurs and must be negotiated with P&O to keep it as low as possible. Similarly, coach tour operators either own their own fleet of coaches or negotiate terms with a coach operator.

Duty office

Smaller tour operators may not have a dedicated duty office, but they always have a designated member of staff on call outside office hours. The duty office provides an essential link between the UK and the resorts. The office deals with any non-routine occurrences, for example medical problems where an insurance company has to be contacted. If delays occur at airports, they will make sure that passengers receive the information, meals or even accommodation that they require.

Package holidays include the services of a representative. The representatives are employed directly by the tour operator in areas where the operator has a large programme with many holidaymakers. In other circumstances, representatives are hired from local companies and will take care of people on holiday with several different tour operators. This latter group is more likely to be made up of local people.

The staff are in communication with the UK and receive daily information updates, for example passenger manifests and special requests. Sometimes the resort staff have to allocate accommodation where customers have booked late at a discount for 'allocation on arrival'.

Health and safety

The representatives will have a degree of responsibility for health and safety. Under the Package Travel Regulations, the tour operator, not the hotel, is responsible for the customer's health and safety. If the representative notices any breach of health and safety or is informed of one by a customer, they must ensure it is put right.

Emergencies

In addition, the representatives must deal with emergency situations. A good tour operator lays down procedures to be followed in such cases. Most emergencies are health-related or involve crimes. The worst scenario involves someone's death; this is a terrible situation for all concerned, but it is not unusual for representatives to have to deal with it and there will be procedures to follow.

Crisis management

The most demanding situation for a representative is dealing with a crisis that affects a lot of customers. Examples include mass food poisoning, a bus crash or a hurricane. In such situations there should be a crisis management procedure that can be put into operation, but representatives would also expect senior management to oversee these procedures. An incident control centre would be set up at head office and would liaise with staff in resort. The head of incident control would issue a carefully considered company policy statement on any incident to try to minimise concern or even panic and to maintain good public relations. The representative would be expected to adhere to company policy and to remain contactable at all times.

Quality control

Quality control is ensured by different methods. Surveys are often undertaken asking for customers' views on their holiday. You might have noticed these on the return flight from a package holiday. Representatives in resort complete a series of reports if customers come to them with problems and they are monitored in resort by senior staff.

Customer service

Tour operators provide routine customer service departments. They may be divided into pre-departure customer service and post-holiday customer service.

Before departure, the customer service agents deal with enquiries and provide information. They may give information about passports, visas and vaccination requirements. They will also deal with any booking amendments and pass on details to reservations.

After the holiday, the customer service department mostly deals with any complaints. The agents answer telephone, e-mail and postal complaints. The large tour operators computerise these systems and scan all correspondence into an individual customer file saved on the system.

Targets are set for responding to complaints and letters are automatically generated as far as possible, although obviously some complaints require a unique response. The aim is always to solve the complaint as quickly and as cheaply as possible. The customer service department's workload is much reduced where overseas representatives are empowered to resolve complaints in the resort as far as possible. The tour operator will try to resolve any further complaint to the customer's satisfaction and to avoid possible legal action. However, many people complain after their holiday because they simply had expectations that were too high, or experienced poor weather, and the tour operator has to respond to such complaints although there is no obligation to provide any form of compensation.

Timescales

Planning a package holiday takes up to two years. The following case study explains why a company has an even longer-term plan and what stages are gone through before the holiday is ready for sale.

Case study: Vintage Travel

Vintage Travel is a villa holiday specialist tour operator. One of its key areas is Croatia. Its operations director explains how the programme in Croatia was set up.

Planning is very important to our business and we have a five-year plan so that we know the direction we are heading in. We can be reasonably accurate with our three-year planning and definite plans are put into place about 18 months before the season. Thus, we are working on May 2009 from December 2007. When we decided to go into Croatia, the perceptions of the country were poor. It was associated with the war and prior to that it had been an area of mass tourism.

We made four or five familiarisation visits seeking out suitable properties to rent. All the villas we let have pools so we had to persuade owners and developers to build pools in order to let their houses. Houses come to us in several ways:

- existing owners tell others about us
- tourist boards are a source of villa owners
- we look for villas ourselves.

Once we have found the villas we negotiate contracts with the owners. A fully guaranteed contract means we guarantee an amount for the whole season. This involves us in financial risk as we have to pay the owner whether the villa is let or not. However, for a particularly good property it may be worth the risk. A minimum guarantee contract means we guarantee to pay for a fixed number of weeks within the season. This gives us less commitment and outside of our

weeks the owner is free to take direct bookings or we may book it if there is demand and it is still free. An ad hoc contract means we pay the owner only if we let the villa.

Our brochure is priced for accommodation only, although extras can be added. This keeps pricing relatively simple and means customers can take advantage of low-cost flights or drive to Croatia. When we set the prices, we use past experience to guide us, particularly comparing with Catalunya or France.

We employ representatives – they are people who live in the area so they have local knowledge. We sell via our website or by telephone. We give a personal service and have excellent product knowledge.

1 **Draw up a flow chart explaining the stages in planning, selling and administering a villa rental programme. As the holidays are to be sold as packages you should include contracting of flights and transfers. Your chart should indicate which activities are sequential and which have to be done at the same time. Give an indication of timescales. Make sure the chart is suitable for display. Add explanatory notes as appropriate.** **P3**

2 **Describe how the villa holiday programme is operated. You may need to do some further research on other villa holiday programmes to help you.** **P4**

In this section you will be given the opportunity to work on two examples which allow you to practise planning and costing a package holiday. You must bear in mind that you are unable to access the negotiated rates that large tour operators can achieve. Nor will you be able to find out the costs of chartering an aircraft. These figures are negotiated for each deal and are not in the public domain. However, you will be able to carry out research and go through a process which is similar to that of a small operator.

Planning and costing

The first example is a specialist tour operator which is bringing out a new product and brochure called 'Spa Bliss'. The product is to be based on hotels all over the world, each one very special, exclusive and offering a full range of spa therapies. Most of them have been sourced and contracted, but the owner wants one more to finish off the programme. Your role is to find an extra special spa hotel in an exotic location and then create a package around that hotel.

How do you do this?

Planning

1   Destination and accommodation

Decide on the destination and the spa hotel. The easiest way for you to do this is to search on the internet for spa hotels. You cannot get the information from another package holiday brochure as you need to access the hotel's rates, so you need to visit the hotel's own website. Search for 'spa hotels' and find one that is suitably exclusive and luxurious for the 'Spa Bliss' programme. Make sure that no prohibitive factors apply to the destination – that is, no political or environmental factors would prevent people from travelling there. Select some photos that you could use in your brochure. Check prices, particularly of a twin room per night.

What type of board will you offer your customers? Check what the hotel offers, from bed and breakfast to all-inclusive. Check rates again.

2   Transport

Decide how customers will get there. Find out what scheduled flights serve the destination – make sure there is a direct flight. Start by searching British Airways. Check prices and try to find an average price.

3   Additional services

Decide which treatments and activities will be included and which will cost extra. List everything. Check prices.

4   Contract

What kind of contract will you arrange with the hotel? This is a new venture and you don't know how many bookings you will get, so perhaps the first season should be on a 'sale-only' contract.

5   Transfer

Decide how you will transfer your customers from the airport to the hotel. If they are paying a lot of money, they will expect a taxi. How much will that cost? Try www.holidaytaxis.com for quotes.

6   Fixed costs

You have an office with three staff in the UK. Allow fixed costs of £8000 per month for running the office.

You are ready to start costing this project – as you are buying rooms, and seats on scheduled aircraft, you do not need to worry about load factors.

Costing

1   Load factor and mark up

The load factor refers to the ratio of paid passengers to the total capacity you have available. Ideally you would like a 100 per cent load factor and tour operators aim for this, but you should do your calculations on a load factor of about 80 per cent. This means as long as you achieve the 80 per cent you will still make your margin. The mark-up on luxury holidays is higher than on mass-market holidays, and you need to get a speedy return on investment, so go for a relatively high mark-up. Start with 20 per cent – this will be in off-peak, and you can price up from that for shoulder and peak times.

2 Fixed and variable costs

Fixed costs are those which do not alter and will have to be paid no matter how many bookings you take, for example the price of a charter flight. Variable costs are those which change according to number of bookings, for example catering costs and hotel rooms.

Note in a table the costs of everything you want to include in your package. Do this for a 7-night and a 14-night period. Remember you will get commission from the suppliers on everything you book. Assume this is 10 per cent and take this off. Add on your mark-up. The figure you have left is the basic price.

At this stage you should look at some other spa packages and see how your basic price compares. Is it realistic?

3 Currency conversion

Decide on the season, perhaps November to April. Divide the season into peak, shoulder and off-peak periods and adjust the prices. You also need to convert prices into sterling if you are quoted in another currency.

Collate a list of supplements, activities and excursions with the prices you will charge for them.

Keep all your notes from each stage so that you are able to explain how you arrived at your package. Put your information together as a brochure page. Present your proposal to your tutor.

Profitability

The tour operator has to maximise the profitability of the planned package holiday programme. There are various means of achieving this. Let's examine them.

Methods of contracting

Negotiating a more flexible contract with a supplier means that if insufficient bookings are made they can be cancelled without penalty. Remember: a fixed contract means that rooms or plane seats have to be paid for whether they are filled or not.

Consolidations

Two underbooked flights may be put together to save money on charters. The extra administration costs must be taken into account.

Currency exchange

Rates of exchange should be monitored and currency should be bought when the rate is favourable and banked until invoices have to be paid. Speculating on currency exchange in an attempt to reduce risk is known as 'hedging'.

Cancellation charges

Tour operators' terms and conditions include details of cancellation charges. If a customer decides to cancel their holiday they must lose a percentage of the cost of their holiday. This increases on a sliding scale the nearer to the departure time the cancellation is made. The tour operator is free to resell the holiday. You can find details of these charges in the terms and conditions of the holiday brochure.

Late sales

Holidays are perishable – once the flight has departed the opportunity to sell that holiday is gone. Late sales mean that at least some contribution to costs is made even if no profit is made. Tour operators prefer to avoid late sales. They deplete an already very tight margin. If forecasting of demand is accurate, then late sales can be avoided.

Commission

The tour operator pays commission to travel agents but can negotitate this. They also receive commission from third parties whose products and services they sell, for example car hire and insurance.

Interest

Customers pay deposits on their holidays and pay the balance about six weeks before departure. Paying for holidays upfront helps the operator's cash flow and allows them to earn interest on sales before they have to pay suppliers.

Excursion sales

These are a very valuable source of income and an important part of the representative's job is to sell them.

They can often be bought prior to departure.

Now try another example on your own in the following activity.

Assessment practice

In this activity you are setting up business as a French villa tour operator. You will start the season with a handful of properties, but need to describe only one for the purposes of the activity. Tour operators would travel to the region of France in which they were interested, visit properties and contract them. You will have to work through the internet.

You need to find individuals who are renting villas rather than companies; try www.villadata.com.

1 Choose a villa that you will offer in your brochure for a period of June to September.

2 Decide what type of contract you will arrange.

3 Find suitable transport for your customers by plane or car and ferry.

4 Decide what will be included in the package.

5 Produce a costing for the package, showing your mark-up and load factor.

6 Put all the information together as a brochure page with prices.

7 Show your costing separately from the brochure page.

8 Be ready to present your proposal and explain how you arrived at it. **P5**

9 Explain ways of maximising the profitability of this package. **M3**

10 Recommend, with justifications, what other products and services might be added to appeal to the customers of this villa holiday programme. **D2**

Knowledge check

1 Why are UK residents taking more trips abroad than ever before?

2 What are the benefits of integration?

3 Identify the associations that support tour operators.

4 Give examples of environmental influences which might affect tour operation.

5 Explain how tour operators charter aircraft.

6 Define a package holiday.

7 Explain why ancillary products are important to tour operators.

8 What are the different kinds of contracts between tour operators and suppliers?

9 Describe the different pricing strategies used by tour operators.

10 What is an e-brochure?

11 What are the functions of a duty office?

12 Describe the main provisions of the Package Travel Regulations.

Preparation for assessment

After finishing your BTEC course you have found a job with a medium-sized, independent tour operator specialising in packaged ski holidays, called Especially Ski. You work in the reservations department. You really enjoy your work but you are keen to learn about other departments and make career progression.

At your appraisal, you discuss this with your line manager, who asks you if you would like to be involved in a project that the press office team has suggested. The press office is constantly receiving requests for information from students who want to know about tour operating and about how the company operates. The press team acknowledges that it is important to help students, but they find they are spending a lot of time answering questions and sending out information.

Their idea is to compile a student pack that can be posted on the internet. It will be a series of downloadable fact sheets so that students can choose the ones they need. The press team has put together a list of the most frequently asked questions that they receive and they want each sheet to be a response to one of the questions.

Carry out the necessary research to allow you to produce a detailed response to each of the questions, and put together an information page for each question. The pages must be suitable for inclusion on a website.

Frequently asked question 1

What kind of tour operator is Especially Ski, and how does it compete with other kinds of tour-operating businesses? **P1**

1   Describe the different types of tour operators and how they link with other sectors of the travel and tourism industry and the environment in which they work.

2   Describe the various trade associations that support tour-operating organisations.

3   Explain the impact of integration in other tour operators on Especially Ski.

Grading tip

Different categories should be described, with at least three named examples of each of the listed categories. Links with travel agents, providers of transport, accommodation and ancillary products and services should be shown, together with the relationship tour operators have with trade and regulatory bodies. The relevance of key regulations, laws and licensing should be described.

Frequently asked question 2

What products and services are provided by Especially Ski? How do they meet the needs of its target market?

4   Describe the products and services provided by different categories of tour operator. **P2**

5   Analyse how Especially Ski's products and services meet the needs of its target customers. **M2**

Frequently asked question 3

What challenges face the tour operating sector?

6   Explain the challenges facing the tour operating sector. **M1**

Grading tip

Include challenges such as dynamic packaging, new distribution methods, effect of low-cost airlines and the trend towards independent travel.

Frequently asked question 4

Can you tell me about problems caused by challenges that tour operators have had to deal with and how well they managed it?

7   Research newspapers, trade magazines and websites and find specific examples of challenges affecting tour operators' programmes. They could be examples of the factors you have described. Describe the situations and analyse the effectiveness of the tour operator in dealing with the situation.   **D1**

Grading tip

You must include at least five different recent examples.

Frequently asked question 5

How do tour operators plan, sell, administer, and operate their package-holiday programmes?

8   Describe the different aspects of planning, selling administering and operating the package-holiday programme including:
   - planning
   - marketing
   - administration
   - operations
   - customer service
   - timescales.   **P3** **P4**

Frequently asked question 6

What new packages are coming up for Especially Ski? How did you decide on them?

9   Design, plan and cost a package for inclusion in Especially Ski's new brochure. Describe each stage of the process.   **P5**

Frequently asked question 7

How would Especially Ski maximise the profitability of their package holiday programme?

10   Explain ways of maximising the profitability of the planned package holiday.   **M3**

Frequently asked question 8

How does Especially Ski ensu.. '' attracts new customers?

11   Recommend how Especially Ski could adapt its range of products and services to appeal to a new market.   **D2**

Grading tip

Make sure you justify your recommendations.

Grading criteria

To achieve a pass grade the evidence must show that the learner is able to:	To achieve a merit grade the evidence must show that, in addition to the pass criteria, the learner is able to:	To achieve a distinction grade the evidence must show that, in addition to the pass and merit criteria, the learner is able to:
P1 describe the tour operations environment **Case study page 40**	**M1** explain the challenges facing the tour operating sector **Case study page 43**	**D1** evaluate the effectiveness of tour operators in responding to challenges facing the sector **Assessment practice page 48**
P2 describe the products and services provided by different categories of tour operator for different target markets **Case study page 50**	**M2** analyse how a selected tour operator's portfolio of products and services meet the needs of its target market(s) **Case study page 50**	**D2** recommend, with justification, how a selected tour operator could expand its range of products and services for its current target market or adapt its range of products and services to appeal to a new market **Case study page 50**
P3 describe how tour operators plan, sell and administer a package holiday programme **Case study page 64**	**M3** explain ways of maximising the profitability of the planned package holiday **Assessment practice page 67**	
P4 describe how tour operators operate a package holiday programme **Case study page 64**		
P5 plan and cost a package for inclusion in a tour operator's programme **Assessment practice page 67**		

Roles and responsibilities of holiday representatives

Introduction

Most students look forward to finding out about the role of the holiday representative. You have probably seen representatives at work when you have been on holiday and thought that it looked like an exciting life. It can be a very interesting and fulfilling job but you should realise that it is often very hard work too. It is a job that gives you great experience of customer care and organisational skills and allows you to live abroad if you choose. It can be a fun temporary job in a gap year or after leaving education, or it can be a serious career path leading to other positions within a tour-operating company. Many of the people at the very top level of tour operation started out as holiday representatives.

The role of holiday representatives is to look after holidaymakers whilst they are on holiday either in the UK or abroad. In this unit you will find out about the different types of holiday representative and their roles and responsibilities.

You will find out how a holiday representative deals with customers and carry out some practical activities to deal with customers in a range of situations. We will look at the the legal responsibilities of holiday representatives and their role in ensuring holidaymakers have a safe environment.

After completing this unit you should be able to achieve the following outcomes:

1   Know the roles and responsibilities of different categories of holiday representatives
2   Understand the legal responsibilities of a holiday representative
3   Understand the importance of health and safety in relation to the role of the holiday representative
4   Be able to apply social, customer service and selling skills when dealing with transfers, welcome meetings and other situations.

Talking points

Many young people take jobs as holiday representatives as it is an exciting way of learning about different places while working in a holiday environment. It is an opportunity to develop customer service skills that can be useful in any future job. Many people see it as a temporary career but in fact there are lots of opportunities in travel and tourism for progression for representatives, as this extract from Thomson explains:

And it doesn't end there. If you're looking for a long-term career in travel and tourism, we can open countless doors for you. In our beach programme roles like Team Leader, Resort Team Manager, Area Managers and many more are available. It gets better – if you want to try something different, then there are the airline, retail and ski businesses too.

(Source: http://www.thomson.co.uk/jobs/overseas-jobs.html)

Resort representatives

There are many different types of holiday representative. The most common example is the overseas resort representative, in uniform and working for one of the large tour operators.

There are many others. Camping and holiday home operators employ a lot of seasonal representatives who spend their summers under canvas. Some overseas representatives look after customers from several tour operators at once and are employed by local companies and, of course, there are holiday representatives working in holiday parks and hotels in the UK looking after domestic and inbound tourists.

In this first section of the unit we will find out about the roles and responsibilities of the different types of representative and consider where they might be located. Their responsibilites are not just to the customers, but to their organisations and to suppliers such as the hotels they work in.

Property representatives

A property representative is responsible for customers in a number of different hotels, apartments or villas in a resort. This role typifies that of a holiday representative and most people employed by the major tour operators have this role. They live in the resort, usually in separate accommodation from the guests but with other representatives. First, we are going to examine the general role and responsibilities of a property representative.

What do property representatives do?

■ Role

- Represent the tour operator – the property representative may be the only person from the tour-operating company that the holidaymaker meets. Therefore, the impression presented by the representative is of vital importance. A poor representative can lose many customers and do great harm to the company's image.
- Give customer service – the representative is there to make sure that the customer has an enjoyable holiday and any problems are swiftly solved.

■ Responsibilities

- Conducting welcome meetings for new arrivals
- Preparing an information file about the resort for guests' use
- Keeping the notice board in the hotel or apartment block updated
- Visiting properties every day to answer guests' queries
- Selling and booking excursions
- Handling payments
- Keeping paperwork up to date
- Booking hire cars etc. for guests
- Guiding tours
- Doing airport transfers according to a rota
- Participating in entertainment for guests
- Checking properties for health and safety
- Liaising with hotel management
- Dealing with problems and emergencies

The representative will receive training and be given a uniform. They are also provided with accommodation and a basic salary. Commission is earned on the excursions sold.

You can see that there is a lot to the job and, of course, the representative has to be on call in case of emergency, although when there are several representatives in a resort they have a rota for this. Problems may range from overbookings to serious illness or even death. You will have an opportunity later in this unit to consider some of the problems that you might face as a representative and see how you would deal with them.

Case study: First Choice

The following extract from www.firstchoice4jobs.co.uk summarises the role of the representative. If you look at the website you can see all the different types of representative jobs available and even apply online.

What you'll be doing

For our customer

You will provide excellent customer service and promote relevant excursions to ensure guests have a fantastic holiday. A fountain of holiday and resort knowledge, you'll ensure that every one of our customers has the time of their life and be a key ingredient in ensuring the success of their holiday.

For our company

It's a big commitment – a holiday experience that stands out from the rest requires real commitment to customer service and a personality that truly shines. Add to that a flair for sales and teamwork, and you'll leave a lasting impression of First Choice. This formula will enable you to meet customer service and financial targets whilst using your creative ideas to generate extra income.

(Source: http://www.firstchoice4jobs.co.uk/fe/tpl_firstchoice01.
asp?s=enPmSXuHfWlnKkWfc&jobid=23855,6568652371&
key=5476869&c=211565233423&pagestamp=seuleqytckiycwqxpr)

Take a look at www.firstchoice4jobs.co.uk and make some brief notes on the types of representative jobs available.

The role and responsibility of the representative vary according to the type of property and holiday brand the representative is working with. We are going to look at some of the variations on the property representative role.

Holidays for 18–30s

Representative work for companies such as 18–30s, 2wentys and Escapades is often very appealing to young people, as there is a great deal of partying! These representatives have to party almost every night even when they don't feel like it. In addition to the usual duties of a representative, they are expected to take their guests out and to arrange games and drinking competitions so that they go home having had a wonderful time. Representatives need to have lots of energy and stamina as there isn't much time for sleep and they need to be able to keep sober and sensible when all around are not. They must have initiative because with the kind of nightlife that is going on there may be problems of sickness, injury or theft to sort out. They also have to be young so that they fit in with the age group of the client. These positions are seasonal and the representatives can expect to be employed from May to September or October. There is a lot more demand for 18–30-type holidays in the peak summer season so there are more jobs for representatives in that period which means this job can fit in with studying. These representatives work in major summer holiday resorts all over western Europe.

▼ **Figure 14.1 Holiday representative with a group of young people at a party**

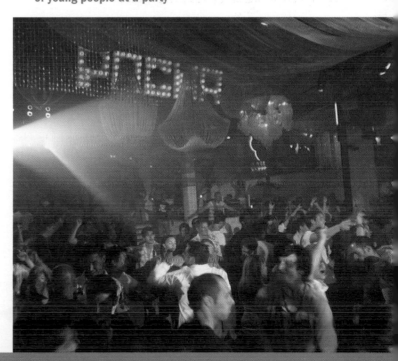

Theory into practice

Do some internet searching and find an advertised job for an 18–30s-type holiday representative. Produce a fact sheet outlining the roles and responsibilities of the job.

P1

Over- 50s representatives

Most tour operators have brands that are aimed at older or more discerning customers. You can imagine that these customers are expecting a different kind of holiday from the 18–30s customer and so a different personality of representative is needed. Sovereign, the tour operator, looks for representatives with more maturity, good communication skills and a second language, as shown in the following extract from its website. Some tour operators deliberately target more mature people in their recruitment as they think their older clients will be more comfortable with a more mature representative. They do have to abide by laws on age discrimination, of course. Note how Sovereign gives these representatives a special title to give them enhanced status.

Sovereign Service Executives

Sovereign is renowned for delivering outstanding levels of service. Through acting as a source of information on the local area, offering excursions or simply advising customers on how they can get the most out of their holidays, you'll exceed our customers' high expectations.

Over 21 with a very mature approach, you have excellent interpersonal and communication skills and ideally a second European language. You can manage your own time easily because of your outstanding organisational ability and will also need a current driving licence.

(Source: http://www.careerintravel.co.uk/sovereign.htm)

Ski-resort representatives

Ski resorts offer lots of seasonal jobs and if you work successfully as a ski-resort representative you should not have any problem getting a transfer to warmer climes in the summer. Tour operators prefer to keep trained and proven staff. Ski-resort representatives do the same job as other property representatives. They are allocated a number of hotels or chalets and visit their guests, solve problems and sell excursions in the same way. They are likely to be keen skiers or snowboarders as that is all there is to do in free time.

In addition to the property representative you will find chalet hosts and assistants in the ski resort. A chalet for 12 people will typically be run by two chalet hosts. They are expected to clean daily, order food and cook it for the guests. If they become very efficient they can get their morning breakfast and cleaning routine finished by late morning. Then they are free until it is time to cook the dinner at about 5 pm. This gives a good few hours skiing a day and is definitely the perk of the job.

Figure 14.2 Representative with clients on ski slope at ski resort ▶

The chalet hosts are expected to give excellent customer service but don't book excursions or do airport duty. They can call on the property representative if they have any problems.

Assessment practice

The following description outlines a ski-resort representative job for Thomson Holidays.

Resort reps

Life's a riot when you're a Rep. Skiing, snowboarding, socialising – you'll get to experience it all in one of Europe's nicest resorts without having to part with a single penny. That's not to say it isn't hard work, though. We'll expect you to make sure our guests have the holiday of a lifetime – and that's a big responsibility. Whether you're making welcome visits, helping out on the slopes, selling extra packages or dealing with resort admin, you'll always find there's plenty to be getting on with. Organised and practical, you'll have a winning way with people and some previous sales and customer service experience under your belt already.

(Source: http://www.shgjobs.co.uk/job_descriptions.asp#13)

Produce a flyer for recruitment purposes that describes in detail the role and responsibilities of the ski-resort representative job illustrated above. Present the information in a way which is appealing for potential applicants. **P1**

Transfer representatives

■ Role

Transfer representatives meet and greet holidaymakers at the airport and take them by coach to their hotel. If passengers are travelling by taxi or hire car they are welcomed and sent on their way. The job of the transfer representative is possibly the least appealing of the representative jobs as the hours are long and there is little variation in the work. You might be interested in this work if you really like a challenge, because transfer representatives face all the problems and angry customers caused by delayed aircraft. Property representatives often take turns to do airport duty to share the load.

■ Responsibilities

The responsibilities of a transfer representative include:
- meeting and greeting guests arriving at the airport
- checking arrivals against manifest
- directing guests to coaches or taxis
- accompanying guests on the coach
- giving welcome speech and commentary
- checking guests into hotel
- collecting guests from hotel at the end of their stay
- accompanying guests to the airport
- directing guests to check-in
- staying at check-in until all guests are checked in.

Some ski operators such as Crystal and Thomson offer a more unusual form of transfer representative job. This is the job of ski-train representative. The job involves working weekends and accompanying customers on the ski train from the UK to France. The representatives have to welcome customers as they check in for the train and show them to their seats or beds. If necessary they issue tickets and deal with paperwork. They sort out any problems and maintain a high level of customer service. They also have to speak French.

Children's representatives

A children's representative usually needs to hold an NNEB or NVQ Level 3 in Childcare and have some experience of working with children and a First Aid certificate. A Criminal Records Bureau (CRB) check will be required, as it is whenever someone works with children.

Duties involve looking after groups of children for several hours a day and organising activities for them. There is usually different provision made for different age groups. The following extract from Canvas Holidays' website shows that they have four different levels of free club activity, a good selling point for families. At Canvas the children's couriers are expected to help with other duties if needed. Canvas do not ask for a specific childcare qualification but do require formal experience of working with children.

Figure 14.3 Canvas Holidays children's representative ▶

▼ Figure 14.4 Canvas Holidays web page

Our toddler-friendly campsites typically have play centres, baby bathing cubicles, cots and high chairs, swings, sandpits, paddling pools and a free Toddler Club for under 4's.

View further information ▶

Families with children age 4-11

Hoopi's Club for 4-11 year-olds operates on 51 campsites and is open during the Easter holidays and throughout the summer.

View further information ▶

Families with teenagers

Buzz Club is an organised programme of sport and social events designed especially for teenagers.

View further information ▶

For all the family

Wild & Active is fun for all the family. Located in areas of outstanding beauty, where the entire family can join in and get closer to nature.

View further information ▶

Disneyland Resort Paris and other themeparks

Many of our campsites are close to the best themeparks in Europe. Go for a short break, or stop en route for a holiday with a difference.

View further information ▶

(Source: http://www.canvasholidays.co.uk)

Assessment practice

The following extract has been taken from Canvas Holidays' children's courier job description:

Job title: Children's courier

Reports to: Area Manager, Site Manager, Site Supervisor, Senior Courier

Liaises with: Camp Proprietors, Operations Department, Warehouse Personnel

General function:

To ensure that every aspect of our customers' holiday is of as high a standard as possible by participating in montage & demontage and, in the role of Children's Courier, by being fully committed to providing excellent Customer Service through the regular organisation and supervision of safe and fun children's activities on site.

This will be measured through feedback from Customer Questionnaires and Area Managers.

Duties and responsibilities

- Participate in montage and demontage as and when required, ensuring compliance with Health and Safety guidelines and in accordance with laid down procedures and standards.

- Assist the Campsite Courier, as per duties and responsibilities laid out in Campsite Courier job description as and when required.

- Organise and supervise a regular programme of events for children, aged 4–11 years, 5 hours per day, 6 days per week, ensuring that the programme is advertised in a way that Canvas customers are kept aware of the programme of events and timings.

- Ensure the safety of all children whilst attending Hoopi Club.

- Encourage participation of all Canvas Holidays' customers' children, regardless of nationality, to be achieved by the use of all available resources such as noticeboards, flyers, Welcome Sheets and daily customer visits.

- Maintain staff accommodation unit and the unit/equipment supplied specifically for the children's Hoopi Club, ensuring hygienic and safe living and play conditions for themselves and their clients.

(Source: http://www.canvasholidays.co.uk)

Produce a flyer for Canvas Holidays for recruitment purposes, describing in detail the roles and responsibilities of children's couriers. Present the information in a way that is appealing to potential applicants.

Compare and contrast the role and responsibilities of the Canvas children's courier with those of the ski-resort representative you studied earlier. You can produce this comparison as a separate flyer.

Taking it further

Analyse the contribution that the children's representative can make to the customer's overall holiday experience. Present this as an information sheet to give to Canvas's recruitment manager. **D1**

Campsite representative

These representatives are often students who want to work abroad for the summer. Besides all the usual tasks described above, couriers are responsible for cleaning the tents and holiday homes in between clients. This can be quite a task – depending on how customers leave their accommodation. The couriers are provided with tents in a staff area of the campsite. The downside of this kind of work is that the guests know where you live and will find you!

Resort managers

It is important that you realise that there is a career structure within holiday representation, especially in busy resorts. There is likely to be a resort office supported by administration and financial staff and a management structure. Experienced representatives may be promoted to supervisory roles and eventually to resort manager.

The responsibilities of the resort manager are to:

- manage sales, operations and customer service
- represent the company to customers
- monitor, train and develop the team of representatives
- to deliver excellent customer service.

Theory into practice

If you want to find out about holiday representative jobs there are careers sections and links to jobs on all the major tour operator websites. Just search for the name of the tour operator that interests you. TUI (Thomson) has a dedicated jobs website for all its brands at www.shgjobs.co.uk

14.2 Understand the legal responsibilities of the holiday representative

Early in 2004, holiday firms were told by the Office of Fair Trading (OFT) to offer consumers a fairer deal. New guidance was issued on unfair terms in package holiday contracts.

Denying liability after a short period of time or unfairly limiting compensation when a holiday goes wrong are among the acts deemed unfair. The guidance came about because of numerous tour operators having contravened the Unfair Terms in Consumer Contracts Regulations 1999 and the Package Travel Regulations 1992.

Key term

Office of Fair Trading – the government office set up to oversee trading practices of organisations and individuals in the UK.

EU Package Travel Regulations 1992

As far as the holiday representative is concerned, their most important legal responsibilities are covered by the EU Package Travel Regulations.

Regulation 15 covers unsatisfactory holiday arrangements.

Regulation 15 imposes a strict fault-based liability on the tour operator for the proper performance of the obligations under the contract by their third-party suppliers. This means that the tour operator is responsible for anything that goes wrong in the hotel or other accommodation and during transfer and has to compensate the customer for any faults. The holiday representative has responsibility for carrying out health and safety checks in properties and reporting any faults.

Regulation 14 covers alternative accommodation arrangements.

Regulation 14 states that if after departure a significant proportion of services contracted for is not provided, the organiser will make suitable alternative arrangements, at no extra cost to the consumer, for the continuation of the package and will, where appropriate, compensate the consumer.

For the holiday representative this means that in the case of overbooking or accommodation being unavailable, they must offer the customer alternative accommodation of at least the same standard.

There are requirements under the Package Travel Regulations for the customer also. If a customer has a complaint they should report it in resort so that the representative has an opportunity to resolve it. If they need to write to the tour operator to complain, this should be done within a reasonable period (usually 28 days).

Supply of Goods and Services Act 1982

The Supply of Goods and Services Act 1982 (amended 1994) says that the tour operator must ensure that the contract for the holiday should be carried out using 'reasonable skill and care'. Also the holiday should comply with any descriptions and be of a satisfactory standard. Some holidaymakers take their holiday brochure with them. This means they can easily check whether the holiday has been described accurately. The operator may also have committed a criminal offence under the Trade Descriptions Act of 1968 if there is a misdescription.

Health and Safety at Work Act 1974

Safety and security factors must be considered in resort, and legislation such as the Health and Safety at Work Act 1974 must be adhered to. Specific regulations also apply where food is served or where there are chemical hazards, for example in a swimming pool. All these requirements are important.

Trade Descriptions Act 1968 and 1972

The purpose of this Act is to control the accuracy of statements made by business about goods and services. It is an offence to apply a false trade description to goods, or to supply goods to which a false trade description is applied. The Act also applies to services like holidays but is difficult to prove as the false statement must have been made 'knowingly' or 'recklessly'.

Disability Discrimination Act 1995

A person with a disability is anyone who has a physical or mental impairment which has a substantial or long-term adverse effect on their ability to carry on normal day-to-day activities.

This Act makes discrimination against people with disabilities unlawful in respect of employment, education and access to goods, facilities, services and premises. The relevant part for the representative is ensuring access to facilities, services and premises.

Contractual responsibilities

Each representative is issued with a contract which lays down their responsibilities and the terms and conditions of employment. These will include place of work, hours of work, holiday entitlement and notice periods to be served.

Booking conditions

Booking conditions are laid out in the brochure or provided to the customer before departure. They are based on the requirements of the Package Travel Regulations but written in plain English so that they are easily understood.

The booking conditions are fairly lengthy and will run to two or more pages. The extracts below, from the Thomson Al Fresco brochure, illustrate the refund and compensation arrangements if booked accommodation is unavailable.

Major changes to your holiday

Occasionally we have to make major changes to your transport or accommodation making up your holiday with us. If we tell you about any of these changes after we have confirmed your holiday booking you may either:

– accept the new arrangements offered by us; or

– accept a replacement holiday from us of equivalent or similar standard and price if one is available; or

– cancel your holiday with us and receive a full refund of all monies paid.

Either way we will pay you compensation … unless the change is for reasons beyond our control … and we will always refund the difference in price if the replacement holiday is of a lower standard and price.

(Source: Thomson Al Fresco Summer brochure 2007; http://mag1. olivesoftware.com/ActiveMagazine/print.asp)

The representative would ensure that these conditions were met and set in motion the paperwork to arrange compensation.

The second extract illustrates how Thomson accepts its liability for the facilities and services of its suppliers being below acceptable local standards. Again this relates to its responsibility under the Package Travel Regulations.

Our responsibility for your holiday

We will arrange for you to receive the services that make up the holiday that you choose and that we confirm. These services will be provided either directly by us or through independent suppliers contracted by us. Except where we are a Booking Agent we are responsible for making sure that each part of the holiday you book with us is provided to a reasonable standard and as was advertised by us (or as changed and accepted by you). (If any part of your holiday is not provided as described and this spoils your holiday, we will pay you appropriate compensation …. Also if you buy a local excursion or tour through one of our official respresentatives, we will pay you reasonable compensation if it is not as advertised in our literature.

We have taken all reasonable care to make sure that all the services which make up the holidays advertised by us are provided by efficient and reputable businesses. These businesses should follow the local and national laws and regulations of the country where they are provided. However, overseas safety standards are generally lower than in the UK, for example few hotels yet meet EC fire safety recommendations even in Europe.

(Source: Thomson Al Fresco Summer brochure 2007; http://mag1. olivesoftware.com/ActiveMagazine/print.asp)

Documentation

Holiday representatives have to deal with quite a lot of paperwork to make sure they help the tour operator comply with the legal requirements. This is in addition to paperwork for excursions and sales. In training, the representatives are shown how to complete all the forms. Paperwork will include reports and accounts. Examples include sales of excursions and expenditure. Standards are set for completing paperwork and will include:

- recording dates in full
- using a 24-hour clock for times
- writing names in full
- giving full resort details
- only reporting facts and not opinions
- deadlines for completion.

Reporting and recording

The holiday representative will also have to complete forms if there are customer complaints and if any compensation is given. Customers and representatives will both sign these forms. An example of a customer complaint form is given later in this unit. Accident reports are another type of documentation that the representative is responsible for.

Resort representatives are usually part of a team managed by the resort office. They are able to contact their line managers at this office should any situation arise where they need help. If a problem cannot be resolved in resort then the customer service department in the UK will be notified and take over on receipt of full reports. The resort representative will also liaise day to day with the resort office and the UK office to keep up to date on passenger manifests and arrivals. In addition, there is always someone contactable in the UK duty office in case of emergency.

14.3 Understand the importance of health and safety in relation to the role of a holiday representative

A direct responsibility is placed on tour operators for the safety of their customers under the Package Travel Regulations. Tour operators are legally responsible for the components of the package – transfers, hotels etc. if negligence is proved. As the holiday representatives are in the resort they are in a position to carry out regular health and safety checks on behalf of the tour operator. Before a property is contracted the tour operator will carry out a full survey of health and safety and make recommendations to the hotel management about any changes to be made. The tour operator must make sure that suppliers make adequate health and safety provision as the tour operator, not the supplier, is liable if something is wrong. This means it is of vital importance that any incidents are fully logged by the representative at the time. They should collect full details and photographs, diagrams and statements.

Health and safety risks and hazards

The following are some of the things the representatives might check.

■ Accommodation
- Quality standards should be met
- Gas and electricity should be provided safely
- Hygiene standards will be checked

■ Facilities
- Swimming pools should have notices with depths marked

Information is given to customers in brochures and leaflets before they go on holiday. This could include information on health and safety issues such as safe sunbathing, use of pools or even crime. This is repeated during airport transfers and in resort on noticeboards and in information books. The representative attempts to reach those who choose not to read about these issues by raising them again at the welcome meeting.

Representatives carry out regular health and safety checks and complete reports on the findings. In addition, they complete reports on any accidents and incidents and return them to head office.

Health and Safety Defect Report

Property _____ Company _____ Area _____

List other participating companies: _____ Date _____

The summary below should be completed at properties where any health and safety issues have been highlighted on the health and safety audit.

DEFECT DESCRIPTION	REPORTED TO	DATE	ACTION TO BE TAKEN	TARGET DATE	ACTION TAKEN	DATE
Management Effectiveness						

I confirm that a representative of Fabulous Holidays has reported the defects, detailed above, to me.

COMPLETED BY _____   SIGNED _____

▲ Figure 14.5 Health and Safety Defect Report

Health and safety check forms are issued and if defects are found these must be reported. An example of a defect form is given in Figure 14.5.

Theory into practice

Make up your own health and safety defect form and carry out a health and safety check of an area of your school or college.

Theory into practice

Imagine you are taking a group of children on an outing in your locality. Design a form similar to the example in Figure 14.6 and carry out a risk assessment on the area to be visited. Discuss your findings with your group.

Holiday representatives will sometimes have to carry out risk assessments, for example a children's representative often takes children on outings and they must make sure that the new environment is safe. Figure 14.6 shows an example of a form that can be used for wildlife activities.

Reporting incidents

An incident is something that happens that is not presenting immediate danger but should still be dealt with. All incidents are logged by the representative and transferred onto a form which is handed into head office, usually monthly. The most important role of the representative in reporting an incident

WILDLIFE ACTIVITY RISK ASSESSMENT

Activity name	Activity on/off site (delete as applicable)
Assessed by	Distance of walk
Date of Assessment	Recommended age group

For off-site walks please write a description of the intended route:

Please note:

✓ All supervised walks must use public and not private land/footpaths
✓ Children must be accompanied by parent/guardian on all off site activities
✓ Activities just for children are always based on the property
✓ Before taking a group off site inform your fellow couriers of your route

Don't forget:

✓ Phone numbers of nearest emergency services
✓ Office phone number
✓ Your consent forms

For the activity you intend to carry out please consider and identify any hazards and what safety measures you will take. Prior to the activity check out the route/venue. Using the form, mark the hazards you see. Write down whether the risk is LOW, MEDIUM or HIGH and note what safety measures you will take. Fill in any additional hazards. Remember, these may relate to the environment, people, nature of activity and any tools or equipment you plan to use.

HAZARD Here are some hazards you may find/look for others	RISK Low, medium or high	SAFETY MEASURE What can I do to reduce the risk?
Mud and debris		
Uneven/holes in ground		
Steep slopes		
Fallen trees		
Litter		
Stinging/prickly plants		
Poisonous plants or fungi		
Water		
Wild animals		
Stinging/biting insects		
Adverse weather		
Possible diseases		
Medical conditions		
Clothing of participants		

Other risks:

▲ **Figure 14.6 Wildlife Activity Risk Assessment**

is to gather information and pass it on to the right people. It is also important for the representative to stay calm and in control of the situation as customers look to the representative for help. An emergency requires immediate assistance and must be dealt with straight away. In the case of serious illness or death the representative would call in a manager. However, the representative would have to liaise with the resort office and deal with family and friends. Medical report forms would be completed and sent to the resort office.

Accident reports

If an accident occurs the representative will fill in an accident report. Figure 14.7 provides an example. Note that it includes guidelines for completion.

REPORT OF AN ACCIDENT OR DANGEROUS OCCURRENCE

Notes on how to use this form are included at the end of this form

A. **Person making the report**   **Property** _____

Name _____

Your role on the property _____

B. **Date, time and place at which the accident took place. It is important that you be as precise as possible in completing this section.**

Date of Accident _____ Time _____

Address where the accident took place: _____

Specific location where the accident took place: _____

Was a photograph of the location taken: **YES/NO**

Normal activity carried out at this place: _____

Why was the injured person there at the time? _____

C. **The injured person**

Name _____ Ref. No. _____ Pitch No. _____

Address _____

Nature of injury or conditon and part of the body affected: _____

D. **Witnesses**

Name _____   Name _____

Address _____   Address _____

E. **Describe the event and how it happened. Please refer to the note below. Draw a sketch if appropriate.**

_____

_____

_____

_____

_____

_____

_____

_____

NOTES ON HOW TO COMPLETE THIS FORM
1. Please be as clear and precise as possible when completing this form.
2. In section E, you are asked to state only the facts relating to the incident, not opinions as to who is at fault. Details you must include are: what happened; information relating to any police involvement in the matter; and action taken by yourself or any other person involved in this matter. You should also include a sketch of what happened, in the space provided on this form.
3. Fax one copy **immediately** to the Operations Department and one copy to your Area Manager.

 Figure 14.7 Report of an accident or dangerous occurrence

Activity

It is very important to have records of accidents as there may be insurance claims later. Design your own form or copy the one in Figure 14.7 and fill in a report for the following accident.

You are a representative in Fuengirola in Spain. You happen to be visiting a hotel when an accident occurs and you are called to the scene. A child has slipped while running near the pool and fallen into the water. The child was rescued from the water by Jo, the lifeguard, and seemed to have a slight concussion and a broken leg. The lifeguards called the ambulance and the child went to hospital escorted by her parents.

Theory into practice

Explain the legal responsibilities of representatives in each of the following situations. For each one, explain how you, as the representative, would deal with the situation.

1   You are a transfer representative. One of your customers is wheelchair bound. They have arrived safely at the arrival airport but they are upset because of an incident at the departure airport in the UK where they were told no-one was available to help them board. Eventually a fellow passenger was able to help them. The airline is one of your sister companies.

2   A couple arrive in the hotel where you are the representative. They had booked a suite but one is not available and they have been allocated a standard room.

3   You carry out a routine safety check in the hotel where you are the representative and notice that a fire door is locked.

4   A family on holiday complain. They point out that the hotel, where you are the representative, is advertised in the holiday brochure as four star. However, a sign on the front of the hotel and all its literature show that it is a three-star hotel. **P2**

Federation of Tour Operators guidelines

The Federation of Tour Operators (FTO) has devised a code of practice which gives advice on health and safety matters including:

- fire safety
- food safety
- pool safety
- general safety
- beach safety
- *Legionella* management (*Legionella* is a bacterium that causes a form of pneumonia called Legionnaire's Disease)
- children's clubs
- incident management.

The FTO also provides a safety-training video and courses on health and safety.

Theory into practice

You are responsible for the well-being of guests with your company in five hotels near to Palma. Individually, produce a list of four health and safety issues that a representative might come across in the course of a day. Pass your list to a colleague. Discuss the issues together.

Think about how you would deal with each issue and what knowledge you would need to have in order to deal with it. Produce a fact sheet which covers the health and safety issues raised and the actions that a representative could take to ensure health and safety. **P3**

Social skills

You know if someone has good social skills. They have a knack of making everyone feel at ease in their presence and give out a warmth that makes other people feel important. It is true to say that some people do this naturally – it's their personality – but we can all learn to do it. Those who have poor social skills are often concerned about what people are thinking of them and feeling shy. This fear prevents them from opening up and talking to others. If you haven't got good social skills, you will not be a good representative.

Why are social skills needed ?

- To create a rapport and provide a welcome when you meet your customers.
- To provide a helpful and friendly service.

These tips will help you develop your social skills.

- Don't worry about what people think about you.
- Concentrate on making others feel comfortable.
- Smile at people.
- Ask people their names, remember them and use them.
- Listen positively to others.
- Use appropriate language.
- Adapt your approach according to the type of customer, e.g. a child.
- Ask people questions about themselves.

Creating rapport and providing a welcome

All customers should be properly greeted. A smile and a handshake will give a warm impression. Representatives can ask questions to make their customers feel comfortable, for example 'Have you settled in?', 'Have you been here before?' Customers can be asked what they are looking forward to on their holiday. These types of questions demonstrate an interest in the customer.

Empathising

This is done by trying to put yourself in the customer's place and understanding how they feel.

Providing a helpful and friendly service

This is achieved by taking time to listen to the customer's needs and find positive solutions while maintaining a calm and friendly manner.

Choice of language

More formal language should be used with customers. Don't call them by first names unless invited to do so. Don't use slang and never swear.

Dealing appropriately with different customers

Representatives should be aware of the appropriate manner to adopt with different customers. For example, 18–30 customers will accept a less formal approach than prestige customers. Children may be spoken to in a less formal way too.

Customer service skills

Social skills and customer service skills are both needed to provide memorable service but it is possible to have one without the other. For example, a holiday representative can be charming and make customers feel very welcome but if they don't do anything about any problems that arise, they have not fulfilled their customer service role.

On the other hand, a representative might provide a new room immediately when a guest is unhappy with the first one, but if they are surly and off-hand the guest will be left feeling uncomfortable about complaining.

The customer service skills that a holiday representative will need include the following.

Product knowledge and providing information

A representative routinely supplies knowledge by preparing an information file and a welcome meeting.

Identifying and meeting customer needs and dealing with queries

When you deal with queries you might be asked for non-routine information that you have to go and find out about or you may be given a request for something out of the ordinary.

You have explored these skills in detail in Unit 4. Now you can practise them with the following role-play.

Assessment practice

You have just conducted a welcome meeting at Albufeira in the Algarve. Among the guests are the Jenkins who have arrived for a five-week winter holiday. This is their first trip abroad and they are very unsure about what to do and where to go. They ask you several questions.

- The couple want to hire a car but neither has brought their driving licence. Suggest other forms of transport.

- Mr Jenkins has some escudos that his daughter gave him. Explain that he cannot spend them and that euros are needed in Portugal. Tell him how to get some.

- The Jenkins have booked a half-board package. Explain what this means and where they can eat.

- The Jenkins are Roman Catholic and want to go to mass on Sunday. You have no idea where the Catholic church is. Explain that you will find out and let them know.

- Find out if there is anything else the Jenkins need.

You should divide into groups of four for this activity. Two students play Mr and Mrs Jenkins, one plays the representative and the other observes and evaluates the performance of the representative. You can change roles to repeat the role play. **P4 P5 M2 M3**

Theory into practice

Try some practice exercises in dealing with problems and providing information.

1 You are a holiday representative in Florida. A guest has a terrible accident, falling off the top of the water slide by the pool. They need to go straight to hospital. Explain what you would do, remembering to deal with insurance and documentation as well as the customer.

2 A guest has been robbed. They left their bags on the beach whilst they were swimming and when they returned the bags were gone. What would you do for them? What information would they need?

3 A customer in Paris wants to go home early. They do not have a specific complaint – they just want to go home and will pay for a new flight. You are their representative. How will you help them?

Deal with these situations and complete any necessary documentation. **P5 M3**

Handling complaints

Complaints are very challenging but they provide an opportunity for representatives to find out how their service can be improved to ensure satisfied clients.

The process for handling complaints is as follows:
- Listen
- Empathise – show you want to help and don't make excuses
- Ask questions to get the facts
- Agree a solution
- Follow up.

■ Listening skills

The first part of the handling complaints process is listening. When you are communicating with an individual you should make sure you are listening as well as talking. In order to listen properly you must be totally focused and maintain eye contact. Show that you are listening by using the active listening techniques you have learnt about. If you don't listen you will not understand what the customer needs.

■ Finding solutions

It is important that the solution is realistic and within the power of the representative. You can ask the customer what they want and if you can't do it, tell them why. Always make sure that you do what you said you would.

Presenting a positive image

Holiday representatives are the face of the company and the way they present themselves reflects the company image. The tour operator will provide a uniform for their representatives and this should be worn during working hours. It should be worn with appropriate accessories and should be clean and ironed. Even if the uniform is informal, for example shorts and a T-shirt, these guidelines still apply.

Image is not just about what is worn. It is also about grooming and bearing and the attitude you have towards the customer. Being well groomed means always being clean and fresh smelling. This seems obvious but is more difficult to maintain in hot climates and in stressful situations. Nails should be clean and unbitten. If varnish is worn it should not be chipped. Hair should be neat and clean. Long hair should be tied back for work.

Bearing is about the way people hold themselves. It is about presenting positive body language and showing confidence (even when a situation is difficult). Holiday representatives have to learn to present a calm and controlled bearing even if things are going wrong.

The holiday representative should show respect for their customers, colleagues and their company and never speak in a denigrating way about any of them. It is also important that the holiday representative treats everyone equally regardless of their accent, race, religion, age or gender. The holiday representative can be a role model for young people on holiday who have ambitions to be a representative in the future.

Communication skills are an important aspect of customer service so we will explore them further.

Informal and formal communications

If you are presenting a welcome talk or a speech on a tour, you will be communicating formally. When you are chatting with colleagues or customers you will use informal communication.

Theory into practice

Can you tell the difference? Look at these phrases and say whether you would use them in a formal or informal situation with customers.

- Good morning and welcome
- On behalf of Malibu Tours
- I went to the pub with my mates last night
- Hi! How are you doing?
- You mean Phil? The other representative – he shouldn't have told you that, he's new
- I do apologise for the delay
- I would like to wish you a pleasant flight home
- See you then

Consider this

If you have an accent, that is fine – you do not need to try to change your accent to communicate formally, you just have to use the correct language and tone.

For some holiday representatives there may be few occasions where formal communication is needed. If you were an 18–30s-type holiday representative, the emphasis would be on informality with customers. However, if a complaint or difficult situation arose the representative might have to adopt formal communication to underline the seriousness of a situation.

Children's representatives have to communicate with children and would not expect to use formal communication with them. They should be especially aware of the tone of their voice and ensure it is not too strident, which could be construed as angry and thus frightening by small children. It is important to speak clearly and in plain English. A representative is likely to have children of different nationalities in their group. They might not understand English so the courier has to be quite innovative and imaginative to help them understand, using tone of voice and body language.

■ Voice natural and amplified

If you are talking to a group of people you will need to use a microphone or project your voice. On a coach a representative would expect to use a microphone. At a welcome meeting it is likely that you would have to project your voice to be heard. Both need practice and a representative's training will include this. You should always begin by making sure everyone can hear you.

■ Using visual aids

Visual aids help to make a talk more interesting. They can make a point and help the representative remember what they have to say. They can be used in a welcome meeting and might include handouts, welcome packs, leaflets and videos.

Communicating with groups and individuals

Individuals the holiday representative deals with are holidaymakers, hotel employees, airport workers, drivers and tourist guides. They should be treated with courtesy and consideration at all times. Sometimes the representative will be communicating by telephone and should remember the individual might not speak English.

Elizabeth had to speak to suppliers every day as part of her job as a chalet host.

I had to order food for the chalet from our local suppliers. I had to do this every day so the food was fresh and I had to do it by telephone – in French. Well, it was good practice. It was much

more difficult to understand people when I couldn't see them. There were no non-verbal clues that you normally have. My list of food would be in English so before I picked up the telephone I made sure that I had looked all the words up I didn't know and written down the French. After a few days I knew the name and voice of who I should speak to so that made it easier. I always started with 'This is Elizabeth from Chalet Juliette' so they knew who I was. After we got the wrong quantities a couple of times I asked them to repeat the order to me at the end so I could check it.

Good techniques for telephone communication are important – even in English!

- Prepare what you want to say – write it down if you need to
- Introduce yourself
- Make sure you are speaking to the person who can help you
- Speak clearly
- Speak slowly
- Listen
- Don't forget to smile

Non-verbal communication

It's not what you say, it's the way that you say it. Our body language gives a lot away. Holiday representatives have to assume that they are always on view. Even if on a day off at the beach there may be customers around so they have to think about the image that is being presented. On a property visit even before they meet the customers, they should be walking tall and looking ready for business. In presentations on the coach or at the welcome meeting all eyes are on the representative so it is important to give the right signals. Remember the following body language points:

- head held high
- good posture
- no hands in pockets
- no fiddling with jewellery or hair
- make eye contact
- smile.

Written communication

Completing forms, writing reports and putting information together are all part of the holiday representative's job. One aspect of written communication with customers is the notice board.

FABULOUS Holidays

Departure details
Flight BL 2031

Please note for those people leaving on Monday 3rd February, the coach will be arriving at the hotel to pick you up at 9.20.

Please leave your cases at the reception desk ready for transfer by 9.00 that morning.

▲ Figure 14.8 Example of a notice

■ Notice boards

This is situated in a central location such as the reception area of the hotel or apartments. If a guest needs to find out how to contact the representative or remind themselves of the visiting times, they should find the information on the notice board. The representative can use the notice board to give details of excursions and to advertise special events. Guests will also use the notice board to check details of their return transfer and flight, even though these details should also be communicated individually to each customer.

The presentation of the information on the board gives an impression of the representative and the company. If it is poorly presented with spelling mistakes and scraps of paper then the company does not look professional.

The following are some points to remember when presenting a notice board:

● word-process information
● use a clear font
● use colour
● use headings
● make sure spellings are correct – if you have any doubts, use a dictionary or check with someone reliable
● do the same with punctuation
● laminate posters and information sheets
● take down out-of-date information.

■ Information books

This file of local information is prepared by the holiday representative at the beginning of the season. It is time consuming to produce but if it is done well it saves the representative work as the guests can find useful facts and information without having to contact their representative constantly. The file is kept in a reception area for easy reference.

A tour operator may have a set style of presentation for the file and will probably state what information should be in it. The following are some general guidelines for contents:

- representative details including contact numbers and visiting times
- any local regulations
- local transport
- beach distance and directions
- shopping information
- sunburn warnings
- medical contacts
- currency and exchange
- telephoning instructions
- excursion details
- brief history of the resort
- recommendations for restaurants
- departure details
- useful expressions in the local language.

A representative may not have to start from scratch to find this information. Previous representatives will have put together an information file. The internet can be used to find the local tourism website. Guidebooks and the local tourist office are also sources of information. Representatives should get to know the resort and investigate restaurants and local haunts. It is a good idea for a holiday representative to do research before they go to their resort so that they are well prepared.

The same points for presentation apply as for the notice board.

Activity

As before, you are working as a holiday representative in San Antonio. Produce an information book suitable for guests aged 18–30 staying in the Hotel Florida. Make sure you include everything listed above. Limit the number of excursion details to four trips.

Activity

Complete the following worksheet and decide which of the communication skills you are good at and which need improvement.

Communication skill	Evidence of the skill	Why I need improvement
Formal presentation		
Informal meeting and greeting		
Tour guiding		
Body language		
Eye contact		
Writing letters		
Writing reports		
Completing forms		
Creating posters		
Writing informative leaflets		

Discuss your results with a colleague.

Improving customer service skills

As with social skills there are ways of improving customer service skills:

- deal with questions immediately – don't put things off
- try to anticipate customers' needs before they ask
- do research so that essential information is at your fingertips
- if you don't know say so but also say you will find out straightaway and do so
- make sure you know how to deal with non-routine situations, e.g. medical emergencies
- if you refer a situation to a colleague or supplier, follow this up and make sure the outcome was satisfactory.

Selling skills

Selling is difficult at first. The holiday representative has to sell the excursions in order to earn commission and fill up the tours. However, the guests do not want to sit all day listening to detailed talks about tours. A meeting which is too long is counter productive and it should be limited to 30–45 minutes. The best way to sell the excursions is to present guests with a leaflet with full details of excursions so that they can refer to it later. The representative should give a brief outline of the various excursions, in an enthusiastic and interested manner. The representative might point out those tours which sell out quickly and need to be booked early. This is a good closing technique. Having done this the representative should allow guests to leave the meeting and invite those who want to book excursions immediately or get more information to stay behind.

Unit 4 covers selling skills in detail but remind yourself of the different stages of a sale.

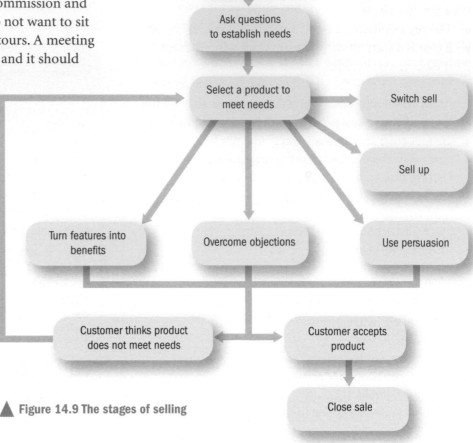

▲ Figure 14.9 The stages of selling

Transfers

Preparation

- The representative ensures they have a copy of the departures and arrivals and details of customers' accommodation.
- Checks the documentation and times of pick-ups at the hotel.
- Puts departure information on the notice board.
- Checks which transfers they are responsible for.

Arrivals

- Goes to arrivals and checks status of arriving aircraft.
- Checks coach numbers for return to resort.
- Greets arriving passengers, checks them off list and directs them to coach.
- Makes their way to assigned coach.
- Checks that the right people are on the coach and that they are safe and comfortable.
- Gives welcome and information commentary during transfer.
- Promotes the welcome meeting and excursions.
- Explains the accommodation check-in procedure.
- Checks everyone into their accommodation.
- Says goodbye to the driver and finishes.

The content and structure of the speech should follow the guidelines below.

- The representative introduces themself and the driver.
- Extends a warm welcome from themself and from the company.
- Gives the local time, route and how long it will take.
- Explains safety features of coach.
- Gives out welcome packs.
- Gives some local information.
- Provides information about weather conditions, changing money, drinking water, sunburn.
- Gives information about checking in at the hotel.

Consider this

What information do guests want or need to know when they are on the coach after arrival?

■ Microphone technique

Using a microphone takes practice. Some people have a tendency to raise their voices as they would when talking to a coachload of people without a microphone. It is important to talk in a normal tone so that you are not shouting at the customers.

- Arrives at the first pick-up point in good time and in correct uniform.
- Meets the driver and checks the coach is clean and tidy.
- Gets off at each pick-up and goes to reception to greet and check off departing guests.
- Introduces themself.
- Checks passengers have paid bills, returned keys etc.
- At the last pick-up does a head count as an extra check.
- Gives information about how to check in and flight details.
- At the airport thanks the passengers for holidaying with the company and goes to find out where the check-in desk is.

- Informs passengers of location of check-in desk and makes sure passengers take all their belongings.
- Stays at check-in looking after any problems until everyone is through.

Case study: Sophie's transfer

Sophie has been working in Ibiza until very recently but has just moved to Marbella to work as a transfer representative. This is the transfer commentary she gave on the way from Malaga airport to accompany guests on their way to Marbella. The guests are all staying in four- and five-star properties.

'Hello everyone I'm Sophie and this is your driver' (talks to driver to ask his name) 'and this is your driver Jaime.

'Has anyone been to Marbella before? Come on shout out if you've been before!

'Welcome to the Costa del Sol on behalf of The Luxury Holidays Company.

'It's 5 am here so set your watches. We'll be in Marbella in about 40 minutes so you've got time for a bit of shut-eye if you're tired after your journey.

'There is an emergency exit at the back of the coach and one at the front and there are safety belts on the seats. Please use them.

'I'm going to come around with your welcome packs now.' (Sophie distributes the welcome packs which are personalised – she gets to a young couple half way down.) 'I don't seem to have one for you – are you on the right coach?' (They reply that a representative directed them to this coach and Sophie soon realises they are on the wrong coach). 'I'm going to put you in a taxi to your hotel at the first stop. I am sorry – she was a silly cow wasn't she?'

(Back at the front) 'OK everyone just a few bits of information about life on Ibiza – great fun, loads of clubs, do put the sun lotion on, It gets very hot. Don't drink the water, stick to vodka' (laughing).

'What about a bit of a sing song before we get there?'

1 **Comment on Sophie's commentary and say how you would change it.**

2 **Role-play the scene and show the right way and the wrong way of doing the commentary.** P4 M2 D2

Welcome meeting

The welcome meeting normally takes place the morning after the guests arrive. They will then have recovered from their journey and be eager to learn about their new surroundings. The meeting will take place in a hotel lounge or bar and complimentary drinks are usually served, depending on the time of day.

It is important to be well prepared for the meeting. The representative should do the following:

- give out invitations on the transfer
- be there in good time in correct uniform
- make sure the room has a suitable layout with enough chairs (see Figure 14.10)
- have promotional materials ready
- have resort and accommodation information ready
- ensure drinks are ready
- have cue cards and visual aids ready
- have any documentation ready including booking forms and tickets
- know which guests to expect.

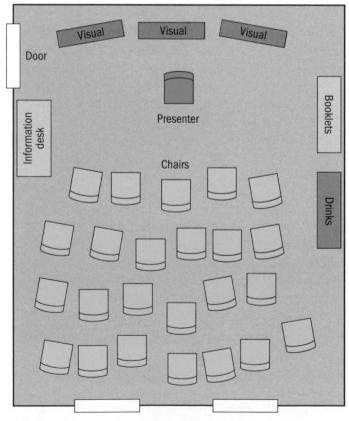

▲ Figure 14.10 Floor plan of welcome meeting venue

■ Content and structure of presentation

The following points should be covered in the meeting:

- the representative introduces themself, welcomes the guests and makes sure they know customers' names
- makes sure refreshments are served
- asks if everyone has settled in
- distributes information sheets on excursions
- provides information on hotel facilities, e.g. changing money, swimming pool, restaurant times, safes
- provides local information, e.g. transport, beaches, restaurants, shopping, telephoning and medical information
- tells guests about location of notice board, information file and representative's visiting times and contact details
- explains the programme of excursions and sells
- takes bookings for interested parties
- extends thanks and farewell
- answers individual questions.

Assessment practice

Prepare and carry out a welcome meeting for a resort of your choice. One or more of your group should carry out a critical evaluation of your meeting. Swap roles and repeat the exercise. **P4 P5 M2 M3 D2**

Dealing with complaints

People on holiday are likely to complain if facilities do not match up to their expectations or if something goes wrong. Remember that representatives are expected to solve as many complaints as they can in the resort so that the customer is satisfied and does not pursue the complaint once they get home. Companies do work hard to minimise complaints but there is no doubt that every representative will be on the receiving end of many complaints whoever they work for, particularly if the weather is poor. ABTA says it receives over 18,000 holiday complaints per year – in theory these are the complaints that were not resolved by tour operators and customers went to ABTA. However, some customers may go straight to ABTA without writing to their tour operator, as the organisation is so well known. Tour operators keep records and statistics on complaints but these are not in the public domain.

Customers are told in booking conditions that they should report complaints to their representative and then the representative has an opportunity to resolve the complaint.

The complaint, if handled well, is an opportunity to give excellent customer service and turn the complainant into a very happy, loyal customer.

- The representative should listen to the complaint, remembering active listening techniques.
- Complaints should not be taken personally, they are usually not about the representatives themselves but about situations.
- The complaint should be summarised and reiterated to the customer to make sure it is understood properly by the representative.
- The representative should empathise with the customer's situation without admitting any liability for the complaint.
- The customer should be told what the representative is going to do about their complaint and when.
- It is essential that the representative stays calm and professional.
- A solution should be agreed with the customer.
- Appropriate records should be made.

Common complaints

Here are some common complaints with possible solutions.

■ Complaints about the hotel

There could be a range of complaints about the hotel – about rooms, the pool or the restaurant food and service. All these complaints can be resolved by the hotel so the representative needs to establish a good relationship with the duty management and with the respective heads of housekeeping, restaurants etc. and report problems to the appropriate department. Representatives should ensure that the customers are satisfied with the response to their complaint.

Case study: dealing with complaints

I won't go into the exact details, all I will tell you is that the service was appalling and one of the restaurant 'specials' was spam in gravy … enough said! Anyway … after about four days of horrible food and service I complained to the rep in our resort. She was very helpful and said that she would sort things out with the restaurant manager. In spite of that, even though she tried, the restaurant situation still didn't improve. We then wrote out a customer complaints form (you have to do this in resort if you intend to complain when you get home – you need your rep's signature).

1 **Could the representative have resolved this complaint so that it was not pursued on return to the UK? If so, how?**

2 **What would the representative do if she thought the customer's complaint was not valid?**

■ Complaints about travel

The most common of these is flight delay, which is beyond the control of the representatives. The best way to handle it is to apologise for the delays without admitting any liability on behalf of the company, for example 'I am sorry your flight was delayed, you must be very tired.' Passengers should be kept fully informed of delays and the reasons for them. Representatives can also ensure that passengers receive food and drinks according to entitlement under the Denied Boarding Compensation Regulations.

Other complaints might be about length of transfers. In this case, the representative should reassure passengers that the holiday will be worth the journey.

Key term

Denied Boarding Compensation Regulations – these regulations offer compensation for cancellations, delays and overbooking by airlines. They were new in 2005.

HOTEL FACILITIES COMPLAINT FORM

- Please complete this form AS SOON AS POSSIBLE following a customer complaint regarding the facilities.

- It is essential you bring the matter to the attention of the hotel management with a note of any action to be taken.

- The hotel management must sign this form in acknowledgement of the complaint.

Property _____   Date _____

Brief Summary of Complaint _____

_____

_____

_____

_____

Customer Name: _____   Ref. No: _____

_____   _____

Reported to member of Hotel Management: _____

Action to be taken with agreed Timescale: _____

_____

_____

_____

_____

Signed on behalf of the Hotel: _____

Signed Staff Member: _____   Date: _____

▲ Figure 14.11 Hotel Facilities Complaint Form

■ Complaints about excursions

Again customers have different expectations. If everyone complains about an excursion, then it may be that it really was poor value or badly managed and in this case it might be appropriate to give a refund. If customers complain about too few stops then the representative can ask the driver to make more or explain politely that there is not enough time.

Most tour operators allow their representatives to give compensation in resort for complaints to allow them to resolve as many situations as possible. Monetary compensation is avoided but not forbidden. Representatives should be allowed to make changes of accommodation where necessary and to offer free excursions or car hire as compensation for valid complaints.

Assessment practice

Role-play the following situations ensuring you use appropriate social and customer service skills. Take it in turns with members of your group to play representative and customers. Your aim is to deal effectively with the situation and end up with satisfied customers.

1 You are working as a holiday representative in a ski resort, La Plagne, which is located in the Alps in France. You are holding your welcome meeting and it is going very well but you are aware of a couple whose body language indicates that they are unhappy about something. They are not smiling or showing any enthusiasm about anything you say. When you have finished talking about the excursions and invite questions, they begin to complain loudly about their chalet, in particular the standard of cleanliness and the attitude of the chalet hosts. They say that their pillowcases were used and they found sweet wrappers under the bed. The rest of the group is listening with interest. What will you do?

2 You visit one of your assigned chalets in La Plagne to find that a member of the party has a leg in plaster. It seems he broke his leg and was airlifted off the mountain. It was day one of a seven-day holiday. He does not want to go home but he needs you to help him with his insurance and suggest things for him to do for the rest of the week. You must also complete an accident form. Deal with this situation.

3 Some of your guests stay in a hotel and you make a visit most days. You are unhappy to see Mrs Allan waiting for you on your arrival. She has already complained twice about the sauna in the hotel. She likes to have a sauna when she comes off the slopes and on three occasions in the last week it has not been working. You have reported it to hotel management twice but nothing has been done. Your task is to appease Mrs Allan and to fill in a complaint form. **P4 P5 M2 M3 D2**

Knowledge check

1 Describe three different kinds of representatives.

2 Why might a company prefer a more mature representative?

3 Which piece of legislation is most important for a representative to know about?

4 Name two other Acts which representatives should be aware of.

5 What kind of things are checked in a health and safety check?

6 Who is liable for negligence, the tour operator or the supplier?

7 What points relating to body language should a representative consider at a welcome meeting?

8 What information should be included on a notice board prepared by a representative?

9 What is the purpose of a welcome meeting?

10 Why is image important for representatives?

11 What is meant by social skills?

12 What would happen if a representative gives poor customer service?

13 What forms of compensation might a representative give to a customer when they have made a valid complaint?

Preparation for assessment

Part 1

No more reps?

Reps everywhere are wondering how safe their jobs are as tour operators search for more cost-cutting measures. Is the service of a rep really essential? Aren't customers confident enough to look after themselves on holiday? After all many of them are managing to book holidays over the internet without using a travel agent. Can't they book their own excursions and hire cars as well?

At the moment it's just accommodation-on-arrival deals that seem to be targeted, with both Thomson and Cosmos suggesting they might do away with reps on these deals. But where will it end? Surely some customers choose well-known tour operators just because they offer excellent service through their reps. What about the legal aspects of the rep's job? Who is going to check health and safety in the resort? Some tour operators are arguing that late bookers tend to be less well off and have lower expectations than other customers – so they don't need reps – or they don't pay for them.

(Source: *Travel News* 21 September 2007)

You work as a holiday representative for a tour operator and your boss is horrified at the tone of the article. She has been asked to respond at a forthcoming Travel Market, a trade exhibition where she will be giving a presentation to members of the trade including tour operators. She needs to present the case for holiday representative services and you are to help her by preparing her notes. The notes can be in the form of cue cards with supporting notes or in the form of information sheets which she can then form cue cards from.

You are to cover:

- a detailed description of the role and responsibilities of a property representative, a children's representative and another type of representative **P1**
- a comparison of the roles and responsibilities of two of the representatives **M1**
- the representative's legal responsibilities in the following situations:
  - a hotel is overbooked and alternative accommodation is needed for a family of four
  - a flight is cancelled and the passengers have to wait 12 hours for another flight (the airline is part of your operation)
  - a guest points out that the beach is much further away than described in the brochure and demands a daily taxi from the company
  - a safety rail is missing from the balcony of a second-floor apartment.

For each scenario, explain what the responsibility is, what action should be taken and complete any necessary documents. **P2**

Describe the role played by the holiday representative in creating a safe and healthy holiday environment. **P3**

Give arguments for the case that holiday representatives contribute to the overall experience of the customer's holiday. **D1**

Learning Zone
City of Westminster College
North Wharf Road
London   W2 1LF

Part 2

Your boss is so pleased with the work that you did for her for her presentation that she agrees to post you to your chosen resort for the summer season – Palma, Majorca!

You are expecting a very busy season and these are some of the duties you are faced with.

1   Part of your role is to collect guests from the airport and transfer them to their hotel. Prepare and carry out the transfer speech you will give on the coach.

2   Prepare and carry out a welcome meeting for your guests.   **P4** **M2**

3   A customer wishes to book an excursion by coach to the local market. It costs 10 euros per person and there are three people in the party. Complete the booking form. NB Your tutor will provide the booking form.   **P4**

4   A customer is unhappy with her accommodation. She says the room is not clean and is too small and she does not consider that it reaches the standard of a four-star hotel which it claims to be. The hotel is full. Decide what to say to this customer and deal with her. Complete a complaint form.   **P5** **M3** **D2**

5   The lifeguard has pulled a child, one of your customers, from the pool. The child is alive but almost blue. His mother is hysterical. You have been called from the lounge where you were meeting some other guests. Deal with the situation and complete an incident form.   **P5** **M3** **D2**

NB. These situations should be role-played.

Grading tip

To reach Pass level you must use social and customer service skills effectively and complete appropriate documentation.

To reach Merit level in Part 2 you must consistently deal effectively with a range of customers in different types of situations and complete all the relevant documents.   **M3**

To reach Distinction level in Part 2 you must consistently project a confident, professional image when dealing with customers in different situations.   **D2**

Grading criteria

To achieve a pass grade the evidence must show that the learner is able to:	To achieve a merit grade the evidence must show that, in addition to the pass criteria, the learner is able to:	To achieve a distinction grade the evidence must show that, in addition to the pass and merit criteria, the learner is able to:
P1 describe the roles and responsibilities for three different categories of holiday representatives **Theory into practice page 76**	**M1** compare the roles and responsibilities for two categories of holiday representatives **Assessment practice page 79**	**D1** analyse how the roles and responsibilities of the holiday representative can contribute to the overall holiday experience **Assessment practice page 79**
P2 identify and explain the legal responsibilities of holiday representatives in four different holiday situations **Theory into practice page 87**	**M2** demonstrate effective social, customer service and selling skills when delivering a transfer speech and welcome meeting **Assessment practice page 89**	**D2** consistently project a confident, professional image when dealing with customers in different situations **Case study page 95**
P3 describe the role played by holiday representatives in creating a safe and healthy holiday environment **Theory into practice page 87**	**M3** deal effectively with customers in different situations and accurately complete all relevant documentation **Assessment practice page 89**	
P4 use social, customer service and selling skills to deliver an arrival transfer speech and plan and deliver a welcome meeting, completing appropriate documentation **Assessment practice page 89**		
P5 use social and customer service skills to deal with customers in different situations, completing appropriate documentation **Assessment practice page 89**		

16 Events, conferences and exhibitions

Introduction

In this unit you will examine the event, conference and exhibition industry and how it relates to travel and tourism. You will also look at the trends and issues affecting the industry by researching and by visiting travel and tourism exhibitions if at all possible.

You will learn about the different kinds of events, conferences and exhibitions, their venues, and the personnel involved in organisation and buying. You will decide which venues are suitable for different types of events.

You will learn how to produce an event, conference or exhibition programme for a given client brief. You will also produce costings for your event. Planning and staging an exhibition, conference or event will help you to develop your organisational, teamwork and problem-solving skills, and to show your initiative.

You will have to think about the different factors which can affect the organising of an event, conference or exhibition and build contingencies into your planning. You may even get the opportunity to stage a real event and practise your organisational and teamwork skills.

After completing this unit you should be able to achieve the following outcomes:

1   Understand the event, conference and exhibition environment in the UK

2   Know the types of venues utilised for events, conferences and exhibitions

3   Be able to produce an event, conference or exhibiton programme for a given client brief, taking into account significant factors

4   Be able to produce costings for an event, conference or exhibition.

Thinking points

The conference industry gives people the opportunity to communicate face to face. The overall estimated value of the industry in 2005 was £10.5 billion according to the British Conference Venues Survey. However, young people are very comfortable with remote communication such as e-mailing, text messaging and so on. Do you think that the rise in remote communication could lead to the demise of events, conferences and exhibitions?

Types of event

Corporate hospitality

Corporate hospitality refers to the provision of hospitality and entertainment to customers of a company. It is done to develop good relationships with customers and to encourage new business. For example, a company might hire a marquee at Wimbledon and invite business guests to watch the tennis and have drinks and strawberries and cream in the marquee.

Many sporting venues provide facilities for corporate hospitality and it is a lucrative market for them.

Team-building events

These are usually arranged as staff development exercises to bond teams and get them to work more effectively. When we think about team-building events, outward bound, physically demanding courses come to mind. These are fun but not suitable for everyone. Other types of team-building activities are available and there are companies which specialise in running them.

Case study: 'Game, set and match to corporate hospitality'

At Wimbledon, fans can queue up and get tickets on the day – or can they? At a match last season, thousands of seats were empty and yet fans who had been queuing in the rain did not get in. Only 500 seats had been reserved for those who queued. The rest of the seats, they were told, were full. Officials blamed the bad weather for the empty seats but critics said corporate hospitality was to blame. The seats are bought by companies and given out to their customers. If it is raining they don't turn up. A marquee at Wimbledon costs thousands of pounds but companies think it is worth the expense to entertain their top clients.

Choose a sporting venue in your area, for example the football club. Find out what corporate hospitality

▲ Figure 16.1 Centre Court at Wimbledon

packages are on offer and what they cost. Make notes and comment on whether they represent value for money.

The following case study gives an example from a team-building events company, Sandstone.

Case study: Romanbar

Probably our most 'out and out fun' team building activity. Certainly a very popular one!

When you want a session with some real team building flavour, why not try a full-bodied business simulation? In a Romanbar session, product sampling isn't the only aspect that involves the participants! In the idyllic setting of Oldetown, Devashire, each team starts a wine bar within the franchised Romanbar family.

Collectively, they must be competitive enough to wrestle business away from the pre-existing competition. Individually, each team will want to be the best.

Teams make their first decisions and the venture begins! Their deliberations are computer analysed and the results fed back on a 'weekly' basis in the form of financial statements and general information on the state of the business.

But no business or service is only about facts and figures, of course. It's also about knowledge, skill and application. Our wide range of activities allow you to:

- Learn bar flair from our speciailist trainer. Watch those bottles fly!
- Mix 'traffic light' cocktails and learn about many more.

- Volunteer for your bar's cheese rolling team and take on the other bars.
- Have a fantastic time *and* take away real team improvements. Brilliant!

Your new-found expertise converts prospective customers into revenue.

Can you demonstrate an understanding of the marketplace as a whole. Can you collaborate with the other Romanbars? They are, after all, part of the same organisation …

This is a popular team simulation that highlights issues and decisions that affect all organisations. It is ideal when you want to mix business with pleasure in a challenging and motivating activity that people will really enjoy. And if you want to spice the competition up a little, we recommend the use of prizes for the winning team.

Bottles of wine, of course.

(Source: http://www.sandstone.co.uk)

1 **Determine the objectives of a Romanbar team-building activity for a team of staff who work for a reservations call centre.**

2 **What advantages does this kind of activity have over a physical team-building session?**

Theory into practice

You could organise a team-building event for your group. You can find out about activities in your local area. What about devising your own team-building course and running it for another group of students?

Incentives

Incentives can be used for employees or for customers. Offering incentives for employees is a way of rewarding staff for hard work or loyalty and motivating staff to improve performance. Similarly, customers can be rewarded for loyalty or encouraged to make future orders through incentive events. These may take the form of corporate hospitality or travel or even gifts.

An annual National Incentive Show is held at the National Exhibiton Centre (NEC) in Birmingham. The following are some examples of what is exhibited:

- Achievement awards
- Business gifts
- Competition and game prizes
- Experiences
- Incentive travel
- Promotional merchandise and clothing.

Fund raising

Some organisations hold fund-raising events and donate the funds to their chosen charity. Such events have several benefits:

- they raise money for charity
- they allow staff to work together for a common cause
- they get useful publicity for the company.

Some charities are proactive in using tourism to help them raise funds. The charity 'Mind' organises, alongside travel professionals, a series of treks, for example in Cuba. Participants raise money from sponsors to pay for the trip and to donate money to the charity.

A fund-raising event is one of the easiest events for you to organise. If you do, make sure it is linked to travel and tourism in some way.

Product launches

Events are held to launch new products or new company names or to raise awareness of existing products. The following is an example From South West Tourism on Water Saving Action.

08 March 2007 – South West Tourism Action Of The Year Water 2007 Launch Event

All South West Tourism members are invited to the launch of Action of the Year Water, on Tuesday 20 March at Plymouth Marine Aquarium.

Using the setting of an underwater hotel reception, the key messages and water saving actions for Action of the Year Water will be unveiled. Our new Action of the Year Water fact sheet packs, staff training presentations and towel agreement cards will all be available at the event, which will be supported by a number of trade and industry

related display stands. A number of discounts on water saving devices have also been negotiated for all those who take part in the Action of the Year.

Programme

10.30 *Welcome and launch. Setting up an underwater hotel reception, divers dressed as hotel staff will unveil the key messages and water saving actions associated with Action of the Year – Water and illustrate just how much water the tourism industry uses.*

10.50 *Guest speaker – Chris Hines*

11.00 *Introduction to Action of the Year*

11.10 *Envirowise – practical environmental advice for businesses*

11.30 *Coffee and Pastries*

(Source: http://www.swtourism.co.uk/html/08_march_2007__south_west_tourism_action_of_the_year_water_2007_launch_event.asp)

Theory into practice

You could put on a launch event as a means of raising awareness locally about new programmes or courses at your school or college. Hold a discussion about how you would do this.

Types of conference

Political conferences

The most famous are the party political conferences held each year by leading political parties. Popular venues for the main parties are Brighton, Blackpool and Bournemouth. It is not mere coincidence that they are held in these seaside towns. The seaside resorts heavily rely on conference business outside the summer holiday season. Political conferences related to travel and tourism include those held by the World Tourism Organisation. A full list of its events can be found on its website. Examples include a Summit of Ministers of Tourism and Environment of Latin America and the Caribbean and an

▲ **Figure 16.2 Political party conference**

International Seminar on tourist marketing planning and evaluation of promotional activities

Business meetings

Many business meetings are held on work premises as part of the working day. However, there are occasions when this is unsuitable:

- when a group of staff need uninterrupted time to discuss policy or issues – they may hire a room in a local hotel
- when a supplier needs to meet a customer – if only two or three people are involved in a meeting they can meet in the lounge of a hotel or airport without any charge.
- when everyone needs to come together for a full meeting such as an Annual General Meeting.

Annual conferences

Annual conferences may be held by a single company to bring their employees together or they may be organised to bring interested professionals together to discuss industry issues.

Travel Insight is an example of an industry conference. It is aimed at travel marketers and discusses a number of key marketing topics, for example consumer behaviour. Delegates or their employers pay to attend and are attracted because high-level speakers attend the conference.

Types of exhibition

Trade fairs

Key term

Trade fair – an exhibition held for people working within a particular industry. It gives an opportunity for people to meet and do business together and see what new products and services are on offer.

The World Travel Market is held annually in London and is probably the best-known travel-related trade fair. It attracts visitors from overseas as well as the UK. In recent years it has moved to the ExCeL venue in east London. Trade fairs provide an opportunity for industry members to meet up and conduct their business. They also give an opportunity to find out about latest developments in the industry.

British Travel Trade Fair is held in Birmingham in the spring at the NEC. British Travel Trade Fair promotes itself in the following way:

British Travel Trade Fair is the established exhibition dedicated to showcasing travel and tourism products and services from the UK and Ireland to a domestic and incoming audience.

BTTF fits ideally within the business cycle, offering face-to-face opportunities for both larger and small companies and destinations, to generate business, contract, network and gather information.

Held annually, over two days at the NEC Birmingham in March, British Travel Trade Fair is organised by Reed Travel Exhibitions, global leaders in travel trade exhibitions on behalf of Visit Britain in conjunction with VisitScotland, the Wales Tourist Board and Tourism Ireland.

(Source: http://www.britishtraveltradefair.com)

International Confex is a trade fair about trade fairs! It is billed as the UK's leading event exhibition, bringing together event organisers, venue providers and support services in the UK and abroad.

Consider this

Restricted student attendance (in groups and with a tutor) is allowed at travel trade fairs on some of the days. These are useful events to attend to carry out research and learn how the industry networks.

Promotion

Most exhibitions have the aim of promoting new sales and attracting potential customers. Examples in travel and tourism include the Travel Technology Show. Such a show would not be of interest to the public but would attract trade customers who need to update technology in their business. This particular event boasts over 100 suppliers exhibiting.

Further examples of exhibitions are the holiday and travel shows held annually in Glasgow and Manchester. Visitors at these events are potential holidaymakers, from the general public. These are known as consumer exhibitions rather than trade shows.

Many people attend shows on products or themes which interest them as a leisure activity. An example is the Ideal Home Exhibition. With this in mind, exhibitors provide entertainment, free samples etc. to attract more visitors, but the ultimate aim of the exhibition is to sell.

Theory into practice

20 February, 2007

Aboriginal tourism highlighted in roadshow

A two-week 'Indigenous Experience' roadshow highlighting Aboriginal and Torres Strait Islander tourism experiences in Australia kicks off this week.

The roadshow is the first of its kind for Tourism Australia and starts in London on Thursday (February 22) before travelling to Milan, Paris, Utrecht, finishing in Berlin on March 9.

A delegation of 15 Indigenous tourism operators will run a series of trade and media workshops led by Aden Ridgeway, executive chair of Indigenous Tourism Australia.

Australia House in London will be the venue for appointments followed by a consumer event with celebrity Australian chef Mark Olive and the Nunukul Yuggera dance troupe providing entertainment.

The roadshow has been timed around tourism trade events including BIT in Milan this week and ITB in Berlin on March 7–11.

(Source: http://www.travelmole.com/stories/1115976.php?mpnlog=1)

1 What are the advantages of putting on this event as a roadshow rather than a one-location event?

2 How else might it be run?

Consider this

The website www.exhibitions.co.uk lists all the trade fairs and exhibitions in the UK. Have a look and see if you can find travel and tourism exhibitions.

Roadshow

An exhibition is a roadshow if it travels around different locations. This is costly as, of course, all the equipment and exhibits have to travel with it.

Organisations

Venue-finding agencies

Most organisations involved in venue-finding offer the service as part of an extended range of services. Once the venue has been confirmed and booked for the client, they will offer a conference-organising service too. Venue-finding agencies build up databases of contacts and find suitable venues to match the clients' requirements. They do not charge clients for the venue-finding service as they earn their fees on commission from the venue. However, they need to offer more services than venue-finding, as it is easy for customers to trawl the internet themselves and find suitable premises.

Some Tourist Information Centres offer venue-finding services. They have excellent knowledge of local venues and can advise on suitability. The service allows them to make some extra revenue in commissions and they can offer other services to organisers and delegates, for example souvenirs of the area, visits to attractions or walking tours.

Conference organisers

Around one-third of conferences are booked by a professional conference organiser or venue-finding agency. Organising an event or conference is very time-consuming and within a company it may be that a busy member of staff has this task on top of their normal duties. Conference organisers take the stress away from companies, who merely tell the organiser what their requirements are and allow them to do all the work. The service they offer will include:

- offering a choice of suitable venues
- putting together a delegate package
- making all bookings
- liaising with the venue
- organising catering
- organising signage
- booking accommodation
- arranging speakers
- booking transport
- arranging audio-visual equipment.

Exhibition organisers

There are several large exhibition organisers in the UK. UK-headquartered Reed Exhibitions is the world's leading organiser of trade and consumer events.

The following is how Reed explains its role on its website.

Reed Exhibitions excels in creating high profile, highly targeted business and consumer exhibitions and events to establish and maintain business relations, and generate new business.

Every year we run over 460 events in 34 countries, bringing together over 6 million active event participants worldwide. With 2,400 employees in 37 offices around the globe we serve 52 industries worldwide.

Our network of offices and promoters extends to 65 countries. With more market-leading events than any other organiser, nobody delivers more business contacts than Reed Exhibitions.

(Source: http://www.reedexpo.com)

There are also smaller companies successfully operating in exhibition organisation. An example is John Fish Exhibitions Ltd which was formed in 1992 and has annual exhibitions on holidays and travel in Manchester and Glasgow attracting 77,000 and 50,000 visitors, respectively.

Event-management companies

These companies are experts in organising and managing events to a given client brief. Everything they do is tailor made to fit that client's needs. They will have a network of venue providers, caterers and entertainers to call on to provide services at competitive rates. They save the client a lot of time and anxiety in putting on an event.

Customers

Corporate

Customers at exhibitions and events fall into two main categories. First, there are the exhibitors. These are the buyers of space and stands and they are the main source of income for the exhibition organisers. Secondly, there are the people who attend the exhibition and usually pay an entrance fee. This is the second strand of income for the exhibition organisers.

The exhibitors may be companies, government organisations such as VisitBritain or trade associations like the Federation of Tour Operators. Of course, the nature of exhibitor depends on the type of exhibition.

Those attending the exhibition may be corporate customers or members of the public or a mix. Again this depends on the type of exhibition or event.

The customers for a conference are the delegates who attend – they are usually corporate customers as they represent their companies.

These customers may be domestic, that is UK-based, or international. The UK conference market's international customers are mainly from the USA, Germany and France. Emerging markets are China because of 'approved destination status' granted to the UK and other European countries. Central American countries such as Panama, Nicaragua and El Salvador have had rapid growth in their economies and are likely new customers for UK conferences.

Associations

Customers can be associations, for example ABTA, who wish to put on a conference or event for their members. The Association of British Travel Organisers to France holds an annual conference for members – in 2007 it was held at Futuroscope in Poitiers.

Governmental

Government departments, agencies and local authorities are often customers of conferences and corporate events. Conferences may be held to discuss policy on tourism or other matters.

Private individuals

Many leisure exhibitions are open to the general public and attract individuals. Examples are the Ideal Home Show and the Boat Show.

Theory into practice

The Business Travel Show is organised by Centaur and the London show takes place at Olympia. Identify the different categories of customers for Centaur.

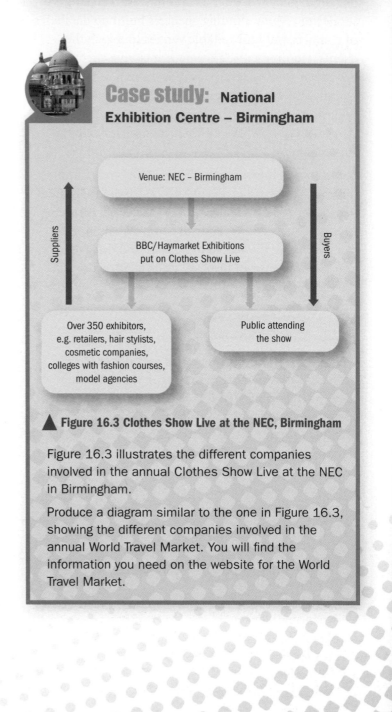

Case study: National Exhibition Centre – Birmingham

Venue: NEC – Birmingham

Suppliers

Buyers

BBC/Haymarket Exhibitions put on Clothes Show Live

Over 350 exhibitors, e.g. retailers, hair stylists, cosmetic companies, colleges with fashion courses, model agencies

Public attending the show

▲ Figure 16.3 Clothes Show Live at the NEC, Birmingham

Figure 16.3 illustrates the different companies involved in the annual Clothes Show Live at the NEC in Birmingham.

Produce a diagram similar to the one in Figure 16.3, showing the different companies involved in the annual World Travel Market. You will find the information you need on the website for the World Travel Market.

Trends

Popularity of unusual venues

According to the British Conference Venue Survey of 2006, there were an estimated 1.58 million conferences in the UK in 2005 – an average of 452 per venue. The most popular venues for conferences are hotels, universities and other academic venues.

However, organisers of corporate events are looking for more unusual venues where an event can be organised around a particular theme and customers or employees can enjoy a more unusual experience. Some of these more unusual venues are introduced in the next section.

Growth of venue-finding and event-management companies

An internet search will find hundreds of these companies. There is a trend to use them as they are experts and save time for busy managers. Although they usually charge a fee for their services, the overall cost of the event is not necessarily increased as they are able to get services at good rates.

Impact of video-conferencing

Key term

Video-conferencing – system that allows two or more people in different locations to link up and communicate by video.

The advent of video-conferencing did not have the expected impact on conferences and business meetings. It seems that people still prefer to meet and talk face-to-face. With video-conferencing, the camera focuses on the person who is speaking so it is impossible to gauge reactions of the rest of the meeting and to get an instinctive feel for the meeting. It is least suitable for large meetings.

Growth of budget meeting facilities

There is a trend for meetings to become smaller and shorter. The reasons are so that companies can control spending, so that more frequent and flexible meetings can be held and because employees are reluctant to spend long periods of time in meetings they feel are not always relevant to them. This trend has led to companies choosing smaller and cheaper venues for meetings and often seeking out the more unusual venues.

Increasing security procedures

Some events have been cancelled because of terrorist fears in major cities. Organisers must have sufficient security procedures in place to reassure delegates and customers. People attending exhibitions may be subject to bag searches and other security procedures.

■ Security personnel suppliers

For an event, security personnel will be needed and there are specialist agencies who provide security. They can take charge of crowd management, car parking, entry control, front-of-house security and other safety issues. At a large event it is worth getting a specialist company to oversee security as they will also be able to advise on what is required for a particular event.

Assessment practice

Study a city or major town in your own area and describe the event, conference and exhibition environment. Give examples of provision in each category. Explain what trends and issues affect the provision of events, conferences and exhibitions in the area. **P1 M1**

Taking it further

Consider the potential for growth of events, conferences and exhibitions in the area. This could be in terms of attracting new customers or increasing revenue. **D1**

Venues

Purpose-built centres

Purpose-built centres are the least popular venues for conferences. However, national exhibitions are held in purpose-built centres as they are so large and they need to be in venues that can accommodate large numbers of visitors and are accessible by all modes of transport.

There are several purpose-built exhibition and conference centres in the UK. We have already mentioned the NEC in Birmingham, the biggest venue. You may have heard of Olympia and Earls Court in London and GMEX in Manchester. In Glasgow, there is the Scottish Exhibition and Conference Centre.

Consider this

Up to 4 million people visit the NEC each year. The NEC has several venues within its complex, suitable for large exhibitions, events such as the Clothes Show and International Motor Show and even concerts by top rock and pop stars. Conference rooms for smaller groups of people are also available.

Hotels

Hotels are the most popular venues for conferences. The average number of conferences held per year in hotels is over 500. All hotels want to cultivate the business market and will provide conference and meeting facilities. In addition, local sales exhibitions are held at hotels. Examples include wedding fairs and property exhibitions. Hotels are also suitable for many events as catering and entertainment facilities are readily available.

Academic venues

Academic venues are ideal for conferences and meetings as they have all the necessary facilities inbuilt. Student rooms can be used to accommodate delegates and catering facilities are readily available. Lecture theatres provide room for large numbers of people with audio-visual facilities for speakers. Universities and colleges are pleased to have the opportunity to hire their premises and facilities outside term time.

Sporting venues

We have already mentioned sporting venues in terms of corporate hospitality. They often provide conference and meeting facilities in order to make use of the facilities when sport is not taking place.

Theory into practice

Manchester United is known as an organisation with great business acumen. Part of its business activity involves a complex of function rooms for social or business use.

Visit the Old Trafford website and find out what kind of facilities are offered and what they cost. Decide on an event you might hold there and write some notes on the products and services you would hire.

Unusual venues

Many venues not traditionally used for conferences and events are vying for the lucrative conference trade. The advantage of holding a conference at a more unusual venue is that it adds an extra incentive for the delegates to attend and the conference can be combined with corporate hospitality. Examples include Xscape, a snow centre where conference rooms and facilities are available and delegates can go skiing as well, and London Zoo, where events or conferences can be hosted. Boats are popular on the Thames and even in York where Yorkboat offers tailor-made cruises for conference organisers and delegates.

Civic venues

Civic buildings usually have board rooms and meeting rooms where council meetings are held. When not in use for these purposes they may be hired out to local businesses for meetings.

Facilities

Hospitality

Most venues, particularly hotels, have in-house catering supplies and will not allow organisers to use outside contractors. Where such services are not on offer the organiser will have to seek another contractor.

Large exhibition centres provide different kinds of catering, for example at the ExCeL Exhibition Centre in London a number of sandwich bars, cafés and restaurants are provided on site for the benefit of visitors and exhibitors alike. In addition, stand catering is available, where exhibitors can order catering items for their stands from an on-site shop. The shop delivers the goods directly to the stands. The shop will also offer coffee machines, napkins, cups etc.

Accommodation is often required at conferences which is why hotels are a popular venue. Hotels open near exhibition centres to benefit from the visitors' custom.

Licences

Venues must have licences to play live music, to provide entertainment and to serve alcohol. As these are the responsibility of the venue, the organiser need not worry about them.

As a result of the Licensing Act 2003, responsibility for licensing the provision of alcohol, entertainment and late-night refreshment has been passed from magistrates to local councils.

If a one-off event is held then a temporary event licence can be applied for. This applies if less than 500 people are attending and the event lasts for no more than 96 hours.

Equipment

For meetings and conferences the venue usually supplies any audio-visual equipment or projection equipment required. Sometimes more sophisticated equipment and technicians are needed and then a specialist company may be hired. Venues or conference organisers have contacts with such companies or they can be found easily on the internet. The services they offer may include:

- video conference production
- set design (where a themed event is desired)
- graphics
- multimedia presentations.

Assessment practice

Describe the different types of venues available in the local area you chose in the last assessment practice. Try to include examples from all the categories discussed in the text. **P2**

Choose two of the venues, each one from a different category with different types of facilities, and arrange to visit them as a group. Compare the facilities provided at these venues. **M2**

Programme

Objectives

The objectives of the event, conference or exhibition must be clear from the outset. In the case of a conference it is usual to communicate the objectives to the delegates. The objectives should be tested against the SMART theory to make sure they are feasible.

SMART objectives stands for:

Specific – clear and concise

Measurable – how will we know if we achieved them?

Achievable – must have the skills and resources to achieve them

Realistic – not overly ambitious

Timed – deadlines.

Case study: organising a day trip

One group of students organised a day trip to a go-cart track. They had all managed to find sponsors based on the number of laps they managed to achieve. They had to organise transport and the entrance to the track. They managed to have the track to themselves as they were a group. They took lots of photos and wrote a press release which they sent to the local newspapers. The funds raised were donated to charity.

What do you think were the objectives of this event?

Target market

When you produce an event you must know who it is for so that you can invite the right people or advertise in the right place to reach potential delegates.

Time constraints

Everyone involved in planning an event must know exactly what they are responsible for and work to agreed deadlines.

Preparation will vary depending on the type of event but will include:

- venue liaison and booking
- administration
- finance
- fundraising
- marketing
- catering
- contracting speakers
- planning layout, delegate flow, signage etc.
- methods of gathering feedback for evaluation.

In addition, people will have particular responsibilities on the day of the event. These may include:

- welcome and registration
- setting up the room(s)
- food preparation
- guiding delegates and speakers
- taking photos
- meeting press
- hosting the event
- introducing and thanking speakers
- gathering feedback
- taking everything down
- clearing up.

Theory into practice

Imagine you are going to organise a talent show at your school or college and you need to allocate tasks to different members of your group. Consider the strengths and weaknesses of group members when deciding who will do what and who will work well together in small groups. Decide whether you would have a chairperson for the project.

Timings

Personnel will set up the day before where possible, otherwise they have to arrive in good time to set up. When delegates or visitors arrive, they will gain a poor image of the company or event if preparations are still underway. Delegates attending a conference must be informed of programme timings and time of registration before the event. Visitors to an exhibition must be aware of opening times. It is good manners to provide speakers with a full programme of speeches, not just their own, and a list of who the other speakers are.

Minimum numbers

Minimum numbers relate to costs and cost-effectiveness. If the event, conference or exhibition is meant to be profit-making, then a breakeven point will be calculated for a minimum number. If that number is not reached it may be necessary to cancel the event.

Booking methods

People may be able to book a place at a conference online or by post. Tickets for an event or exhibiton may be bought online or at the venue. The organiser should plan what details should be captured on the booking form. It is advisable to collect e-mails so that people can be added to a mailing list. You would also want to know about any special dietary needs.

Figure 16.4 shows an example of a booking form for a conference.

▼ Figure 16.4 Conference booking form

Conference Booking Form 2007

The conference fee includes all meals, tea and coffee and evening events. Standard accommodation at one of the colleges can be booked using this form. Information about hotel accommodation is available from the Tourist Information Office.

Title _____ Name _____

Address _____

Email _____

Tel. _____ (wk) _____ (home) _____

Affiliation _____

Three-day conference fee (including lunch, dinner, tea and coffee)
          Full fee (£155) _____   Postgraduate fee (£125) _____

Conference accommodation:

Bed and breakfast (August 15) standard (£30) _____

Bed and breakfast (August 16) standard (£30) _____

Bed and breakfast (August 17) standard (£30) _____   Total _____

I am a vegetarian _____   Other dietary or access needs _____

For any further information about booking meals and accommodation please contact the conference organiser.

Payment:

By cheque   Cheques should be made payable to Conference Services plc.

By credit / debit card

I would like to pay by Visa _____   If other, please specify _____

Card number _____   Expiry date _____

Issue no. (if applicable) _____   Security code _____

Name on card _____

Address of cardholder _____

Please debit from my account the sum of: _____ _____

Signed _____   Date _____

Payment methods

Note the payment methods available in the booking form shown in Figure 16.4. How would you pay if you booked online?

Registration format

At a conference there is an attendance list which delegates should sign to confirm their presence. Badges should be provided for delegates as it cannot be presumed that they all know each other and they will hope to network – which badges enable them to do.

At exhibitions it is usual to collect all details of visitors. At a large event like the World Travel Market a system of pre-registration online or by post enables visitors to arrive with tickets. This means reception halls are not clogged with people filling in forms, although there is a provision for people to resister on arrival as well.

Agenda

For a meeting or conference an agenda will be required. These will be prepared in advance and can be as simple as a sheet with times of speakers and activities and locations of seminars or meetings. For an exhibition, a full catalogue of exhibitors and their location within the venue will be provided. These catalogues can be sold to provide extra revenue. They sometimes carry advertising.

Refreshment and catering

Organisers will have a budget for catering or it will be included in a delegate day rate. At exhibitions people will buy their own refreshments but they will expect facilities to be provided. At conferences you would need to find out any special dietary requirements and cater for them. You should include times of refreshment breaks on your agenda.

Venue

The following venue factors must be considered when planning an event, conference or exhibition:
- capacity

- accommodation and quality
- facilities
- availability for specific dates
- access for visitors
- parking
- cost.

Once a venue has been chosen, the size of room needed must be determined and the organiser will also be given a choice of layouts for the room. Different layouts are suitable for different degrees of formality in meetings. Conferences for large numbers of delegates will need theatre-type layouts to ensure there is room for everyone and that they can all see speakers. Venue suppliers and suppliers of services contracted will require a contract to be drawn up with the particulars of what has been ordered and the terms of the contract.

Consider this

One group of students borrowed a whole theatre for a day and put on a fashion show. Another group organised their event for children in a local primary school. The local council allowed another group to put on a Christmas fête in a hall at the local Guild Hall.

Equipment

At a conference the basic equipment needed is presentation material, that is, a flip chart, markers and an overhead projector. Many speakers arrive with PowerPoint presentations and they will expect a screen and projector to be provided. They may require internet access. It is usual to provide pens and paper for delegates and water should be on the table.

More sophisticated equipment like video-conferencing or computer networks will have to be specially ordered.

At an exhibition or event, all kinds of special effects may be required from lighting to graphics. These could be provided by a specialist company.

Theory into practice

Make a list of all the equipment you would need for a student conference in your organisation. You could ask your marketing department if they have any college pens or diaries that they could give you? If you wanted to have a display you might need to borrow boards or stands within your school or college.

Additional services available to delegates

The venue may not be able to provide everything needed, or the organiser may just want something different. In that case the organiser will look to outside contractors to provide extras. They might order:

- flowers
- food and drink
- transport, e.g. taxis or buses to shuttle delegates from one venue to another
- accommodation – may be provided at hotels nearby the venue in a separate arrangement
- use of a business centre or gym – this could be requested by the organiser.

Signage

Signs may be needed at various points around the building, particularly in venues where several events are taking place at the same time. Organisers should remember that signs may also be needed to guide people to a venue.

Factors

There are several things which might affect the success of an event, conference or exhibition.

High or low delegate numbers

If too many people turn up on the day it may affect health and safety requirements so you must be aware of maximum capacity of your venue. If too few turn up it will be too late to cancel so you will have to carry on.

Venues are costed per delegate so when planning you have to determine the break-even point for delegates. That means you have to determine the minimum number of delegates attending to cover your costs.

Staff

Staff are needed to meet the visitors and establish their needs at an exhibition and then to sell. At a conference an administrator will be needed to register people and see to any last-minute issues. Catering staff are also needed. At exhibitions and events security staff are needed. If an exhibition has stands booked from different companies they will provide the staff for their own stand.

ICT requirements

These should have been planned in advance but IT can often go wrong. It is essential to have back-up for IT equipment. Most venues provide ICT facilities but you do need to check what is available and whether there is an extra charge. Sometimes wireless internet is available but delegates need their own laptops to access it.

Delays

Speakers may not turn up or may be delayed. You should always have a contingency plan for this. Either move another speaker forward and finish the day earlier or have a member of staff prepared to step into the breach with something.

Transportation

Delegates or visitors may be held up by transport problems. You have to decide whether to wait for latecomers or start on time. It is usually better to start on time rather than risk frustrating those who have arrived.

Weather

Poor weather can affect the success of an event. For example, recently heavy snowfall meant only 10 people turned up at an event for 40. The event had to be held again at great cost. However, the original 10 enjoyed a very good day and learned a lot.

Assessment practice

Your group has decided to put on a Higher Education (HE) Fair at your school or college. The event will last one day at the beginning of July and will take place in the main hall. You are to produce a full programme for this event. This should be an individual piece of work, although you may carry out group discussions. **P3**

The following information will help you although you may add any other details you think are appropriate:

- objectives – to provide potential HE entrants with information about HE establishments, locations and choices of courses
- target market – all students in the schools and colleges in the area who may be interested in entering HE in the next two years – you cannot expect them to pay to attend
- exhibitors – you will need to invite HE establishments to attend – you will not have to pay them
- room layout – must allow visitors to look round all stands in safety – determine maximum capacity
- equipment – consider stands, tables, chairs for exhibitors, lighting

- catering – you should provide drinks and possibly lunch for exhibitors. You could have drinks and snacks on sale for visitors (consider contracting to your cafeteria)
- promotion – invitations to exhibitors with response forms, marketing to schools and colleges, press release
- decoration of hall and signage needed
- budget needed
- programme for visitors listing exhibitors and location
- timings for the day
- evaluation methods needed.

Explain how your programme meets the brief and how it takes into account factors which may affect its success. **M3**

Taking it further

Swap your programme with that of one of your colleague's. Evaluate their programme, stating its strengths and weaknesses and make realistic recommendations for improvement. **D2**

Budget

Going over budget can affect the outcome of an event creating a loss rather than a profit.

All of these factors can be planned for in contingency planning which is discussed above.

Promotion

Unless the event is a very small conference or meeting, it will require publicity or advertising. The two are often used together in a campaign. The advertising for an event has, of course, been planned in advance, and hopefully press releases have resulted in press interest and they have turned up to the event. This should never be assumed and it is a good idea to put on some pressure

by reminding the press a couple of days before that the event is happening.

Even if press do not attend, a photographic record of the event can be made and a further press release sent out with photos after the event. This would still be useful publicity. The photos can be posted on a website.

Promotion could include any of the following:

- Advertising
- Direct marketing to exhibitors
- Invitations to VIPs
- Public relations
- Discounts.

Discounts might be given for block bookings from companies rather than individual bookings. Early bookings might also merit a discount.

We will consider some examples of promotion for different types of events.

A conference for company staff

All this requires is an internal e-mail or invitation for staff to attend. Posters and leaflets advertising the event can be distributed throughout the company.

A national conference for travel professionals

It is necessary to inform potential delegates of the event. This can be done by placing advertisements in professional travel journals. Press releases with information about the event can be sent to journals too. These have the benefit of generating free publicity – if they are used. A delegate's pack can be sent to each person with details of the location, accommodation and agenda. Pre-conference reading can be included.

A national trade exhibition, for example the World Travel Market

As soon as one of these major trade fairs finishes, work begins on planning the next. A website is constantly updated, giving information about dates and exhibitors. Press releases are sent out to all the travel trade press, particularly in the weeks leading up to the fair. These give news updates and information about competitions to entice visitors. Advertising is placed in travel trade journals. Mailshots are sent to all the people who attended the fair in the previous year with their pre-registration information.

A national consumer exhibition, for example Clothes Show Live

This is a very popular, successful show and therefore can afford a large adverting budget. Money is spent on television advertising as well as press advertising. Mailshots are sent to schools and colleges who have previously sent groups to the show. In addition, a publicity team generates press releases and news items to create press interest. Celebrity presenters are an added attraction.

The following example shows an extract from the advertising and public relations campaign for 'The Hotel Show' held in the United Arab Emirates.

The Hotel Show advertising and public relations campaign

Direct mail campaign

The Hotel Show Preview Magazine was mailed, together with a personal invitation, to 12,000 industry contacts throughout the Gulf.

Email invitations were sent to 3,000 key managers in the hotel and hospitality sector.

Newspaper/magazine advertising

The direct advertising campaign involved the placing of 36 advertisements in 18 publications. These publications were circulated to an audience of approximately 683,000.

Internet coverage

The Internet media published 20 articles on The Hotel Show.

Radio coverage

Three half-hour live interviews with Hotel Show exhibitors were broadcast on Dubai FM during the three days of the exhibition.

Bernard Walsh and Joanne Evans were interviewed about The Hotel Show on both Dubai FM and Emirates Radio 2.

Television coverage

The Gulf Business Channel ran a 10-minute interview with Bernard Walsh, along with a review of the show.

Pubic relations/newspapers/magazines

An extensive Public Relations campaign was run throughout the Gulf region by Total Communications and this resulted in the exhibition receiving coverage in 186 press articles. These appeared in both the English and Arabic press throughout the Gulf region and the Middle East reaching a circulation of approximately 2.6 million.

(Source: The Hotel Show)

Theory into practice

Prepare a press release for a sponsored run which is being held at your school or college to raise money for charity. Use headed paper and include a picture that a newspaper could print. Make sure you have all the details of:

- what is happening
- where it is taking place
- the date
- the times
- contact details for further information.

Evaluation

It is very important that the issue of evaluation is not left until the end of the event or conference. At this stage it is too late to request feedback or design a questionnaire. For this reason, decisions on evaluation must be incorporated into the planning stages. The criteria for evaluation have been determined throughout the process of planning. Aims and objectives have been set. The team of organisers meet following an event and go through every detail and analyse it. They are very critical and look for areas which can be improved next time.

Feedback methods

■ Questionnaires

These are a useful tool for gathering feedback. They have to be prepared well in advance and the usual rules of questionnaire design apply. The organisers must determine who the respondents of the questionnaire will be, for example, at a large exhibition it would not be feasible to ask everyone to complete a questionnaire but a sample could be completed.

■ Statistics

Quantitative information about numbers of visitors is easily acquired and allows organisers to make comparisons with the same event in previous years or with comparable events.

The following example shows a section of a report analysing the International Luxury Travel Market Fair held annually in Cannes. Statistics provide an overview but are then broken down further and analysed in a post-show report.

> *There were over 80 countries represented at the show, with a 100 new exhibitors attending the event for the first time. During ILTM 2006 over 42,000 appointments between exhibitors and the world's top buyers took place.*

> *The research also highlighted the key reasons for attending ILTM. Most important was its role to generate new business as 97% of exhibitors and buyers see ILTM as a key method to source new contacts. It also highlighted areas of geographical interest; exhibitors were most keen to speak with buyers from the UK and North America, whilst buyers' favourite destinations to source new product were Italy, Greece and the Mediterranean.*

(Source: http://www.iltm.net)

■ Feedback cards or forms

It is customary for delegates at a conference to fill in an evaluation form. The example shown in Figure 16.5 is from a seminar organised by local government to encourage sustainable business practice. You can see that the format is very simple but gives the organisers a clear idea of the success of the seminar.

Staff and resources

The organiser should consider using feedback from different groups of people and not just the organising team. In this way, different points of view are aired.

Clients or suppliers invited to an event such as corporate hospitality can be invited for their views on how it went. Of course, having been invited they can be expected to be complimentary but observation of behaviour and enjoyment during the event will give a good indication of how it is going. At an exhibition, visitors and suppliers can participate in a questionnaire or can complete feedback forms provided around the venue. They will probably require different questionnaires as they will be evaluating different aspects of the exhibition.

Tourism SustainBiz
Gales Brewery – 12th October 2004

Name: _____   Company: _____

If not, why? _____

Please tick the appropriate box:	V. Good	Good	Average	Poor
1. Booking arrangements				
2. How effective was the seminar format?				
3. Presentations & content				
4. Topic relevance				
5. Standard of delegate packs				
6. Standard of catering & refreshments				
7. Overall event				

Would you be willing to discuss ways around some of these problems in a small group in the months following this meeting?

Yes ☐   No ☐

Following today's seminar, do you feel better equipped to make practical changes to your business in order to make it more sustainable?

Yes ☐   No ☐

Further Comments:

▲ **Figure 16.5 Tourism SustainBiz**

(Source: East Hampshire District Council)

Ongoing dialogue

Meetings of planning teams following the event will aid a critical evaluation of its success. Points for consideration include the following.

- Were the objectives met?
- Objectives relating to numbers of visitors are easy to measure. It is more difficult to measure issues such as 'raising awareness'. Delegates can be asked if they consider that the objectives of the conference were met on their feedback forms.

- Was the venue suitable and the event well designed?
- Were the roles and responsibilities allocated appropriately?
- Were legal requirements met?
- Was the budget met?
- How were my own performance and skills?
- Was the programme suitable?
- Was the evaluation system a success?
- What were the areas for improvement?
- What improvements are recommended?

Health and safety

The Health and Safety at Work Act 1974 lays out a duty of care towards members of the public visiting an establishment. Thus, a conference or exhibition organiser must ensure, so far as is reasonably practicable, that visitors are not exposed to health and safety risks. In addition, the Occupier's Liability Act 1984 places a duty of care on occupiers to see that a visitor will be reasonably safe in using the premises for the purposes for which they are invited or permitted by the occupier to be there.

If an organiser brings in outside contractors to a venue, for catering, for example, then the organiser must make sure that the contractor complies with health and safety legislation.

The following are some of the points relating to health and safety that should be considered.

Risk assessment

The Management of Health and Safety Regulations 1999 have specific requirements regarding risk assessment and it is necessary to carry out a risk assessment in relation to persons visiting an establishment.

When carrying out the risk assessment the following points should be considered.

Who is at risk?
- people attending the event
- organisers
- outside contractors working at the event

What are the possible hazards?
- tripping or slipping
- manual handling injuries
- bad housekeeping

- electrical problems
- fire hazards from heaters or smoking
- food hygiene

How can the risk be minimised?
- remove the hazard, e.g. no lit candles, no blocked gangways
- minimise the hazard, e.g. provide fire extinguishers, train in lifting techniques

For example, at the Leeds Festival organised by Mean Fiddler, no campfires are allowed on site. This reduces the risk of fire and is a condition of the festival licence from Leeds City Council. Patrols are carried out to make sure fires are not lit and there are fire observation towers.

What is the level of risk?
- very low
- low
- medium
- high
- very high

A risk assessment form should be completed and kept.

Delegate numbers and flow

Every conference or exhibition room has a maximum capacity which should be displayed in the room. The capacity is determined by the size of the room and by ability to exit in a fire. A room with many fire exits will be allocated a larger capacity than a room with only a few. Organisers must make sure the maximum capacity is not exceeded and bear in mind that if there are many wheelchair users then the overall capacity is reduced.

Entrances, exits and reception areas must be able to cope with numbers of visitors arriving at the same time. Consideration should be given to the movement of people around the building, to toilets, dining rooms etc. If necessary, people should be guided in smaller groups.

Fire safety

When designing the room layout make sure that everyone will be able to get out if necessary. Make sure that exits and gangways are not blocked and that there are no obstacles for people to fall over. Ensure that fire exits and procedures are signed and made known to delegates at conferences.

Guidance on fire safety is provided by an HMSO publication called *The Guide to Fire Precautions in Existing Places of Entertainment and Like Premises* (known as the 'Yellow Guide').

Organisers have to consider access for people with impaired mobility or other special needs. The Disability Discrimination Act 1995 should be taken account of as well as fire safety.

Security

Delegates or visitors should have secure places to leave their belongings. Rooms should be locked when not in use.

Contingency plans

Key term

Contingency plan – a plan you have ready to deal with things that go wrong.

The risk assessment will identify some hazards but there are many things that can go wrong which do not fall into the category of hazards. When planning a conference, exhibition or event it is always best to think of everything that could possibly go wrong and prepare for it. The most common problem at conferences is the late arrival or cancellation of speakers. Good planners confirm with their speakers the week before and the day before the conference and make sure times and transport details are confirmed in writing. It is such attention to detail that may prevent problems. At a very large exhibition it may not be so noticeable if one or two exhibitors cancel. However, exhibitors may have problems if their products, props or outside contractors let them down.

Activity

Imagine you have invited a group of 15 eight-year-olds to participate in an afternoon of games in your sports hall. Carry out a risk assessment under the headings 'Hazard', 'Risk level', 'Safety measure', 'Who is responsible?'.

Activity

Think about each of the following problems and discuss with your group what you might do about them. Also think about whether a contingency plan would have helped. If so, what would the contingency have been?

1 You have organised a conference and half of your delegates haven't turned up. There is a traffic problem on the motorway and you think they will arrive later. In the meantime your first speaker is ready to begin.

2 One of the delegates has a mobile telephone and has taken three calls by lunchtime in the middle of the conference.

3 The conference has four key speakers and the third one hasn't shown up.

4 One of the delegates is taken ill. He appears to be having a heart attack.

5 You are holding a fashion show and plan to sell wine in the interval. You didn't realise you needed a licence and the health and safety officer at your college is refusing to let you sell it.

6 One of the exhibitors at your tourism event has placed their stand in front of a fire exit.

7 You are delighted when the press arrive to cover your event. Unfortunately, one of the exhibitors who had a big problem with their equipment is talking to the reporter at length.

The contingency plan should be written and available. It allows organisers to check contingency procedures and gives them confidence. Organisers need to know when the contingency plans come into play, that is, what the trigger is. For example, if an event is to move indoors in case of rain, does a shower trigger the move or should you wait until it becomes a downpour? Absolutely every detail of an event should be written down and everyone should know where the plans are and what the timetable for the day is.

Client brief: preparing a bid and delivering a tender

When preparing a bid you need to read the client's brief carefully to make sure you fully understand what they require. Think about the purpose of the event, what does the client want to achieve? What practical requirements do they have? For example, do they need a location that is close to rail and road links or do they need overnight accommodation? Think also about their budget limitations, what are they prepared to pay? You should contact the client to clarify any of the requirements that are not clear.

Once you have a clear understanding of what is required you can start putting your programme and bid together. The programme will provide details of the event as discussed. The bid will provide details of why the client should choose you to deliver the programme: what can you offer that others can't? The tender may be a written document or could be a meeting where you present your bid and the client can ask you questions. You must make sure that you have all the necessary information and documentation to hand. You might want to have the key points on PowerPoint slides so you can easily show the client and they can act as reminders of what you want to say. There should also be a written document that contains all the details. The client will be judging you and your work so you should ensure that all your documents have been proof-read and spell-checked and that your personal appearrance and presentation is suitably professional.

Evacuation

This only takes place in case of emergency but if you are organising any event you must be aware of the evacuation route and be prepared to lead your delegates to safety. It is good practice also to warn people if there is to be a fire alarm test so that they are not ready to evacuate when it is unecessary.

Environmental factors

Event organisers must ensure the comfort of their delegates or visitors by arranging suitable ventilation or heating as appropriate for the season.

If you were employed as an organiser of events, conferences or exhibitions you would be working to a given client brief.

Have a look at the brief given in the following assessment practice for an example.

Assessment practice

You work for the Institute of Travel and Tourism as an adminstrator. The Institute wants to organise a training event for travel agency managers in the South East. The brief is as follows.

- Event to take place on a Friday in June in a Central London venue
- One main room to seat 50 cabaret style
- One breakout room
- Data projector and laptop required
- 2 flip charts required
- Lead trainers = 3
- Travel agency managers to be invited = 50
- Invited speakers = 3 x 30 minutes each
- Workshops of 90 minutes led by trainers; each one will run twice so that the group can split into two smaller groups to attend workshops
- Buffet lunch to be served in a restaurant
- Coffee mid-morning and afternoon tea
- Registration and badges required

1 Produce a bid which must include a programme for the event. **P3**

2 Describe factors that will affect the success of this event. **P4**

3 Suggest ways in which this event could be promoted and evaluated. **P5**

4 Explain how your programme meets the client brief, and how it takes into account factors that may affect its success. **M3**

5 Give reasons why the client should choose your bid.

Be prepared to present your bid to the client as written documents or orally.

Costings

Calculations per delegate

Venues calculate rates for delegates on a day basis or on a residential basis. Such rates will usually include accommodation, meals and use of facilities if at a hotel. Conference organisers may add a percentage onto these rates to add to their profits and to apply for additonal services.

The average daily delegate rate achieved by venues for conferences in 2006 was £43 and the average 24-hour/ residential rate was £136. The packages can always be enhanced when extra funds are available.

Exhibition space rates

When booking space at an exhibition, suppliers have to take into account the cost of stands and space. The best positions, for example at the top of escalators, cost more as do the larger stands. Companies have a budget allocated annually which must cover all the shows at which they wish to exhibit. This budget must cover the cost of hospitality on the exhibition stand as well as any props.

A holiday home company exhibiting at the National Holiday Home Show has the following costs to consider:

- cost of stand
- wine and appetisers on the stand to offer to customers
- props inside the holiday homes
- purchase of garden chairs, table and parasols to add ambience to the stand
- hire of greeters (to meet customers and direct them to sales personnel).

In addition, the company is likely to provide corporate hospitality in the evenings in terms of dinners out and entertainment.

▲ Figure 16.6 Customers at a large exhibition

Case study: Ernst Hotel

You are going to use the Ernst Hotel for a small conference to discuss the next year's business plan. You have 12 staff but it is not essential that they all attend. However, some may be upset if they are not invited. You have a budget of £2000 for the event.

Decide whether it is to be a day meeting or a residential one and what you will offer the delegates. Draw up a table showing how you have spent the budget. Compare your plan with those of your colleagues.

Week commencing	24-hour delegate rate	Daily delegate rate
January		
Monday 01	£120	£50
Monday 08	£120	£50
Monday 15	£120	£50
Monday 22	£120	£50
Monday 29	£120	£50
February		
Monday 05	£140	£50
Monday 12	£140	£50
Monday 19	£140	£50
Monday 26	£140	£50
March		
Monday 05	£160	£50
Monday 12	£160	£50
Monday 19	£160	£50
Monday 26	£160	£50
April		
Monday 02	£120	£50
Monday 09	£120	£50
Monday 16	£160	£50
Monday 23	£160	£50
Monday 30	£160	£50
May		
Monday 07	£120	£50
Monday 14	£160	£50
Monday 21	£160	£50
Monday 28	£120	£50
June		
Monday 04	£160	£50
Monday 11	£160	£50
Monday 18	£160	£50
Monday 25	£160	£50

Table 16.1 Conference and meeting facilities 2007 delegate rates for the Ernst Hotel

Case study: stand application form

Space and stands are very expensive as the Stand Application Form for the World Travel Market indicates (see Figure 16.7). Those suppliers on a limited budget may opt to share a stand.

1　Who is selling the stand space?

2　What do you think is meant by sponsorship opportunities?

3　Explain the other services on offer.

Discuss your answers with your group.

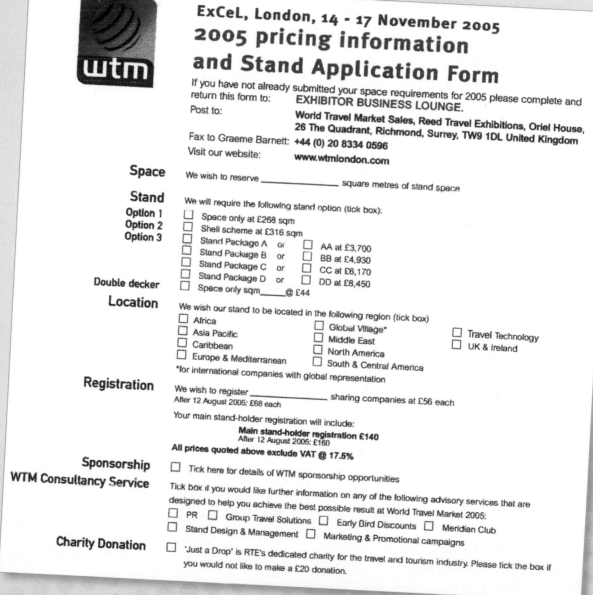

▲ Figure 16.7 ExCel pricing information and Stand Application Form

(Source: Reed Exhibitions Limited)

Calculation of ticket costs

The second strand of revenue for exhibition companies is the entry fee. Exhibition organisers have to decide at what price to sell their tickets. Remember too that many business customers will not be charged for entry to an exhibition as their custom is precious and if they do not attend then the exhibitors do not want to be there. For example, at the World Travel Fair, everyone who pre-registers gets in free. Of course, the organisers then have useful names and addresses for their future mailings. Some exhibitions are targeted at the public and in this case an entrance fee can be charged. The fee will depend on what customers will be prepared to pay and on how many visitors to an exhibition are expected. This is not difficult to calculate for an exhibition which is held regularly as previous visitor numbers are available.

Calculations of additonal services

If the organiser wishes to provide transport or accommodation this cost must be added to the delegate rates when calculating final costs.

Budget and breakdown of costs

A budget must be realistic and include all costs and all sources of revenue. It should include an amount for contingencies.

Below is an example of a budget form for a travel and tourism conference.

What other items would you add to the budget? What other sources of income might there be?

Pre-conference budget

Conference title: _____   Date: _____

Organiser(s): _____

Expected Income

Registrations:

Non-members @ £30   Members/concessions @ £20   Speakers (concessionary rate for 2-day+ conferences) @ £20

Sponsorship (state which bodies you have applied/are applying to)

Fees for stands @ £500 per exhibitor per day   Fees for programme advertisements @ £30 per ad

Other (please state source)

Total Projected Income £

Expected Expenditure

Cost of venue

Travel expenses for speakers (give name of each speaker and where travelling from)

Hotel accommodation for speakers @ £90 per night per speaker

(only where agreed with the Institute and where strictly necessary; please name each speaker involved)

Tea/coffee/biscuits @ £1.25 per person per break

Lunch @ £6.50 per speaker per day

Administration costs @ £250 (one day events)

Any publicity (please state nature and estimated cost)

AV Technical Support @ £35 per hour (weekdays)

Other (please state)

Total Projected Expenditure £

Total Projected Loss/Profit £

_____   _____   _____
Signature   Print Name   Date

Figure 16.8 Budget form for a travel and tourism conference

Assessment practice

Produce a budget for a talent show at your school or college. The target audience will be parents and friends of the students. Estimate all the costs you will have and all the revenue. It is likely that you will be keeping costs as low as possible and using accommodation and facilities in your school or college as far as possible. Will you be able to charge for entry? How much will you charge?

You will have some expenses, for example you might want to serve refreshments. If you have no funds available for your event, consider fundraising activities like sponsored walks and cake sales. Don't forget to ask your school or college if they have funds allocated for student events. **P6**

Sponsorship

Sponsorship is a very good idea as it gives kudos to an event if a well-known brand provides sponsorship and it also relieves the budget. Drinks companies such as Moët & Chandon or Evian or Kronenbourg often sponsor events to promote their brands – but it is unlikely they will sponsor yours!

A sponsor may send a representative to make sure their logo, name and products are being presented properly. The representative should be given VIP treatment at the event. When setting up the event the organiser must consider the sponsor's needs and incorporate them into the room plan.

This example shows how TravelMole runs its 'Fast conference' service by using sponsors. This means that three or four different sponsors pay for the costs of a conference on current issues in travel and tourism and then delegates can attend for free.

Silver Sponsors receive:

- *company logo, 100-word profile and live link to your website from the TravelMole Fast Conferences website (this site will be promoted via email marketing and banner advertising)*
- *company logo and profile of 150 words included in the delegate pack*
- *acknowledgement by the TravelMole chairperson during event opening*
- *free attendance for one company delegate*
- *opportunity to be included in post-event promotion, including editorial summary.*

Package value: £500

(Source: http://www.travelmole.com)

Key term

TravelMole – You should sign up to TravelMole as it is a good source of information about current issues in travel and tourism and student members are welcomed. It is an online community of travel and tourism professionals.

Knowledge check

1 Explain the difference between a trade fair and a consumer fair.
2 Explain what is meant by corporate hospitality.
3 What kind of venue would be most suitable for a national exhibition?
4 Discuss the advantages and disadvantages of academic venues.
5 Explain what a roadshow is.
6 What services do conference organisers offer?
7 Comment on the impact of video conferencing.
8 What is meant by SMART objectives?
9 How is fire saftey ensured in a venue?
10 What is the purpose of a risk assessment?
11 Think of five things that could go wrong at a conference.
12 What is meant by a delegate day rate?
13 Suggest some promotional activities for a national exhibition.
14 What is a contingency plan?
15 Why is it important that evaluation is considered at the planning stage of an event?

Preparation for assessment

Part 1

You recently gave advice to a company named Slovenia Tours who were hoping to set up an office in the UK promoting Slovenia as a destination to UK outbound tourists. They have been very successful in the holiday market and have returned for you for advice once again. They are now interested in the conference, event and exhibition market which is in its infancy in Slovenia. They see the development of their business in organising conferences in Slovenia for international businesses. They want to know how conferences and events are organised in the UK and what issues affect the market. They think that knowledge of the UK experience will help them build their business in Slovenia.

Produce a report in which you:

1 Describe the events, conference and exhibition environment in the UK. Describe different types of venues used. **P1** **P2**

Grading tip

Include examples of events, conferences and exhibitions. Consider who uses the services provided and how their needs differ. Make sure you include trends and issues.

2 Explain how trends and issues affect the conference, exhibition and event environment in the UK. **M1**
3 Compare facilities available at two venues **M2**
4 Assess the growth potential of the event, conference and exhibition environment. **D1**

Part 2

You and your colleagues are to put on a conference. The theme is to be 'Careers in Travel and Tourism' and you will invite all the travel and tourism students at your college or school to attend. There must be at least 50 delegates. You may, of course, invite other students if you wish. Although this is a group activity, all your evidence must be your own individual work and should record your own individual contributions to the conference. Remember to consider evaluation at the early stages and not just at the end.

Programme

1 Produce a programme for the conference which must include:
   - objectives for the conference
   - target market
   - time constraints
   - timings
   - minimum numbers
   - booking method
   - registration format
   - agenda or programme
   - refreshments
   - choice of venue with reasons for choice
   - list of equipment needed
   - health, safety and security measures. **P3**

2 Produce a bid for your programme describing the factors that will affect the success of the event. Suggest ways in which the event could be promoted and evaluated. **P4**

3 Explain how your programme meets the brief and how it takes into account factors that may affect its success. **M3**

4   Prepare costings for the event.   **P5**

Grading tip

Make sure you include all the costs mentioned in the text.

5   Swap your complete bid and programme with that of a colleague and evaluate their bid. State its strengths and weaknesses and make realistic recommendations for improvement.   **D2**

Grading criteria

To achieve a pass grade the evidence must show that the learner is able to:	To achieve a merit grade the evidence must show that, in addition to the pass criteria, the learner is able to:	To achieve a distinction grade the evidence must show that, in addition to the pass and merit criteria, the learner is able to:
P1 describe the UK event, conference and exhibitions environment **Assessment practice page 113**	**M1** explain how trends affect the event, conference and exhibitions environment **Assessment practice page 113**	**D1** assess growth potential of the event, conference and exhibition environment **Taking it further page 113**
P2 describe different types of venues used for conference, exhibition or events **Assessment practice page 115**	**M2** compare facilities available at two different venues **Assessment practice page 115**	**D2** evaluate how their complete bid fulfils the client brief and make recommendations on how the presentation of their tender could be improved **Taking it further page 120**
P3 produce a programme for an event, conference or exhibition to meet a given client brief **Assessment practice page 126**	**M3** explain how their programme for an event, conference or exhibition meets its client brief, and how it takes into account factors that may affect its success **Assessment practice page 120**	
P4 present a bid for their programme, describing the factors which will affect the success of the proposed event, conference or exhibition and how it could be promoted and evaluated **Assessment practice page 126**		
P5 prepare costings for an event, conference or exhibition for a given client brief **Assessment practice page 131**		

The appeal and importance of UK visitor attractions

Introduction

The visitor attractions sector is an important component of the travel and tourism industry. It is the sector that provides the interest, excitement and activity for tourists when they visit a destination or when they venture out on a day trip.

In this unit you are going to find out about the different types of visitor attractions and the products and services they offer. You will explore the interpretation techniques that they use and their purpose in giving the visitor a meaningful experience.

You will investigate the appeal of different types of attraction to different types of visitor. You will determine what it is that constitutes appeal to a visitor at particular attractions and consider how the appeal can be increased. You will also investigate the impact of the attractions on the wider community, in enhancing the appeal of the whole area and creating income and employment.

While studying this unit you will be encouraged to visit as many attractions as you can to aid your knowledge and understanding. You can easily visit attractions in your own locality but don't forget that you may be going on organised visits with your group or going on holiday with friends and family during your studies. Use these outings to take the opportunity to visit more attractions and compare their appeal. You are fortunate too in that almost all visitor attractions have their own websites full of information. Some of them have prepared materials for students which you can download from the internet. Remember that such materials are meant to aid your research and cannot be submitted as your own work.

Completing the assessment for this unit could provide evidence for other units, for example Marketing or Customer Service. Make sure that you plan for this when you go on any visits so that you collect appropriate information.

After completing this unit you should be able to achieve the following outcomes:

1   Know the products and services provided by different types of visitor attractions
2   Know the range and purpose of techniques used for visitor interpretation
3   Understand the appeal of visitor attractions to different types of visitor
4   Understand the importance of visitor attractions to the popularity and appeal of UK tourist destinations.

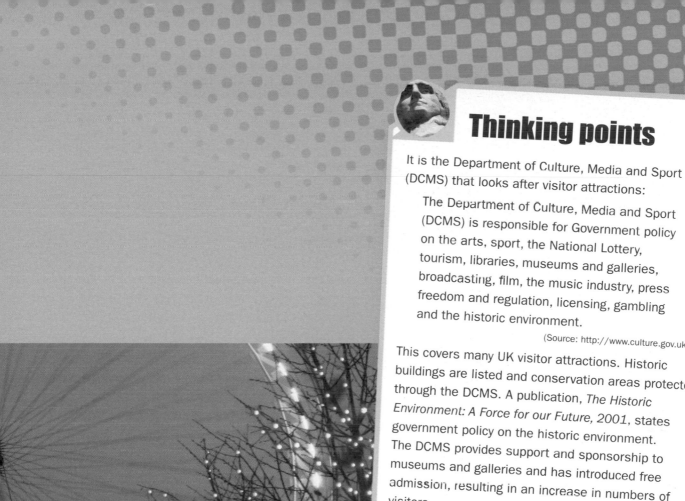

Thinking points

It is the Department of Culture, Media and Sport (DCMS) that looks after visitor attractions:

> The Department of Culture, Media and Sport (DCMS) is responsible for Government policy on the arts, sport, the National Lottery, tourism, libraries, museums and galleries, broadcasting, film, the music industry, press freedom and regulation, licensing, gambling and the historic environment.
>
> (Source: http://www.culture.gov.uk)

This covers many UK visitor attractions. Historic buildings are listed and conservation areas protected through the DCMS. A publication, *The Historic Environment: A Force for our Future, 2001*, states government policy on the historic environment. The DCMS provides support and sponsorship to museums and galleries and has introduced free admission, resulting in an increase in numbers of visitors.

Some visitor attractions may be eligible for EU funding for development. Applications are made to the European Regional Development Fund. The EU is committed to sustainable development and works with the European Community Network for Environmental Travel & Tourism (ECoNETT). This project brings together issues relating to tourism and the environment and provides guidance to tourism businesses.

Why do you think EU funding is given to the development of visitor attractions?

Each of the national tourist boards of England, Northern Ireland, Wales and Scotland conducts an annual 'Survey of Visits to Visitor Attractions' to monitor visitor and other trends.

The following is an extract from the definition of a visitor attraction:

An attraction where it is feasible to charge admission for the sole purpose of sightseeing. The attraction must be a permanently established excursion destination, a primary purpose of which is to allow public access for entertainment, interest, or education; rather than being primarily a retail outlet or a venue for sporting, theatrical or film performances. It must be open to the public, without prior booking, for published periods each year, and should be capable of attracting day visitors or tourists, as well as local residents.

(Source: Survey of Visits to Visitor Attractions England 2005; http://www.tourismtrade.org.uk/Images/Sector%20structure%20and%20visits%20by%20attraction%20category%202005_tcm12-29728.pdf)

Note the main points of the definition:

- it must be feasible for the attraction to charge admission – but many are free

- it must be permanently established – thus, for the purposes of the survey, events such as the Notting Hill Carnival would be excluded

- it must have a primary purpose of interest, entertainment or education – thus, shopping centres are excluded even though they attract tourists

- it must be open to the public for at least part of the year

- it must attract tourists, not just locals.

The top five paid-admission visitor attractions in England in 2005 were:

- British Airways London Eye
- Tower of London
- Flamingo Land Theme Park & Zoo
- Royal Botanic Gardens, Kew
- Windermere Lake Cruises.

The top five free-admission visitor attractions in England in 2005 were:

- Blackpool Pleasure Beach
- British Museum
- Brighton Pier
- National Gallery
- Tate Modern.

Note that Blackpool Pleasure Beach tops the list of free-admission attractions but of course it is only free if you choose not to go on any of the rides. Each ride is paid for individually.

All of the top five paying- and free-admission attractions given here are in England. Each national tourist board compiles its own separate figures on visitor attractions. You can find out what these are by visiting the websites of the national tourist boards.

Theory into practice

Go to the websites of the national tourist boards for England, Northern Ireland, Wales and Scotland and find out what the top five paying and free attractions are in each area. Note them. Check whether the English top attractions are the same as the ones mentioned above. The website addresses for the national tourist boards are:

- www.visitbritain.co.uk
- www.discovernorthernireland.com
- www.visitwales.com
- www.visitscotland.com.

The visitor attractions sector covers many different categories of attraction. These include museums, art galleries, historic houses and castles, churches and cathedrals, gardens, wildlife sites, leisure parks and other recreational facilities. For the purposes of this unit we are going to use the same categories of visitor attractions as the survey of visits to visitor attractions. These are shown in Table 18.1. You can also see how many of each type of attraction participated in the survey in 2005.

Category	Attractions		Visits	
	No.	(%)	(m)	(%)
Country parks	96	5	18.6	10
Farms	72	3	3.8	2
Gardens	140	7	9	5
Historic houses/castles	401	19	23.4	12
Other historic properties	148	7	5.9	3
Leisure/theme parks	39	2	26	13
Museums/art galleries	653	31	53.7	28
Steam/heritage railways	49	2	3.2	2
Visitor/heritage centres	81	4	5.0	3
Wildlife attractions/zoos	112	5	14.5	7
Workplaces	92	4	3.3	2
Places of worship	104	5	9.3	5
Other	124	6	18	9
England	2111	100	193.7	100

Table 18.1 Sector structure and visits by attraction category 2005

(Source: Survey of Visits to Visitor Attractions England 2005; http://www.tourismtrade.org.uk/Images/Sector%20structure%20and%20visits%20by%20attraction%20category%202005_tcm12-29728.pdf)

Products and services

Primary

Key term

Primary product or service the main purpose of the visit, for example the exhibition in a gallery or the rides in a theme park.

Whatever the visitor attraction the main reason for the visit is the primary product or service. If you visit a gallery it is to see an exhibition of art; if you go to a stately home it is to admire the beauty of the architecture and learn about its history. If you go to a theme park it is to have fun on the various rides; if you go to a countryside area it is to admire the landscape.

The primary product or service can change from time to time but rarely changes completely. If it were always exactly the same there would be little reason for visitors to go back. So, museums hold temporary exhibitions to attract people back and theme parks introduce new rides regularly for the same reason. The primary product and service serves to attract visitors but is not always the main source of revenue. In fact, we have already seen that some of our most popular attractions are free to enter. These are usually museums and they do receive public funding but they also have commercial activities to raise revenue. Those attractions that we pay to enter often have special offers with free tickets, sometimes in conjunction with other companies, for example rail companies.

Consider this

If attractions are free or often give away free tickets how do they make money?

Key term

Secondary products and services – products or services which add to the appeal of the attraction and are a means of revenue but do not provide the main draw. Examples include gift shops, restaurants, parking and corporate hospitality.

Secondary

The role of secondary products and services is to provide the services that customers require during a visit to an attraction and to raise money from these services. There are several benefits of providing such services:
- increase in customer satisfaction during the visit
- visitors are encouraged to spend more time at the attraction
- increase in revenue from secondary spend.

All visitor attractions have similar secondary products. They include:

- catering
- services for visitors with special needs
- car parks
- gift shops
- restaurants
- snack bars
- ice cream stands
- minor attractions that cost extra, for example special exhibitions
- children's activities
- photos.

Consider this

Have you been to a theme park? Think back to your last visit and how much you spent on top of the entry fee. What were all the secondary products and services you bought?

Most visitor attractions offer guided tours and/or educational events and hire out rooms for business seminars, special celebrations and even weddings. Although such services are additional to the main product they are a major source of revenue and visitor attractions try to make the most of these lucrative markets.

Types of attractions

In general, visitor attractions can be divided into built or natural attractions. Built attractions include buildings, of course, and other constructions such as the London Eye or a theme park. Natural attractions include National Parks such as the Brecon Beacons and other areas of natural beauty.

We will look at each of the categories from the visitor attraction survey to ensure you know what kind of attractions are included in each category and what their primary products are. We are going to study them in order of their popularity.

Museums/art galleries

According to a report in the London *Evening Standard* (1 December 2006), visitors to London museums have risen 86 per cent in the last five years since museums became free to enter. Some museums were already free and they had a small rise in visitors of 8 per cent.

The most popular museums and galleries in the UK are in London:

- Tate Modern
- British Museum
- National Gallery
- Natural History Museum
- Victoria & Albert Museum
- Science Museum
- National Portrait Gallery
- Tate Britain.

These all offer permanent exhibitions of artefacts and artworks but they differ according to the museum's speciality or leaning.

Of course, there are important museums outside London, such as the Kelvingrove Art Gallery and Museum in Glasgow and the Lowry Centre in Salford.

Nature reserves

Natural England owns or manages 223 national nature reserves. Natural England is a new organisation whose role is to conserve, enhance and manage the natural environment for our benefit and that of future generations. It aims to enhance biodiversity, landscapes and wildlife in all areas,

Case study: the Lowry Centre

The Lowry is an art and entertainment centre which opened at the newly renovated Salford Quays in 2000, an area which has since developed into a tourist destination known as The Quays and including Imperial War Museum North. In addition to its art galleries, The Lowry houses three theatres, including the largest stage in England outside London, with performances of music, dance, drama, musicals, opera, comedy and children's shows. Partner companies include Opera North, Birmingham Royal Ballet and the National Theatre.

The Lowry is home to the work of one of the UK's most beloved artists, LS Lowry, and the Lowry exhibitions regularly change to encourage visitors to return and experience different aspects of his work. Alongside, there are different exhibitions of work by contemporary artists of local, national and international interest. Artists are sometimes commissioned to create work especially for the galleries.

Education is an important aspect of The Lowry's work. A Community and Education team delivers about 1000 sessions a year to all age ranges and covering all art forms.

Within the building there is also a gift shop selling a range of goods, both LS Lowry themed and more general, as well as a restaurant plus bars and cafés.

Building tours and gift vouchers are also available.

As a new building, The Lowry was built with access in mind. There are car parking and theatre spaces for wheelchair users plus free wheelchairs for the public to use, disabled toilet facilities on all levels, infrared facilities for hard of hearing customers, plus regular signed, audio described and stage text captioned performances. The website contains downloadable audio files of its brochure and other information.

The building contains a number of spectacular rooms for corporate hire, including a round, glass-walled room overlooking the waterside of the Manchester Ship Canal, an ideal venue for wedding ceremonies and receptions, and the theatre and gallery spaces are also available for hire.

There is more information, including online registration and booking, at www.thelowry.com.

(Source: http//:www.thelowry.com)

1   **Describe the primary products and services at the Lowry Centre.**

2   **Describe the secondary products and services at the Lowry Centre.**

3   **Explain why there are several temporary exhibitions each year.**

Figure 18.1 The Lowry Centre houses a range of exhibitions to attract visitors

not just the countryside. It also aims to promote access, recreation and public well-being in natural environments.

The strategic outcomes are as follows.

- A healthy natural environment: England's natural environment will be conserved and enhanced.
- Enjoyment of the natural environment: more people enjoying, understanding and acting to improve the natural environment, more often.
- Sustainable use of the natural environment: the use and management of the natural environment to be more sustainable.
- A secure environmental future: decisions which collectively secure the future of the natural environment.

(Source: www.naturalengland.org.uk)

The following are some examples of popular country parks in the UK which attract more than a million visitors a year:

- Strathclyde Country Park, Motherwell, Scotland
- Ashton Court Estate, Long Ashton, England
- Upper Derwent Reservoirs, Bamford, England
- Drumpellier Country Park, Coatbridge, Scotland
- Fairlands Valley Park, Stevenage, England.

Local authorities manage country parks, for example North Lanarkshire Council is responsible for Strathclyde Country Park. They protect different types of landscape such as woodlands, wetlands and lakes and the wildlife that inhabit them.

Entry to a country park and many of its activities is free so visitors can go birdwatching, walking or cycling. However, there are some activities which are charged for to allow funds to be raised for further improvement to the park. Examples include watersports, hire of land and equipment and accommodation on campsites.

Historic properties

The following are some examples of the UK's most popular historic properties:

- Tower of London
- Edinburgh Castle, Edinburgh
- Windsor Castle, Windsor
- Roman Baths, Bath
- Stonehenge, Amesbury
- Chatsworth, Bakewell
- Tatton Park, Knutsford.

The Tower of London is managed by the Historic Royal Palaces Agency, together with other unoccupied royal palaces. The Agency is responsible to the DCMS.

Windsor Castle is one of the UK's royal residences and is held in trust for future generations, so the Queen cannot decide to sell it. The palaces – others are Buckingham and Sandringham – are royal homes, used for state functions and are also open to the public at certain times of the year. Windsor Castle is an official residence of the Queen and the largest occupied castle in the world.

Chatsworth is a beautiful stately home and is the home of the Duke of Devonshire and his family. The house is a major visitor attraction in Derbyshire.

There are two important organisations that look after heritage in the UK. These are English Heritage and the National Trust. There is also a National Trust for Scotland and a Welsh Historic Monuments organisation.

English Heritage reports to the DCMS. It has powers and responsibilities from the National Heritage Act (1983, amended 2002). English Heritage is funded in part by the government and in part from revenue earned from historic properties and other services.

The National Trust is a registered charity and completely independent of government. It relies for funding on donations and revenue from its properties. It has over 3 million members and cares for over 200 historic properties and gardens. The Trust exists to conserve its properties but has to attract visitors to them in order to raise funds to do its work.

It has come up with some interesting ideas to encourage visitors, including touring film locations, as shown by the description of filming at Lyme Park from the National Trust website.

Lyme Park, Stockport, Cheshire

Pride and Prejudice *(BBC)*

The words 'Colin Firth' and 'Mr Darcy' took on new depth in 1996 when the BBC's six-part adaptation of Jane Austen's famous novel hit our television screens. If you were swept up with Darcy-fever, you weren't alone – video sales of the adaptation shot up as people who could not wait for the transmission of the last episode queued to buy. The magnificent Lyme Park, with its 1400-acre deer park and 17-acre garden, is where they filmed the external scenes at Pemberley. (*The internal views were shot at Sudbury Hall in Derbyshire – also a National Trust property.*) The first view of the house is as breathtaking in real life as on camera. The famous pond (where Darcy takes his plunge) and other memorable places can be located with the National Trust's 'Pemberley Trail' leaflet, available at the garden kiosk.

(Source: http://www.nationaltrust.org.uk)

Consider this

Can you think of any other film locations at visitor attractions? The National Trust website has a lot more.

Assessment practice

Go to the English Heritage and National Trust websites and choose one built and one natural attraction in your area.

Describe the products and services provided by each of the attractions. Remember to distinguish between primary and secondary products and services. Include examples of facilities for special-needs visitors, corporate hospitality, guided tours, education and other services

Produce a fact sheet for each attraction.

Leisure/theme parks

The UK market for theme parks reached 13.5 million visitors in 2003. This was an exceptional year and although the general trend in expenditure is still up, 2003 figures have not been met since. Alton Towers is the most popular theme park. It has been visited by 42 per cent of adults. The market was worth an estimated £268 million in 2005, with average spend of over £20 per admission. About 60 per cent of a theme park's revenue comes from admissions, that is the primary product, and the rest from secondary products such as food and retail.

(Source: Mintel, 'Theme parks', March 2006)

The Tussauds Group is the dominant company in running theme parks. The group's responsibilities include the following:
- British Airways London Eye
- Thorpe Park
- Alton Towers
- Chessington World of Adventure
- Warwick Castle.

The Tussauds Group acquired Heide Park, in Soltau, Germany, in 2003 as part of its expansion strategy. Heide Park is one of Europe's top theme parks.

Alton Towers has been transformed by the Tussauds Group and has a reputation for thrilling roller coasters, such as Oblivion, Nemesis and AIR. The Tussauds Group successfully enhanced the product offering at Alton Towers by opening two hotels, Alton Towers Hotel and Splash Landings Hotel. The addition of the hotels meant that Alton Towers became a short-break destination as well as a day-trip destination. Splash Landings Hotel is themed and incorporates a water park. It also incorporates facilities and accommodation for corporate customers. This is of particular importance in the winter months when the theme park is closed.

Theory into practice

Find out more about Splash Landings Hotel and the facilities offered for corporate customers at Alton Towers. Report back to your group.

Key term

Wait time – the percentage of the total time spent in an attraction waiting for access to products or services.

To improve customer service, wait time has to be reduced. These are some of the measures taken:
- signs giving the wait time from a certain point
- information on entry, advising current wait times
- fast pass systems which allow a timed entry to a ride
- virtual queuing.

Gardens

The following are some examples of the UK's most popular garden attractions:

- Eden Project
- Royal Botanic Gardens, Kew
- Royal Botanic Gardens, Edinburgh
- Royal Horticultural Society Gardens, Wisley
- Botanic Gardens, Belfast.

The Botanic Gardens in Belfast is one of the most frequented parks in Belfast with events and band performances attracting visitors as well as the plant collections. It is owned by the Belfast Corporation, who paid £10,500 for it in 1895. There are collections of exotic flowers and plants and a beautiful palm house. The gardens are a famous landmark in Belfast and attract thousands of visitors. The Botanic Gardens at Kew have been designated a World Heritage Site.

Consider this

What do you think the primary product is at a garden?

Wildlife attractions/zoos

The main attractions in this sector are zoos. Examples are Chester, London, Bristol and Edinburgh zoos. Also included are attractions such as 'The Deep' in Hull. Described as a submarium, The Deep celebrates and investigates the world's oceans. The Deep is a good example of a Millennium project. Half of its funding came from the Millennium project, that is lottery funding. Part of its remit is to carry out environmental research.

Farms

Farm attractions suffered immensely from a decline in visitors in 2002 due to the foot and mouth outbreak. However, this part of the attractions sector has demonstrated a strong recovery and the most popular farms attract 200,000 to 300,000 visitors per year.

▲ Figure 18.2 The Donkey Sanctuary provides a refuge for donkeys as well as a source of entertainment for visiting families and other groups

Examples include the Cornish Cyder Farm in Penhallow and the Donkey Sanctuary in Salcombe Regis. Some farms cater specifically for children and attract school visits.

Places of worship

Tourists on city visits frequently visit a church or cathedral but it is not often the sole purpose of the visit. Churches do not usually charge entry as people should be able to go into a church free, but some cathedrals do and either might charge for entry to a tower, for example. At King's College Chapel in Cambridge a charge is made so that the chapel is not overrun with visitors. The dwell time is short in a place of worship: the average is only just over an hour, less than in any other type of attraction. Popular places of worship for visitors are York Minster, Canterbury Cathedral, Westminster Abbey and St Paul's Cathedral.

Visitor/heritage centres

This category of visitor attractions has a variety of attractions within it ranging from Somerset House to Cadbury World and the world-famous Old Blacksmith's Shop Centre, Gretna Green – an exhibition built around the original blacksmith's shop. It houses an exhibition about runaway weddings from the first one in 1754.

The following case study explains the exhibition.

Case study: the Gretna Green Story Exhibition

The Gretna Green Story Exhibition reveals a fascinating chapter in social history. Why did people run away here? What happened when the angry relatives caught up with the eloping couple? When they returned home, were people punished for marrying this way? Intriguing questions. The answers can be found when you step back into Gretna Green's past. The story unfolds through a collection of audio and audiovisual displays along with memorabilia and artefacts from the heyday of runaway weddings. The push-button displays situated along the route of the exhibition bring the story to life as characters re-enact a part of Gretna Green's past.

Who do you think would visit this exhibition?

Workplaces

Some workplace attractions form part of our industrial heritage, like those in Bradford. Others are still working and provide a means of attracting attention to their products as well as making money from admission fees. The following are the most visited workplace attractions in the UK:

- Poole Pottery
- Blakemere Craft Centre, Northwich
- Denbies Wine Estate, Dorking
- Cheddar Gorge Cheese Company.

Steam/heritage railways

Steam railways are probably a type of attraction that particularly attracts enthusiasts. There are still quite a few in the UK, including the North Yorkshire Moors Railway, the Severn Valley Railway and the Great Orme Tramway in Llandudno.

▼ **Figure 18.3 North Yorkshire Moors Steam Railway attracts railway enthusiasts from all over the world**

Key term

Interpretation – a means of imparting information to visitors so that their understanding and enjoyment of the attraction are enhanced.

Interpretation is part of the visitor experience and when it is done well it makes visitors feel enthusiastic and involved with the attraction. They will enjoy themselves and want to come back or tell their friends about the attraction. Visitors will stay longer and spend more money if they are enjoying themselves.

Interpretation techniques

Displays

Static displays are not very exciting but do have a place, particularly in museums and galleries where people sometimes want to stand and admire pieces. Even so, basic interpretation will include signage and labels and information about the artist or piece of work.

Interactive displays are more exciting for the visitor where they can participate and make something happen. Children particularly like interactive displays and learn more through them.

■ Purpose

For security, exhibits are protected by many means, from very sophisticated alarm systems in galleries to roped-off areas and glass. Vulnerable items like tapestries are also protected from light and flash photography. The purpose here is conservation.

Actors

One way of communicating art to visitors is through the use of creative writing or storytelling workshops or performances. These techniques allow the visitor to become connected and emotionally involved with the exhibition rather than just looking at it. Galleries and museums use these techniques constantly and advertise them in their programmes. The London Dungeon uses actors to help horrify the visitors!

■ Purpose

Actors can be entertaining and informative. Visitor attractions often have outreach objectives and actors can help to achieve these, perhaps by visiting a school and putting on a performance relating to the visitor attraction.

Interactive technology

With interactive technology things happen! Computers are used and exhibits work – these kind of exhibits are often used to explain scientific principles in a hands-on way. The extract below describes an example from the Intech Science centre.

New exhibit – Watch your waste

An exciting new exhibit has just been unveiled at INTECH. You can't miss it, it is a 3.5-metre walk-in wheel bin. It allows you to shop using a bar code scanner and it tells you about the waste that comes from the items you have selected.

Visitors follow the instructions on the screens mounted in the wheel bin kiosks. They scan their age group, which allows the information to be displayed at the appropriate level, then they enter the giant bin and scan their selections as they shop for a typical lunch – fruit, drink, sandwiches, sweets and a comic. While in the bin they can also look at what happens to some of the rubbish, rotating displays show the stages of the recycling process. When they leave the bin and scan 'checkout' back at the kiosk the screen shows their score and details about the final destination of the waste that they purchased.

(Source: http://www.intech-uk.com/folders/online_exhibits/
new_exhibit__watch_your_waste.cfm)

▲ Figure 18.4 Interactive technology being used to help people think about how much waste they generate

Consider this

What do you think is the purpose of the 'Watch your waste' exhibit?

Guides and tours

Guides can be written in the form of books, leaflets or maps. All are useful for visitors but personal guides have the opportunity to bring an attraction to life. Guides are usually very knowledgeable and at their very best are performers connecting the visitor to the attraction.

The following features of good interpretation should be taken into consideration when producing a written guide:

- it is targeted at the right audience
- each piece of interpretation communicates a clear message
- it is fun, not dull and boring
- it stimulates different senses
- it is interactive
- it doesn't have too much text
- it is updated and maintained as necessary
- it tries to be different.

Audio guides are increasing in popularity in visitor attractions. They consist of taped information, available through an individual headset, in different languages.

They have many benefits:

- the individual can tour the attraction at their own pace
- they are cheaper than guides
- the individual can elect to hear extra pieces of information at the touch of a button
- special sound effects can be included.

However, it is difficult for the visitor to ask questions when they are plugged into the tape and it is a lonely experience being cut off from the other visitors.

Examples of visitor attractions using audio guides are Buckingham Palace, Althorp, the Churchill War Museum and Milestones' Museum in Hampshire.

The Milestones' Accoustiguide Programme for Primary Schools won an 'Interpret Britain' award for its interpretation of the county's history. Acoustiguides is a brand of audio guide using a listening device which combines narrative, music and sound effects. To encourage good interpretation in attractions, English Heritage holds an annual event 'The Interpret Britain and Ireland Awards Scheme'. The awards recognise outstanding practice in the provision of interpretive facilities at natural and cultural heritage sites throughout the UK and Ireland. The Award Scheme is open to organisations or individuals involved in interpreting a theme, place, site, collection, event or other facility for the benefit of the general public.

Theory into practice

Visit acoustiguide.com and find out the benefits of this type of guide. Make notes. Acoustiguide claims to be an attraction in the way it uses an audio guide. Try to think of your experiences of using audio guides and decide whether you agree with Acoustiguide's claims.

■ Purpose

Guides can be entertaining but their main purpose is education.

Leaflets and maps

All visitor attractions produce leaflets about their products and services. These can be displayed in Tourist Information Centres or in hotels, airports and so on, to get the attention of potential customers. Maps are often incorporated into leaflets to help visitors reach the attractions.

Curators

Curators are people who are on hand to give information about an attraction, usually in a historic attraction like a stately home. They will be well informed and able to answer questions.

■ Purpose

Curators give information but also aid security and conservation as they can monitor the behaviour of visitors.

▲ Figure 18.5 A curator in a stately home provides information and guidance for members of the public

Case study: activities at the Science Museum

Below are some extracts from the education programme at the Science Museum in London. Note all the different interpretation techniques used to enhance learning and enjoyment. Note also special events for children with special needs.

Science Night

Science Night is an all night extravaganza with a scientific twist! Science Nights provide education and fun for children and accompanying adults, through an evening of fantastic activities rounded off by camping in the Science Museum overnight.

Take part in hands-on workshops, lively demonstrations and trails based on our galleries and exhibitions. Explore scientific themes, get a new perspective on science, and see the Science Museum as it has never been seen before.

You will need to bring a sleeping bag, your wash bag and a packed evening snack – perhaps a pillow and your favourite cuddly toy!

Hands-on Bugs!

Get up close and personal with creepy-crawlies from around the world, with an opportunity for the brave at heart to handle some of the amazing creatures.

Leisure and Tourism study day

Monday 5 March, at 10.30

Learn what makes the Science Museum tick in this presentation by the Museum's own industry professionals. The session covers operational aspects such as customer service and health and safety, considers staffing structures and careers in the Museum, and includes a screening of an IMAX film which will be used as a marketing case study.

The Enormous Turnip storytelling

'A brilliant interactive show with fantastic presenters – well done.'

Farmer Giles uses forces and lots of pupil participation to pull up an enormous turnip.

Special Educational Needs events

We welcome pupils with special needs at any time, but on set dates we make particular galleries and activities available specifically for SEN groups.

SEN days in The Garden

Coordination skills can be challenged in the building area, and the gallery as a whole provides opportunities to improve language and social skills.

7 February, 7 March, 25 April, 13 June.

(Source: http://www.sciencemuseum.org.uk/learning/pdf/ ScienceMuseumEducationProgramme.pdf)

Study the extracts and describe all the interpretation techniques used. Visit the Science Museum website and look for some current examples of use of interpretation techniques. **P2**

Signage

We are surrounded by signs and there is a campaign to reduce them! However, signs are important at visitor attractions to show us the way to get to them and to help us round them. It is not only their information-giving quality that is important, signs need to fit in with the theme of the attraction. In one Area of Outstanding Natural Beauty (AONB) in Sussex, 16 different kinds of signs were found. It was decided to design a completely new system and replace them all. New designs were developed in conjunction with the Guild of Sussex Craftmen. These designs used local materials and built on the traditional style of Sussex countryside furniture. Then a new system of waymarking was developed which was designed to fit into the local landscape. The signs are made of rounded oak and give information such as designation, for example footpath, and destinations or distances.

For this activity you need to research two attractions:

- White Cliffs of Dover (National Trust)
- Science Museum.

Bookmark their websites for easy reference.

1 Describe the products and services provided by each of these attractions. **P1**

2 Describe all the interpretation techniques used by these two attractions. **P2**

3 Analyse how effectively the products and services and interpretation techniques at each of these attractions are used to meet the needs of different types of visitor. **M1**

Taking it further

Make realistic and justified recommendations for improvement to the products, services and interpretation techniques used at the Science Museum or at the White Cliffs of Dover, and say how they would meet the needs of different types of visitors. **D1**

Theory into practice

Terminology

Think of definitions for each of the following terms:

Primary product   Dwell time   Secondary product   Interpretation   Corporate hire   Signage.

18.3 Understand the appeal of visitor attractions to different types of visitor

Obviously, different types of attraction appeal to different people. Visitor attractions have to be aware of their target audience and direct their marketing efforts at the right groups. Sometimes there are attempts to target a new audience in order to increase revenue. This could be done by working with VisitBritain to encourage inbound tourists to come to an attraction or by targeting different groups of domestic tourists.

The different types of attraction were described at the beginning of this unit. Now we will consider the needs of the different types of visitor that the attractions try to appeal to and study the features of attractions that might affect people's choice of visit.

We will look at the following in terms of appeal.

- Accessibility – in terms of location, opening times.
- Transport links – in terms of mode of arrival. Where possible attractions will encourage their visitors to use public transport to lessen the impact of traffic on the local community.
- Range of products and services provided.
- Costs of visiting such as admission charges and special offers.
- Image.
- Novelty.

Type of visitor
Overseas visitors

Overseas visitors make an estimated 16 per cent of visits to UK visitor attractions according to the visitor attractions survey.

Visitor attractions need to be aware of the country of origin of their incoming tourist visitors. This helps them to ensure that literature and interpretation are available in the relevant languages and that they know where to market their products and services. UK visitor attractions that depend on inbound tourists suffered a drop in visitors in the early years of the twenty-first century. Overseas tourists, particularly North Americans, were deterred from travelling after 11 September 2001, due to fear of terrorism. They were also put off by a weak global economy, which meant that the UK was expensive for them, and by foot and mouth disease. Happily, the number of visitors is once more on the increase.

Location

London attractions are most popular with overseas visitors as London is the most popular destination for them. Other popular destinations include Edinburgh, Stratford, York, Oxford and Cambridge. Visitor attractions in these areas are likely to receive most overseas visitors.

Opening times

Overseas visitors visit mainly in the summer. Besides being the main holiday season, the summer is when opening times are at their least restrictive, with many attractions opening every day and longer into the evenings.

Transport links

Within London, overseas visitors are likely to depend on public transport and attractions must give clear directions and tube and bus stops on their literature. Overseas visitors require good transport links from gateway airports and ports. They are most likely to visit a particular geographical area first and then select visitor attractions in that area.

Products and services provided

Those attractions with a worldwide reputation are likely to attract overseas visitors, as people prefer to see things they have heard about. Those visitors whose first language is not English will be looking for interpretation in their own language.

Cost of visiting

The price of entry to an overseas visitor varies according to the current exchange rate. In the early years of the twenty-first century the pound has been strong against both the euro and the dollar so that overseas visitors from Europe and the USA find the UK expensive. Some attractions offer special prices for overseas visitors.

Consider this

Without doing any research at all can you think about the attractions in Edinburgh which would appeal to you as a tourist there?

Groups (children)

Educational visitors are usually in groups, although the groups and their needs are very diverse. They may be children from primary schools or university students doing specialist courses. Educational groups are a very important client group for many attractions from theme parks to museums to educational projects. The Eden Project welcomes about 250 children per day and some of them are from as far away as Scotland and France. Eden provides activities and learning materials for primary school children, GCSE and A-level students and special-needs children. In addition, it holds sessions for teachers.

Visitor attractions often employ education officers and hold events to attract students, providing case study and assignment material. At Alton Towers and Chessington, student events are held, linked to different vocational areas such as Travel and Tourism or Leisure Studies. These events bring in revenue when the parks would otherwise be quiet and give them a reputation for helping in education.

Location

Primary school children are usually taken to local attractions. For other student or pupil groups the nature of the attraction is more important than the location.

Opening times

Educational visits take place mainly in term time. However, groups of children may be taken to visitor attractions at other times for party outings.

Transport links

Most domestic school and college visits take place via coach transport. It is the easiest and safest way (in terms of keeping tabs on people) of transporting a group. Group leaders of any kind of group will expect attractions to have access for coaches and adequate parking facilities not too far from the attraction.

Products and services provided

For educational groups, products and services must fit what is being studied. Teachers look for attractions which provide products, activities and learning materials linked to the National Curriculum. College students are taken to attractions which complement their A-level or vocational courses.

For entertainment, children may want parties or story-telling arranged.

Cost of visiting

Price is an important factor for this group as schools and colleges do not fund student visits except in cases of extreme hardship. Parents are expected to pay, therefore prices must be reasonable as transport costs will also add to the price. All attractions offer group price concessions.

Special-interest groups

Visitor attractions which look for a niche market of a special-interest type of customer are in the minority as they are not likely to attract visitors in huge numbers and make much money. However, some have an international reputation and do well by attracting visitors from all over the world. Car enthusiasts, for example, might travel to visit the National Motor Museum at Beaulieu. Many attractions make provision for special-interest groups to attract extra custom outside the mainstream.

The following extract from Woburn's website shows how this is done:

> *There are options for day visits or for short breaks for special-interest groups at Woburn. Tailored packages or tours can be created for groups with special interests in art, furniture, silver or history at Woburn Abbey or conservation at Woburn Safari Park. The three championship courses at Woburn Golf and Country Club provide a tempting challenge for any golfer and the opportunity for a special golfing break.*
>
> (Source: http://www.discoverwoburn.co.uk)

Location

Location is not really relevant if you are a dedicated enthusiast.

Transport links

There may be the possibility of inclusive packages so that the enthusiast doesn't have to consider transport and can meet others with a similar interest.

Products and services provided

For this group of visitors the products and services provided by the attraction are the most important. The only reason that they want to visit the attraction is it represents their interest and they will buy guide books, souvenir picture books etc.

Cost of visiting

Price depends on what the individual can afford, but enthusiasts might pay a premium or look for a package that includes visits to their special-interest attractions.

Corporate groups

Corporate customers have different needs from other groups. They are interested in providing an experience for their customers or employees that is different, even unique. They will be using the visit to the attraction as an incentive for clients to buy their products or services or for loyalty and high regard from their employees.

Location

This depends on the nature of the corporate event. International companies will host events anywhere in the world if it is appropriate. Theme parks are suitable venues for corporate entertainment or conferences. Small companies will look for a local venue.

Transport links

This is not so important for delegates who will be used to finding their way around, although good directions should be provided. Access may be a factor if the corporate customer wants to use the attraction to display their products. They will need space and delivery access.

Products and services provided

These are very important for this group, although not in terms of the attraction itself. Catering, accommodation and possibly entertainment will be needed and should be of high quality. Visits to the attraction will be an added bonus for the delegates, not the main purpose of their visit.

Costs of visiting

Corporate packages are offered by attractions – price is dependent on facilities and services required and on numbers. Corporate customers, while expecting value for money, do not usually base their choice of venue on price alone.

Special needs

Provision for special needs

There are many examples of good practice in provision for people with special needs at visitor attractions. In the Science Museum example above we saw how special events are put on for children with special needs. At the Tate Gallery in London many talks and events offer interpretation for hearing-impaired or visually impaired people.

The 1995 Disability Discrimination Act makes it a legal requirement to provide physical and intellectual access for people with disabilities. Part of the Act relates to rights of access to everyday services. By 2004, service providers, and that includes visitor attractions, had to make the necessary physical adjustments to their premises so that disabled people could access them. Most visitor attractions take this access issue very seriously and publish guides for disabled visitors.

Theory into practice

Choose a visitor attraction and find out what measures it takes to allow access to people with disabilities. Make notes on your findings for further discussion.

Theory into practice

Visit the Eden Project website and find out how its interpretation techniques include provision for people with disabilities. Suggest other techniques that could be used and present your ideas to your group.

The government's Disability Unit has put forward recommendations to help visitor attractions ensure that they provide for the requirements of disabled customers. These include:

- think about the way you treat disabled customers – let them know how to request assistance and have a customer complaints procedure that is easy for them to use
- ensure you respect the dignity of a disabled person when providing them with services
- consider putting in place positive practices that will encourage disabled people and others to use your services
- make sure staff training includes your policy towards disabled people and their legal rights, as well as towards disability awareness and disability etiquette training
- regularly review whether your services are accessible to disabled people.

(Source: http://www.disability.gov.uk)

Location

Location is not as important as the suitability of the attraction to the person's interest and its access.

Transport links

This is of vital importance for this type of customer. If there is no access for people with special needs, they will not visit the attraction. The Disability Discrimination Act now applies and should result in improved access and services for customers with special needs. New purpose-built attractions always have good access as it is factored into the design. Heritage attractions have greater problems. The extract below from a leaflet about Chatsworth illustrates this. Access for wheelchair users is limited and a video of the route is shown in the information kiosk so that wheelchair users don't have to try and get round the actual tour.

Wheelchair access

The structure of the oldest part of the house, which involves 160 steps, limits access to the visitor route. The rooms in the North Wing are accessible via the ramp outside the Orangery Shop; for your enjoyment and safety, we recommend that this area is visited when it is quieter at 11am. A video of the entire visitor route is shown all day in the information kiosk. The garden, farmyard, shops and restaurant are fully accessible – access plan and ifnormation on request. Accessible lavatories are available. There are three scooters and eight manual wheelchairs; please book to ensure availabilty.

(Source: Chatsworth information leaflet 2006)

Products and services

These are an important factor when choosing an attraction, depending on personal interest. Attractions should consider special-needs customers when planning interpretation. There are many visual, audio and physical aids that can be included in interpretation.

Cost of visiting

Price is an important factor for groups who will need to keep costs down – special group prices will be expected.

Theory into practice

Match the visitor types to the attraction feature which is likely to be most important to them.

Visitor type	Feature of attraction
Couple with twin toddlers	Lifts and wide passages
Japanese family visiting London	Quality accommodation and catering
Visitor in a wheelchair	Special working steam train day
Group of schoolchildren	Gallery holding Monet exhibition
Steam train enthusiasts	Activities based on the National Curriculum
Corporate customer wanting a 2-day conference	Interpretation in foreign languages
Student studying Impressionist art	Family pricing, family friendly facilities

Assessment practice

Visit the following London attractions or their websites:

- Madame Tussauds
- Osterley Park and House, Isleworth, Middlesex.

Consider the following visitor types:

- a family of inbound tourists, with children of 12 and 14 years old, from Spain
- a corporate visitor who wants to organise a visit which incorporates entertainment and a meal for a group of 14 clients
- a wheelchair user who is visiting London and its outskirts for a couple of days with a friend.

1 Explain the appeal of each visitor attraction to each of these visitor types. You should think about the following features and indicate the importance of each to that visitor type:

- location
- opening times
- transport links
- products and services specific to their needs
- cost of visiting
- image
- novelty.

2 Choose one of the attractions and explain how it could adapt to appeal to a wider range of visitors.

Attracting visitors from overseas

Popularity and appeal

We know how popular the UK is with overseas visitors from research carried out in the International Passenger Survey and market intelligence from VisitBritain.

Research shows that one of the most important appeal factors to overseas visitors is culture and heritage. These are features of many of our vistor attractions in the UK.

Table 18.2 shows the UK's most important inbound markets in 2004.

Activity

Study Table 18.2.

1   What is more important, numbers of visitors or how much they spend?

2   How does it help vistor attractions to know where most overseas visitors come from?

Visitor attractions can influence the numbers of overseas tourists by working in partnership with VisitBritain to promote their attraction. VisitBritain invites businesses to place their products on the website so that interested visitors can find information on the website and plan their holidays. In fact, VisitBritian says that it has 43,000 tourism businesses on its websites. In addition, VisitBritain organises themed marketing campaigns which feature visitor attractions and again attract more visitors.

One way of increasing the spend of overseas visitors is to persuade them to stay longer. However, short breaks account for 41 per cent of visits to the UK, not leaving a lot of time to visit many attractions.

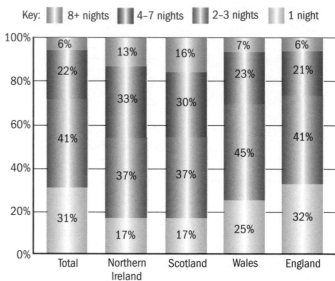

(Source: http://www.tourismtrade.org.uk/MarketIntelligenceResearch/CountryMarketProfiles.asp)

▲ **Figure 18.7 Length of stay of visitors to the UK**

Country	Visits	% of all visits	Country	Spend (£)	% of all spend
USA	3.62 million	13	USA	2.4 billion	18
France	3.25 million	12	Germany	825 million	6
Germany	2.97 million	11	France	769 million	6
Irish Republic	2.58 million	9	Irish Republic	760 million	6
Netherlands	1.62 million	6	Spain	618 million	5
Spain	1.47 million	5	Australia	588 million	5
Italy	1.35 million	5	Italy	523 million	4
Belgium	1.10 million	4	Canada	477 million	4
Australia	787,000	3	Netherlands	462 million	4
Canada	740,000	3	Switzerland	282 million	2

Table 18.2 Top UK inbound markets   (Source: http://www.tourismtrade.org.uk/MarketIntelligenceResearch/CountryMarketProfiles.asp)

Theory into practice

What can be done to encourage overseas visitors to make longer visits to the UK? Discuss your ideas and consider what visitor attractions can do to help persuade visitors lengthen their stay in the UK.

It is also useful for visitor attractions to be aware of the types of overseas visitors we receive in order to cater for their needs.

Group	% of visits
Lone traveller	46
As a couple/with partner	18
Family group	7
Business colleagues	17
Group of friends	5
Tour group	0
Don't know	1

(Source: http://www.tourismtrade.org.uk/MarketIntelligenceResearch/CountryMarketProfiles.asp)

Table 18.3 Travelling groups 2003

Note that 46 per cent of visitors are lone travellers. Explain how visitor attractions can cater for lone travellers.

Stimulating domestic tourism

The importance of visitor attractions in stimulating domestic tourism is demonstrated by the following extract from research carried out by Enjoy England.

The research identified that England excels in the provision of Unspoilt Countryside and History and Heritage. These are also product drivers for the British visiting England. The model has also identified that Local Produce, Arts and Crafts, facilities for Camping and Caravanning, Activities for Children and Myths, Legends and Folklores have high real importance amongst visitors and England is recognised as performing well.

(Source: http://www.tourismtrade.org.uk/Images/England%20UK%20Profile_tcm12-22850.pdf)

Once again, it is evident that visitor attractions are able to provide the features that appeal to tourists, unspoilt countryside, history and heritage. Visitor attractions that understand customers' desire for local produce, crafts and folklore can attract even more visitors if they cater for these needs.

Look at the following extract from the Mountfitchet Castle leaflet and see how history is brought to life for tourists.

Mountfitchet Castle & Norman Village 1066

Stansted Mountfitchet, Essex

HISTORY OF THE CASTLE

Mountfitchet Castle is a unique history time capsule. With its commanding position overlooking the Stort Valley, Mountfitchet Castle is situated on its original site which is steeped in history. This historic site was formerly an Iron Age settlement, a Roman Signals Fort and later a Saxon and Viking settlement before being conquered in 1066 by William the Conqueror who then built his Motte and Bailey castle here. This world famous Motte and Bailey castle enables the visitor to travel back in time to Norman England as it was in the 11th Century. Explore the Castle and roam through the Norman village hidden behind the castle walls, wander in and out of the many houses and view the scenes, smell the log fires burning and experience the ambience of an ancient bygone lifestyle. This castle is truly a living history, hands-on and inter- active experience. Mingle with the many animals that roam freely throughout the castle grounds and listen out for the echoes of long-forgotten voices.

ANIMALS

The animals you see at the Castle are mostly rescued and are the types and breeds which the Normans would have kept for their food and their fur – we have fallow deer, Jacob sheep and several goats. Animal feed available in the shop.

SOUVENIR SHOP

The Castle Shop has a wide variety of souvenirs and gifts on offer to suit every visitor, including books, soft toys, jewellery, preserves, branded gifts, replica weapons and antiques etc.

CATERING

We have a cafeteria that offers a wide variety of hot and cold light lunches and teas including toasted provencette baguettes, sandwiches, a delicious selection of home-made cakes and ice cream. You can either eat inside or outside in the covered picnic area.

ACCOMMODATION

There is a wealth of hotels, guest houses and bed and breakfast establishments in the local area. Visit our website for details (www.mountfitchetcastle.com).

(Source: Mountfitchet Castle visitor information leaflet)

▲ **Figure 18.8 Mountfitchet Castle uses a range of attractions to bring history to life for visitors**

Supporting the regeneration of areas

A visitor attraction can be the means of regenerating a whole area. This was the case with the Eden Project in Cornwall. Since its opening in 2001, it has attracted as many as 2 million visitors per year, settling at 1.2 million most recently. The Project makes a deliberate effort to source food, retail goods, plants and even electricity from local suppliers, thus supporting the Cornish economy. The knock-on spending (multiplier effect) in the local economy from visitors who have come to Cornwall attracted by the Eden Project is estimated to be £700 million since its opening. In the UK, there are several other areas that have been regenerated and now attract tourists. Examples include the Salford Docks area, with the Lowry Centre, and Covent Garden in London, where there are museums, shops and restaurants.

Contributing to the local and national economy

Creating employment

Visitor attractions create jobs. Tate Britain, for example, employs about 800 people. In this kind of institution, many of these employees are highly skilled historians, conservationists, marketers and administrators. They also need fundraisers, building managers and educators.

However, many visitor attractions have few permanent staff. Staff may be employed on flexible contracts so that they can be called upon as needed, posts may be seasonal due to winter closures and pay is often low for unskilled work. Associations like the Association for Leading Visitor Attractions (ALVA) are aware of these problems and are lobbying the government for action and investment in training. In addition, there are a large number of volunteers working in historic properties.

Visitor attractions provide investment in a local environment. The visitors generate wealth in the locality by spending their money in hotels, restaurants and amenities in the area as well as in the visitor attraction.

Case study: visitors and attractions in the south-west of England

Tables 18.4 and 18.5 show the numbers of visitors to, and major attractions in, the south-west region of England in 2005.

Purpose of trip	Trips	Nights	Spend
1 Holiday, pleasure/leisure	11.74	54.18	£2589.25
2 Holiday, visiting friends or relatives	3.57	12.77	£440.81
3 Other visits to friends or relatives	3.04	8.21	£315.99
4 Attend conference	0.22	0.34	£23.76
5 Attend exhibition/trade show/agricultural show	0.13	0.39	£24.20
6 Conduct paid work/on business	1.99	6.14	£394.52
7 Travel/transport employment	0.14	0.19	£10.86
8 Other purpose	0.23	0.76	£24.11
Total trips	21.06	82.99	£3823.50
All holidays (1+2)	15.25	66.44	£3016.04
All visits to friends or relatives (2+3)	6.59	20.93	£758.17
All business travel (4+5+6)	2.50	7.24	£459.01

Table 18.4 Domestic visits to the south west 2005 (millions)

(Source: http://www.swtourism.co.uk/additional/docsys/
UKTS%202005%20SWT%20web_1.pdf)

Attraction	2001	2002	2003	2004	2005	% 04/05
Eden Project	1,700,000	1,832,482 est.	1,404,372	1,223,959	1,177,189	−3.8
Stonehenge	677,378	759,697	745,229	802,811	833,617	3.8
Roman Baths	864,989	845,608	837,457	867,724	824,197	−5.0
Longleat House	361,076	492,807	518,121	692,129	779,488	12.6
Dart Pleasure Craft Ltd	790,480	721,822	713,514	676,973	731,286	8.0
Paignton Zoo	399,586	475,177	457,539	486,728	448,329	−7.9
Woodlands Leisure Park	374,165	400,000 est.	400,000	400,125	400,000	0.0
Bath Abbey	330,000 est.	350,000 est.	350,000 est.	300,000	350,000 est.	16.7
Stourhead House	269,375	305,941	354,893	335,265	334,618	−0.2
National Marine Aquarium	350,000	380,000 est.	330,000	315,000 est.	305,000 est.	−3.2

est. – estimate

(Source: http://www.swtourism.co.uk/additional/docsys/
UKTS%202005%20SWT%20web_1.pdf)

Table 18.5 Major paid attractions in the south west

Study Tables 18.4 and 18.5 and explain how the visitor attractions mentioned attract tourists to the south west.

Taking it further

You may need to investigate the attractions by looking at their individual websites and carrying out research into the annual visitor attractions survey (www.tourismtrade.org).

Evaluate the success of visitor attractions in the south-west in increasing the popularity and appeal of the area, making recommendations for improvement. **D2**

The Natural History Museum attracts more than 3 million visitors a year. These visitors generate a lot of spending in London. *Treasurehouse and Powerhouse*, a report commissioned to look at its economic impact on London and the rest of the UK, said that the Natural History Museum has a greater annual turnover than the Greater London Authority – £52 million – and also generates £190 million for the economy every year

(Source: http://www.nhm.ac.uk/about-us/contact-enquiries/press-office/press-releases/2004/press_release_4250.html)

Promoting cultural exchange

The role of the UK's many galleries and museums is to conserve British culture so that it is there for future generations to see.

There can be no doubt that the British government supports the cultural aspect of the UK's public museums and galleries as they all receive funding via the DCMS, to varying degrees and take on the responsibility of protecting our cultural heritage.

The following extract from the Tate website explains this role:

> *The Tate Gallery first opened on Millbank in London in 1897. It operates as an independent institution under the terms of the Museums and Galleries Act 1992, and is one of the great public museums of the United Kingdom. In common with other museums it presents a perspective on history, but its particular responsibility is to collect objects of our time and places it in the privileged position of creating the frame through which future generations will judge our own culture.*

(Source: http://www.tate.org.uk)

Tate's collection now consists of over 65,000 works of art encompassing the national collection of historic British art from 1500 and the national collection of international modern art.

There is no point in having all these works of art unless the public goes to see them. Thus, it is also the responsibility of the museums to attract different types of visitors and explain the exhibits to them, that is interpret them. The Tate does this via an extensive programme

of activities and entry to the Tate and to other public museums is free. The Natural History Museum welcomes 125,000 school children each year, successfully introducing children to exhibits and learning.

Conservation

In some cases, visitor attractions suffer from their popularity. Historic buildings or sites can be subject to deterioration and erosion. In these cases, measures must be taken to protect the buildings by restricting visits or closing them for periods of time.

Stonehenge is a good example of the need for conservation. The site receives many visitors and the stones have suffered erosion and damage, so a means must be found to preserve it. It is one of the UK's most famous and oldest monuments and a World Heritage Site, but too many visitors over the years mean it needs to be protected while still maintaining access for the public, who see it as part of their heritage. This is underway with the 'Stonehenge Project'. The project involves the building of a new visitor centre and the removal of roads from the site to restore the site to a peaceful location. There are several organisations involved in the project including the DCMS, English Heritage (who manage the site), and the Highways Agency.

In the visitor centre there will be exhibitions and audiovisual presentations to help visitors enjoy and understand Stonehenge. There will also be shops, catering facilities and an education area. Those who wish to visit the stones will walk from the centre. Perhaps fewer people will visit the stones but still get a flavour of what they are about from the visitor's centre by taking a 'virtual tour'. The central circle of stones is already roped off and visitors are not allowed to enter this area. This is not surprising when you hear that some visitors actually chip off bits of stone to take home as souvenirs.

The number of visitors to an attraction can be managed by raising prices for entry or issuing timed tickets – this means visitors buy a ticket and can only enter the building at the time stated. Timed tickets are also used to reduce waiting times during peak periods at theme parks. Customers collect timed tickets for the popular rides and can get straight onto the ride at the time given on the ticket.

There are several organisations which work on conservation projects. Visitor attractions are eligible to join these. An example is the Travel Foundation Forum. Members include some major tour operators. Membership gives the opportunity to share good practice, to influence areas of work and to put forward projects for funding.

Visitor attractions may attract funding from government sources such as the Heritage Lottery Fund for new developments which fit with government policy. The Victoria and Albert Museum has received a £3.5 million grant from this fund towards its £30 million renewal programme. The rest of the funding comes from private donations.

Knowledge check

1 Which are the most popular attractions in the UK?

2 What is meant by 'secondary spend'?

3 Why are some attractions free to enter?

4 Why is secondary spend so important in museums?

5 What is the primary product at a gallery?

6 What is meant by 'dwell time'?

7 What economic benefits can visitor attractions bring to an area?

8 How does the Eden Project support the Cornish economy?

9 Explain what a curator does

10 Why are actors used in museums?

11 What do we mean by interpretation?

12 Describe three interpretation techniques.

13 Give an example of how a visitor attraction can promote cultural exchange.

14 Which 'appeal' factors are most important for school groups?

15 Which 'appeal' factors are most important for families?

Preparation for assessment

Your local newspaper has asked for your help in producing a supplement on local visitor attractions. It does not have the people power to assign a reporter to the supplement so it has invited students to prepare it. The aim of the supplement is to provide information about the visitor attractions in the area. The supplement will be attached to the evening paper and also to the free weekly edition so it will achieve very wide coverage of your area. The newspaper is read by local residents and also by visitors to the area. Your area attracts a lot of inbound tourists who are interested in learning about the visitor attractions available. Some local people worry about the numbers of tourists visiting your local attractions and about the impact on the environment and on their society, so these issues will be covered in the supplement.

Your responsibility is to research two local visitor attractions. One should be a built attraction and one a natural attraction. You should make every effort to visit the attractions to carry out your research. Your work must be individual, although colleagues might be researching other attractions for inclusion in the supplement. You must provide information for the supplement as follows.

1   Give a description of the products and services provided by the two visitor attractions. **P1**

2   Describe the techniques used for visitor interpretation at each of the two attractions. **P2**

Analyse how effectively the products, services and interpretation techniques at the attractions are used to meet the needs of different visitors. **M1**

Suggest new ways in which one of your visitor attractions might improve its products, services and interpretation to meet the needs of different types of visitors. Make sure your ideas are realistic and that you justify them. **D1**

Grading tip

You might make suggestions based on good practice you have seen at other visitor attractions. Make sure you relate your ideas to different types of visitors.

3   Explain all the factors which lend appeal to your chosen visitor attractions for a group of primary school children, a family of Japanese tourists and a retired British couple. **P3**

Make sure you include all the following:
- location and transport links
- opening times and costs of visiting
- products and services provided
- image
- novelty.

Explain how one of your attractions could adapt to appeal to a wider range of visitor types. **M2**

Grading tip

To reach Merit level, think about any products or services that the attraction might offer to appeal to more types of people. For example, they could offer leaflets or tours in different languages or they could introduce an educational programme to appeal to schools.

4 Your supplement will have an article that explains the importance of visitor attractions to tourism. This should be a detailed explanation with examples. **P4**

Choose one area – for example, your town – and explain, in an article, the impact visitor attractions have had on the popularity and appeal of that area. **M3**

Grading tip

The area you choose must have at least three visitor attractions. It would be a good idea to choose a local area that you can visit easily. Statistics on visitor numbers will help you determine the trends. You should be able to get these from the attractions.

5 In your article evaluate the success of the visitor attractions on the popularity and appeal of the area, making recommendations for improvement. **D2**

Grading tip

To reach Distinction level, you could consider factors such as impact on tourism as a whole in an area. For example, do visitors to the attraction go anywhere else to spend their money, and if not how could this be encouraged?

Grading criteria

To achieve a pass grade the evidence must show that the learner is able to:	To achieve a merit grade the evidence must show that, in addition to the pass criteria, the learner is able to:	To achieve a distinction grade the evidence must show that, in addition to the pass and merit criteria, the learner is able to:
P1 describe the products and services provided by one built and one natural visitor attraction **Assessment practice page 143**	**M1** analyse how effectively the products, services and interpretation techniques of a built and a natural attraction are used to meet the needs of different types of visitors **Assessment practice page 150**	**D1** make realistic and justified recommendations for improvements to the products, services and interpretation techniques used by a selected built or natural attraction to meet the needs of different types of visitors **Assessment practice page 150**
P2 describe the techniques used for visitor interpretation at one built and one natural visitor attraction **Case study page 149**	**M2** explain how one built or natural attraction could adapt to appeal to a wider range of visitor types **Assessment practice page 155**	**D2** evaluate the success of visitor attractions to the popularity and appeal of a destination or area, making recommendations for improvement **Taking it further page 159**
P3 explain the appeal of one selected natural and one built visitor attraction to different types of visitors **Assessment practice page 155**	**M3** explain the impact visitor attractions have had on the popularity and appeal of a destination or area **Case study page 159**	
P4 explain why visitor attractions are important to UK tourism **Case study page 159**		

Hospitality operations in travel and tourism

Introduction

Hospitality is central to the travel and tourism industry, since it occurs both as a sector in its own right and as part of many other travel and tourism sectors such as visitor attractions, where hospitality is part of the overall visitor experience and helps to maximise income. You will find out about the range of providers in the hospitality sector and how they operate and what products and services they provide. In addition, you will examine the role of hospitality as a secondary function in other sectors.

You will develop an awareness of how customer needs and expectations affect the provision of hospitality and the level of service.

You will also learn how to plan hospitality provision and you will develop an understanding of political, economic, social and technological issues affecting the sector.

After completing this unit you should be able to achieve the following outcomes:

1   Know the products and services offered by different types of hospitality provision

2   Understand how hospitality providers meet customer expectations

3   Be able to plan hospitality provision for a travel and tourism organisation

4   Understand the factors affecting hospitality operations in travel and tourism organisations.

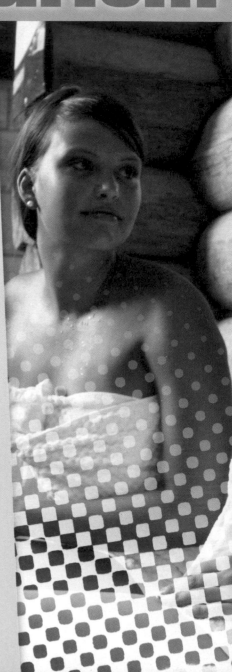

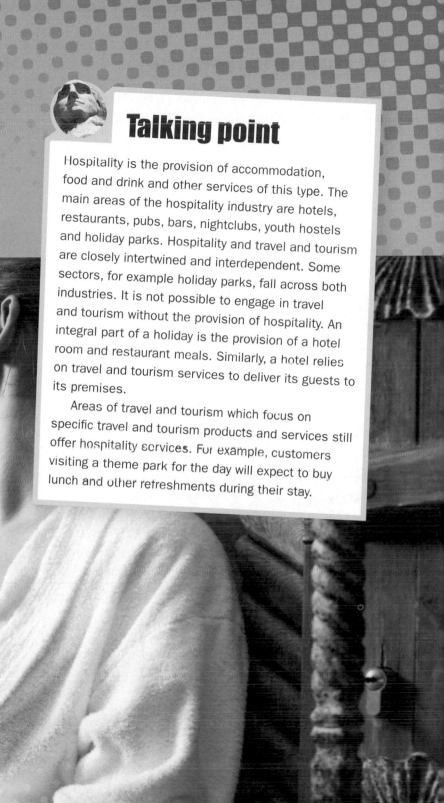

Talking point

Hospitality is the provision of accommodation, food and drink and other services of this type. The main areas of the hospitality industry are hotels, restaurants, pubs, bars, nightclubs, youth hostels and holiday parks. Hospitality and travel and tourism are closely intertwined and interdependent. Some sectors, for example holiday parks, fall across both industries. It is not possible to engage in travel and tourism without the provision of hospitality. An integral part of a holiday is the provision of a hotel room and restaurant meals. Similarly, a hotel relies on travel and tourism services to deliver its guests to its premises.

Areas of travel and tourism which focus on specific travel and tourism products and services still offer hospitality services. For example, customers visiting a theme park for the day will expect to buy lunch and other refreshments during their stay.

Hospitality provision

The nature of the hospitality business is that small, independent companies characterise the market. This is true in the areas of hotels, restaurants, bars and pubs. In contract food services and visitor attractions, the opposite is true and the market is dominated by a few large companies, for example Compass, a food service provider, dominates contract food services.

In this section, we will explore hospitality provision as a main business and as an additional service, looking at examples and case studies from each area.

Products and services

When we think about hospitality in our homes we think about providing people with a welcome and offering them food and drink and possibly a place to stay. This is exactly what hospitality means in hotels, restaurants etc. However, the food, drink and accommodation vary according to the specific needs of the customer. For example, a vegetarian needs to be offered an alternative to meat, families might expect children's meals, cots and extra beds. As we take a more detailed look at different types of hospitality provision, we will take an overview of their products and services. In the following section we will investigate the range of products and services in more detail and relate them to different types of customers and their specific needs.

Key term

Contract food service companies – these organisations provide food service for customers at a range of locations such as offices, factories, railway stations, airports, universities, schools, retail stores and shopping centres. In travel and tourism their services may be contracted at airports, railway stations and in visitor attractions.

Hospitality provision as a main business

This means that the main focus of the business is on hospitality, that is, the provision of accommodation and food. These providers include hotels, guest houses, motels, holiday centres, camp sites and caravan parks.

Hotels

A hotel is an establishment that offers accommodation, food and drink to anyone who is fit to receive these services and is willing to pay for them. Many hotels also provide leisure facilities, conference and banqueting facilities and business services.

	£m
2001	9975
2002	9776
2003	10,070
2004	10,462
2005	10,900
2006 (est)	11,200

(Source: Mintel UK Hotels 2006)

Table 19.1 The hotel market by revenue, 2001–6

There are over 40,000 hotels in the UK. This figure incorporates all sizes of establishments and this includes guest houses. Most of these are independent establishments but there are several large groups, as Table 19.2 illustrates. Table 19.2 rates the hotels by size not by revenue or profit.

Although figures are accurate at the time they are compiled, they change quickly as companies dispose of assets and buy different ones. It is evident from Table 19.2 that Whitbread is the largest group with almost 500 hotels.

Approximately 22,000 hotels and guest houses are registered with the tourist boards, as are 16,000 bed and breakfast establishments. The rest are unregistered. A lot of hotels are run by their owners and the average size of a hotel is 20 rooms. The major groups have a lot of influence on the hotel business.

	Company	Number of hotels	Brands	Number of rooms
1	Whitbread Hotel Company	476	Premier Travel Inn	31,397
2	InterContinental Hotels Group	224	*InterContinental (1), *Crowne Plaza (14) *Holiday Inn (103) *Express by Holiday Inn (103)	30,863
3	Travelodge	279		17,700
4	Hilton Hotels	70		15,500+
5	Accor Hotels	94	*Sofitel (1) Novotel (31), Mercure (1), Ibis (47), Etap (3), Formule 1(10)	13,529
6	Marriott International	75	*Courtyard by Marriott (11) Renaissance (9), Marriott (55)	12,500+
7	Thistle Hotels	48	Thistle (46), Guoman (2)	10,300+
8	CHE Hotel Group	99	*Clarion (4), *Comfort (36) *Quality (53), *Sleep Inn (6)	8,000+
9	Wyndham Worldwide	82	*Days Inn (23), *Days Hotels (10), *Ramada (49), *Ramada Encore (3)	7,980+
10	Britannia Hotels	33		6,729
11	London and Edinburgh Swallow Group**	150+	Swallow Hotels	6,500+
12	Macdonald Hotels	71	Macdonald Hotels (65), Resorts (6)	6,374+
13	Carlson Companies USA	27	*Radisson (8), *Park Inn (12), Park Plaza (7)	6,053
14	Arora Family Trust	11	Arora (4), †Sofitel (1), †Hilton (3), †Express by Holiday Inn (1), †Premier Travel Inn (1), †Radisson SAS (1)	5,500+
15	Jarvis Hotels	42	†Ramada (42)	4,758
16	Rezidor SAS Hospitality	8	†Radisson SAS (8), †Park Inn (12)	4,654
17	De Vere Hotels (AHG)	34	De Vere Hotels (18), Village Hotels (16)	4,646
18	Jurys Doyle Hotel Group	18	Hotels (5), Inns (13)	4,361
19	Millennium Copthorne Hotels	18	Millennium (6), Copthorne (12)	4,163
20	Mitchells & Butlers	113	Innkeepers Lodge (88), †Express by Holiday Inn (25)	4,000+

ˣ Some or all franchised to another operator   † Franchised hotels

(Source: http://www.caterersearch.com/Articles/2006/10/20/44433/industry-data-leading-hotel-brands-in-the-uk.html)

Table 19.2 Top 20 UK hotel brands

Consider this

What are the main hotel groups represented in your area? Are they major chains or independent?

The core products of hotels are the provision of accommodation, that is, hotel rooms, and food and drink. Of course, within that there is a vast range. Hotels may offer basic rooms, executive and deluxe rooms or suites, and family rooms, all at different rates.

In a hotel, the size of the kitchen and restaurant will depend on the size of the hotel and number of guests.

Some hotels have several restaurants open to guests and to the public, others do not have restaurants but only a breakfast room. A hotel which caters for families would have family rooms or adjoining rooms, children's facilities and special meals and meal times. We will look at a specific example in the next section.

Bars may be found in hotels, restaurants or nightclubs or exist in their own right. Bars need cellar attendants to run the cellar and bar staff to serve the customers.

Case study: De Vere hotel group

De Vere used to be known as Greenalls and had a variety of different businesses in leisure, health and fitness, hotels and pubs. In 1999, the group decided to dispose of its pub divisions. It sold Greenalls to Scottish and Newcastle and its Inn Partnership to a Japanese company, Nomura.

Currently, the group has 18 hotels under the De Vere brand, the most famous of which is probably the Grand in Brighton. It also has 16 hotels under the Village brand. The room rates at the Village hotels are less than at De Vere. These are hotels and leisure clubs.

The De Vere Group also owns a chain of health and fitness clubs called Greens.

1 Why do you think De Vere decided to concentrate on the hotel business?

2 How does the health and fitness chain fit in with the core business?

3 What differences would you expect for a higher rate room in a De Vere branded hotel rather than a Village branded hotel?

4 Look at the De Vere website and see if you are right.

Many hotels are part of a franchise operation. This means that although they are independently owned they use the brand name, marketing and reservation services of a group. Of course, they have to pay for the benefits that they receive. This is usually a percentage of revenue.

Case study: Best Western hotel chain

Best Western is an example of a consortium. Best Western International claims to be the world's largest hotel chain with over 4000 hotels worldwide. In the UK, there are more than 290 member hotels. Best Western actively recruits hotels to join the group but carries out extensive quality inspections before accepting hotels.

The benefits of membership are outlined on the website and shown below.

- **Keep full independence**, while being part of an international affiliation
- **Support in maintaining high standards** by undergoing two quality assessments each year
- Represented by the **Best Western Great Britain central reservations service**, open seven days a week and linked to our international reservations centres
- Preferred access to leading **corporate booking agents**

- **Brand recognition**, being part of a national and international brand
- Favoured by over **50,000 Gold Crown Club International** members in the UK and over 130,000 members who are collecting points worldwide
- Best Western is a **non-profit making organisation**. All income is re-invested for members
- **Representation on GDS and web systems**, with online booking facilities
- **Regular media exposure** through brochures, newspapers etc.
- **Full central office support** across all major market segments

(Source: http://www.bestwestern.co.uk)

1 What do you think are the disadvantages of joining a group such as Best Western?

2 Explain how a loyalty scheme such as Gold Crown Club helps hotels.

Budget hotels

A budget hotel caters for visitors on short stays and those who are travelling. This type of accommodation has more or less replaced the motel sector. Motels were one-storey buildings where guests could park their car outside their room and go directly inside. They were built near major road routes so that they were convenient for travellers. Budget hotels are also often built near major routes but there is an increasing trend to build them in cities. These hotels have fewer facilities than other hotels, for example there are few staff, perhaps just one person on reception and no room service. There are no luxuries and usually no catering facilities, although en-suite bathrooms are provided.

This sector is growing because customers realise that the budget hotel sector gives excellent value for money in convenient locations.

There are several companies offering budget hotels. Table 19.3 shows the number of budget hotels and their ownership in 2004.

Budget hotels are such good value that they enjoy a 90 per cent plus occupancy rate. Travel Inn is the UK's leading budget hotel brand, totalling more than 230 hotels. There is a Travel Inn at County Hall, London, on the south bank of the Thames near Westminster and the London Eye. The core product of a budget hotel is accommodation but often a breakfast room and café are provided. Families and people with disabilities are catered for, but only in terms of accommodation and access, as all facilities are quite basic.

Operator/owner	Brand	Number of hotels	Number of rooms	Average rooms per hotel
Whitbread	Premier Travel Inn	457	29,000	63
Permira	Travelodge	270	15,000	56
InterContinental	Express by Holiday Inn	89	8900	100
Accor	Ibis	43	5000	116
Cendant	Days Inn	31	2450	79
CHE Group	Comfort Inns	32	2200	69
Mitchells & Butler	Innkeepers Lodge	78	2100	27
Louvre Hotels	Campanile	17	1230	72
Accor	Formule1	10	746	75
Golden Tulip	Tulip Inn	5	555	111
CHE Group	Sleep Inn	6	530	88
Accor	Etap	2	150	75
Louvre Hotels	Kyriad	1	50	50
Others	Various	25	1,365	55
Total		1066	69,276	65

Table 19.3 UK budget hotel operators, 2004

(Sources: Deloitte, UK Budget Hotel Survey 2004, hotel companies/Mintel)

Case study: Travelodge

Travelodge became the UK's first budget hotel brand when it opened its first venue in the UK in the 1980s. It it is now the UK's second largest player in the limited-service sector (after Whitbread's Premier Travel Inn) and, by bedroom numbers, it is the country's third biggest hotel operator.

It currently operates around 300 hotels with 20,000 bedrooms (including a handful of properties in Spain) in city centres, airports and roadsides and serves more than six million customers a year.

The privately-owned company was bought in 2006 by Dubai International Capital, but it has passed through a number of hands since it was founded during the 1930s in the USA (where the brand is now owned by Cendant Corporation).

Forte bought the brand back in 1973 and the first UK Travelodge was opened in Staffordshire in 1985 by Alan Hearn, cousin of the present Travelodge chief executive Grant Hearn. Subsequent owners have included Granada, contract caterer Compass and venture capital firm Permira.

The group has a long association with the UK's largest roadside restaurant chain, Little Chef, which became part of Forte in 1970. The link was severed in 2005 when Permira sold the 233-strong restaurant chain a year before it exited its investment in Travelodge.

In a bid to woo the one-third of Britons who do not stay in UK hotels and the 85% who view domestic breaks as too dear, the group has priced 1.8 million bedrooms at just £26 a night for 2007.

Travelodge is a vociferous opponent of the proposed bed tax on hotels and collected 90,000 signatures from customers to lobby against the move.

(Source: http://www.cateronline.com)

1 **What are the reasons for the success of Travelodge?**

2 **Describe the products and services offered by Travelodge. You may need to visit its website to help you.** **P1**

Guest houses and bed and breakfast establishments

Usually the difference between a hotel and a guest house is one of size but some guest houses might not provide food and drink whereas a hotel usually does. Most guest houses are family run and only have a few rooms. They are often situated in large houses that would originally have been intended for families.

Years ago people often went to guest houses, or boarding houses as they were known, for their annual summer holiday. Families sometimes returned to their favourite guest houses year after year. They would expect to have a bedroom (a large room might be designated a family room), they would not expect to have a private bathroom but would share with all the other guests. Breakfast would be served at a set time and after that families had to go out, whether it was rain or shine, and not return until early evening. Dinner would be served at a set time in the early evening. Afterwards the family might go for a walk along the promenade or go to a show.

The British seaside was full of houses like this and of course there are still thousands.

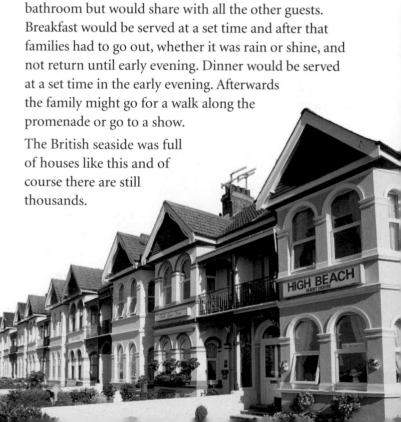

Figure 19.1 An example of a ► typical British guest house

Today the facilities have mostly improved as people's expectations have grown. Many guest houses have rooms with private bathrooms and have lounges for guests to sit in if they wish.

The guest house in Figure 19. 1 is an example of a typical British guest house.

Many guest houses have websites that give information about the accommodation provided and the location. The location of the guest house is often stressed to show that it is suitable for travellers. The websites also give details of room rates and directions for getting there.

The websites are often linked to a national bed and breakfast website. Internet technology has made it much easier for customers and guest house owners to find each other. There are still many guest houses and bed and breakfast establishments who do not have website links and they rely on their local Tourist Information Centre to supply them with clients.

The core products that guest houses provide are the same as those of hotels except that it is very unlikely that full restaurant service is offered. However, many guest houses supplement their income by providing evening meals for guests, often to order.

Holiday centres

These may be camping and caravan parks or purpose-built sites with accommodation, entertainment and leisure facilities. Examples include Pontins, Butlins and CenterParc. They often offer self-catering accommodation.

Many people prefer self-catering accommodation for the extra freedom it allows them in deciding when to eat and controlling the type of food on offer. Self-catering allows a greater level of informality on holidays.

Generally, self-catering properties are suitable for people who want to be independent and do not expect to have the services that would be provided in a hotel such as entertainment, bars and restaurants. However, many holiday centres have blocks of self-catering accommodation where all the facilities of a hotel are available and yet kitchens and cooking facilities are provided.

Camp sites and caravan parks

The UK Caravan Parks and Campsites Directory shows that there are an incredible 2548 caravan sites, parks and campsites in the UK.

Camping and caravanning have become an important sector of the tourism industry both in the UK and throughout Europe. Camping has changed a lot over the years and camp sites have become much more sophisticated and offer many more facilities than they used to.

Customers expect tents to be fixed rather than bring their own, but many prefer holiday homes to tents and in fact many camp sites now prefer to be known as holiday centres and do not allow any campers to bring their own tents or touring caravans. This enables the camp site owners to exert much greater control over the layout and appearance of the site increasing its appeal to visitors. Camp site owners have also increased the level of services and hospitality on offer in line with increased customer expectations.

A wide range of accommodation and food services is on offer at some large camping and caravanning sites including a range of luxury accommodation, bars, restaurants, takeaways and supermarkets.

Hospitality as an additional service

Sometimes businesses offer hospitality to give added value to the range of products and services they provide, but it is not the main focus of their business. The primary purpose of their business may be to transport passengers or to entertain. The revenue gained from customers spent on hospitality in these cases is known as secondary spend. We are going to look at some examples of organisations who offer hospitality as a secondary focus.

Airlines

It is evident that the primary business of an airline is to transport passengers from one place to another. Traditionally, airlines offer hospitality to their customers to enhance the customer experience on board the

▲ Figure 19.2 An air hostess serving drinks on a plane

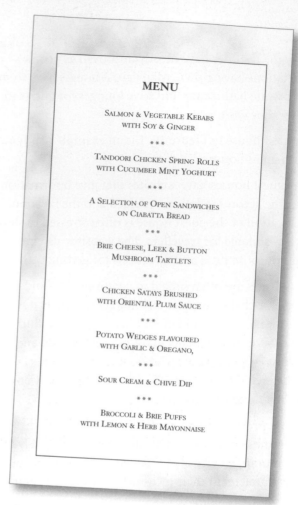

MENU

SALMON & VEGETABLE KEBABS
WITH SOY & GINGER

* * *

TANDOORI CHICKEN SPRING ROLLS
WITH CUCUMBER MINT YOGHURT

* * *

A SELECTION OF OPEN SANDWICHES
ON CIABATTA BREAD

* * *

BRIE CHEESE, LEEK & BUTTON
MUSHROOM TARTLETS

* * *

CHICKEN SATAYS BRUSHED
WITH ORIENTAL PLUM SAUCE

* * *

POTATO WEDGES FLAVOURED
WITH GARLIC & OREGANO,

* * *

SOUR CREAM & CHIVE DIP

* * *

BROCCOLI & BRIE PUFFS
WITH LEMON & HERB MAYONNAISE

▲ Figure 19.3 An example of a finger buffet
for conference delegates

aircraft. The hospitality would take the form of meals and drinks. Today full-service airlines still offer this hospitality and it is included in the price of the ticket. Passengers on a cross-Atlantic flight from an airline such as Virgin or British Airways might expect a choice of meal, an afternoon tea or breakfast depending on time of day and free drinks including alcohol. The catering is provided by a contract food supplier and is specially packaged for airline use. Low-cost airlines such as Ryanair also offer hospitality in the form of snacks and drinks but passengers pay for whatever they choose and this is an important source of revenue for the airline. Thus the purpose of the hospitality for this type of airline is to make money as well as to offer a service.

Conference and exhibition centres

There are several purpose-built conference and exhibition centres in the UK. These include the NEC in Birmingham, Earls Court, Olympia and ExCeL in London. Visitors attending exhibitions will be there for a few hours and will expect to be able to buy food and drink. Hospitality is also essential for exhibitors as they may choose to entertain clients within the exhibition area. Again, the hospitality provision is a source of revenue for the exhibition centre.

Exhibition venues are also used for conferences and catering must be provided for delegates. A catering manager is available to advise conference organisers on menus and catering provision. Menus may range from finger buffets to full dinners.

Attractions

Restaurants, bars and cafeterias are usually provided in visitor attractions. They add appeal to the attraction and encourage visitors to stay longer and spend more money. They are an important source of secondary revenue.

Hospitality at attractions helps keep guests there longer and the management hope that the longer they stay the more money they will spend, not just on hospitality but in the shops and on photos, etc. Some attractions have extended their hospitality provision to the opening of hotels. Alton Towers has two hotels which are themed and help attract visitors to the park.

Customer types

Different types of hospitality are targeted at different kinds of customers. Examples of customers are:

- families
- solo travellers
- corporate
- special needs
- groups.

Customer expectations

Each type of customer has different expectations. First we will take an overview of these in general terms and then we will look at them in relation to specific types of customers. Expectations are in the following areas.

- **Level of service** – of course service is important to everyone but those who are spending a lot of money or corporate customers expect an even greater level of service.

- **Range of products and services provided** – from the core products mentioned in the first section to extras such as spa facilities, theatre and restaurant booking, children's facilities

- **Location** – this is of the utmost importance. For travellers the location must be convenient, hence hotels and budget hotels on major routes and the provision of hotels at airports. Business customers look for city-centre hotels or those located near exhibition centres like the NEC. People on holiday may be looking for a beautiful setting perhaps with sea views.

- **Availability** – consolidators like Lastminute.com and Expedia give lists of available hotels or restaurants in specific locations when dates are entered on their websites. Customers choose the venue on the basis of what is available in their price range.

- **Quality** – many customers are looking for specific standards, they may be guided by reviews such as those at Trip Advisor, word-of-mouth promotion or the classifcation awarded to the facility.

Maintaining level of service

Housekeeping

A large hotel will have a number of housekeepers, usually with responsibility for a floor. They will have cleaners or chambermaids working with them and part of their role is to allocate cleaning jobs to their team. Other responsibilities include:

- making sure high standards of cleanliness are adhered to
- organising and changing guest laundry
- issuing linen
- maintaining stores of cleaning products and bathroom products
- maintaining security procedures
- reporting of maintenance requirements.

Maintenance

Very large hotels may employ their own electricians, plumbers etc. Most establishments employ general maintenance staff who can do most jobs and then experts are called in as needed. Guest houses and bed and breakfast establishments would not employ maintenance staff but would have tradespeople to call on as needed.

Maintenance staff do not have to be very skilled as most of their tasks are minor but would impact on the level of customer service if left unattended.

Portering

Only large hotels have porters and bellboys. Their role is to help guests with luggage and to get taxis for guests. They will also show guests to their rooms. The pay is low and they expect to receive tips.

- **Speed of service** – this factor is more important to some customers. For example, restaurants serving pre-theatre dinners or those in airports are aware that customers have time commitments.
- **Level of hygiene** – a minimum level of hygiene is required by all. Legal requirements ensure that it is adhered to.
- **Value for money** – this does not mean that the hospitality provision must be cheap but that the customer perceives that they have received good service and satisfactory products for the price they have paid.
- **Complementary services** – includes those extras which contribute to a higher level of service and enhance the guest's experience. An example is room service.

Key term

Room service – hotels provide room service, sometimes for 24 hours a day. Guests order from a room-service menu in their rooms. Breakfast is often promoted as a room-service option. It means that all the guests do not descend on the dining room at the same time in the morning and portions can be carefully controlled. Usually room service incurs an extra charge for the guest.

Meeting customer expectations

We are going to look at these expectations in relation to different types of customers with some specific examples. You will then have the opportunity to find suitable hospitality provision for given customer profiles.

First take a look at Table 19.4. It shows the most important facilities selected by 1000 internet users aged 15+ in a survey for Mintel in 2006.

	%
Quality restaurant	62
Flexible meal times	59
Bar	48
Electronic/late check-out	44
Electronic/in-room check-in	36
Satellite or cable TV in the room	35
24-hour room service	33
Internet access in room	32
Additional accessories (e.g. bathrobes, slippers, toiletries)	31
Video or stereo system in room	26
Swimming pool	25
Children's facilities (e.g. playground, baby monitoring)	25
Gym	17
Spa	15
Beauty services	12
Electronic games (e.g. PlayStation)	11
Other sports facilities (e.g. tennis, squash)	8
Golf course	5

(Source: GMI/Mintel)

Table 19.4 Most important hotel facilities, May 2006

Theory into practice

Between your group ask 100 people to rank these same facilites in order of importance. Compare your results with those given in Table 19.4.

Families

Hotels often offer special deals for families. Examples are free accommodation for children sharing their parents' room and meal offers for children. A swimming pool and children's play room are appealing to families.

The extract below is from the website of a superbly located eco-friendly hotel in North Cornwall – Bedruthan Steps. The hotel is situated on a glorious beach and promotes its family-friendly services. The description on its website demonstrates how families are catered for.

Bedrooms

Breathtaking sea views from most rooms. Interconnecting rooms. Spacious family suites, open plan or with 2 bedrooms for larger families. Comfortable and stylish suites for couples.
All rooms have en-suite bathroom, television, telephone, tea-making facilities, cool box and baby listening.

Meals

Breakfast and lunch are family times at Bedruthan. Children dine in children's teas (0–12 years), the children's supper club (during school holidays, 7–12 years) or in the restaurant with parents (7+ years). Dinner is a time for parents to relax, watch the sunset together and enjoy exploring our extensive wine list.

Pools

Children's paddling pool, 3 heated outdoor pools including learners' pool, set in sub-tropical gardens. Outdoor Spa. Swimming lessons for 3–93 year olds. Summer poolside barbecues.

(Source: http://www.bedruthan.com)

▲ Figure 19.4 Bedruthan beach

Theory into practice

Investigate the facilites provided for families at a local hotel. Assess how far they meet the needs of families. Perhaps you can arrange a group visit. **P2**

Solo travellers

People travelling on their own are often business travellers but may be single people on holiday. Unfortunately this type of customer usually fares worst in hotels and restaurants. Single rooms are often small and in the worst location, and they are more expensive per person. Single people in restaurants may also be given small tables which are poorly placed. Many tour operators and travel agents are trying to improve facilities for solo travellers and can arrange rooms without single supplements and means of meeting other people for group holidays. However, these measures do not help business travellers. Women solo travellers sometimes have special facilities such as women-only floors and enhanced security features.

Corporate

Corporate customers may be individuals using the hotel as a base to attend meetings elsewhere. They expect to be offered business services, internet access, food at convenient times for their business needs as well as a comfortable room. They also expect a good restaurant and bar where clients can be entertained. Many hotels now recognise that business customers often require leisure facilities and provide a gym or fitness centre and sometimes a pool. Many hotels offer these services and often they are free for all residents to use.

Case study : Newmarket Racecourse

▲ **Figure 19.5 Newmarket Racecourse**

The prime business of the racecourse is to provide a venue for racing with facilities for race-goers. You might be surprised to learn that races take place on only about 40 days per year. As there are two racecourses at Newmarket, this means that there are a lot of facilities whose use would not be maximised if they were not used for some other purpose. Newmarket racecourse is therefore offered for all sorts of hospitality use including conferences, weddings, parties and corporate events.

On race days a series of packages is available for corporate clients. A business can invite its customers to watch the races from an executive box where they will be able to eat, drink and place bets without leaving the box. Those with larger parties to entertain can hire their own marquee. An example of an executive package at Newmarket racecourse is given opposite.

Find an example of another corporate hospitality package. You might find an example at a venue in your own locality. Otherwise search on the internet. Consider looking at theatres, visitor attractions and sporting venues.

EXECUTIVE BOX PACKAGES

Coffee on arrival

Fine quality champagne and canapé reception

Four-course, four choice meal

Half bottle of fine quality wine per person with the meal

VIP afternoon tea (sandwiches, selection of mini cakes, fruit basket and tea)

Full complimentary bar throughout the day (selection of beers, ciders, wine, spirits and soft drinks)

Exclusive hospitality facility for the whole day

Admission badge for the Premier & Hospitality Enclosures

Car park label (1 between 2)

Official racecard

Complimentary copy of sports newspapers (1 between 4)

£10 Tote betting voucher

Television showing live racing

Totepool betting facility

Dedicated hostess

VIP floral room display

VIP floral centrepiece on each table

(Source: http://www.newmarketracecourses.co.uk)

Corporate customers may be attending a conference. This will be organised by the hotel's conference and banqueting manager. The conference business is very lucrative and the conference manager has targets to meet and must encourage conference business.

Hotels produce sales literature aimed at the conference market and offer delegate packages per day or per number of days. Corporate entertainment is another service offered by venues as our case study shows.

Special needs

Special needs usually relates to the services required by those who are physically disabled. Hotels are aware of their obligations under the Disability Discrimination Act 1995 and most extend a welcome to guests with special requirements. A series of symbols is used to illustrate the extent of wheelchair access and some hotels provide rooms adapted for disabled users.

A charity called Holiday Care is concerned with accessible tourism enquiries. It works with tourism boards and is accredited to inspect accommodation in the UK against 'Tourism for All' National Accessible Scheme Standards. These standards were revised in 2002.

Special needs may also refer to special requirements of customers, for example a special celebration like a wedding. Weddings can take place almost anywhere these days and hotels try to use their facilities for wedding receptions. This dovetails very well with conferences as most weddings are at weekends and most conferences are during the week. Wedding customers can have the services of a wedding co-ordinator. Some weddings are booked and planned a year in advance and the wedding coordinator will offer a range of packages including menus and drinks, evening buffet, master of ceremonies and even advice on wedding etiquette.

In the description below Gemma details a typical wedding and the duties of the banqueting staff on the day. She reminds us that the bride has spent a year planning this day and it has to go well. All the staff understand how important the occasion is even if they have wedding functions every week.

The first thing we do in the morning is put the red carpet at the front of the hotel ready for the bride and groom's arrival. In the function room we lay

out the tables according to the plan that the couple has agreed with our banqueting manager. We have menus and place cards to put on the tables. Sometimes we have little novelties or keepsakes provided by the bride to put on the tables.

When the guests arrive we serve welcome drinks in the function bar and they have photos taken outside in the gardens. Then it's time for the line up. This is where the happy couple welcome their guests in a line.

The meal is served when they are all at tables and we use silver service serving the top table first. We bring in agency staff when we are really busy but otherwise we use just about everyone in the hotel from cleaners to receptionists. They are all trained in silver service.

After the meal, we present the cake and the bride and groom cut it. Whilst they have speeches we take it away and cut it properly.

After the meal there may be an evening party. We clear the room and everyone goes away to their rooms or the bar for a while. We prepare the room for a disco and buffet. More guests will arrive in the evening. The bar closes about 11.30pm and we hope that we've made their wedding day special.

Groups

Groups of customers may be corporate as we have already discussed or they may be groups of leisure travellers, like a group of students going on a residential study trip.

Theory into practice

Consider the expectations of a group like yours for a study trip. What particular needs would you have? What kind of accommodation would you require? What facilites and level of service do you expect? What kind of bars and restaurants would you visit? Discuss this with a partner, make notes and then share your findings with another pair.

Hotel groups are well aware that one brand does not suit all, and they offer branded hotels which may offer similar facilities but at different levels of luxury and service. One such hotel group is the Accor group, which serves as a good example of branding in the hotel business.

The group operates worldwide with nearly 4000 hotels and claims to cover all market segments from economy to upscale. It also has restaurants and casinos. Accor offers several brands but the extent of the range is exemplified by the brands of Sofitel, Novotel and Ibis. Sofitel is extremely luxurious, Novotel is a mid-range contemporary hotel and Ibis is a budget hotel.

The brands can be summarised as follows.

Sofitel

Sofitel is the premium hotel brand of Accor. To establish a top-tier position in the highly competitive deluxe hotel industry, Accor works with leading specialists, from world-renowned architects and top interior designers, to award-winning chefs. In prime business and leisure destinations the world over, discerning international travellers with a penchant for art, culture and luxury know that Sofitel quality will always meet their expectations.

Novotel

Every day, in city centres or just at the outskirts, near major motorways, airports or at the seaside, Novotel hotels throughout the world welcome guests. Novotel is a relaxing spot for people travelling on business as well as for families on weekends or holidays.

Ibis

Ibis hotels offer excellent service and quality at the best possible prices: comfortable rooms with bathrooms, a 24-hour reception desk, a cosy bar area, snack service at any time day or night and usually a varied choice of restaurants. Ibis hotels stand out in their category by their strong concentration in city centres and easy access.

For more information look at www.accorhotels.com.

It is difficult to understand the difference in service and quality between different classes of hotel without experiencing it. A budget hotel such as an Ibis still aims to offer good customer service and a wide range of services but is by no means as luxurious as a Sofitel or similar class of hotel. Read Tamara's accounts of staying in a Sofitel and an Ibis to see the difference.

Staying in a Sofitel

When I arrived at the revolving entrance door of the hotel I was met by a uniformed porter who took my bags for me. The lobby was magnificent and spacious with chandeliers, plush sofas and coffee tables. There were three receptionists in smart navy suits, one of whom greeted me and found my reservation. I was directed to my room and the porter arrived with my bags within five minutes. The room was gorgeous. There was a huge bed with soft quilt and pillows. In one corner was an easy chair. The furniture was dark wood and there were two large and heavy wardrobes. In one hung a fluffy white bathrobe and there were little white slippers by the bed. A television was revealed on opening a cabinet. The two windows had heavy, draped curtains which were fastened back to the wall. The bathroom was equally luxurious – a huge bath and a separate shower. I spent ages looking at the little bottles of toiletries, all of an expensive brand. There was even a sewing kit and shoe shiner. A hairdryer was provided. There were piles of huge white towels. I noticed that there was stationery in the drawers with headed paper and menus available for room service or breakfast in my room.

Back in the lobby I looked around to find the bar. There was a smart cocktail bar as well as a lounge area for guests to sit and read. Newspapers were provided. There was also a lovely French restaurant on the ground floor – it was very expensive but looked good. I wanted to go out that night and went to reception to get some advice. I was directed to the concierge who answered my questions and made a reservation for me.

Staying in an Ibis

When I arrived, I walked up to reception. This was situated on the ground floor with a bar and café area next to it. This was also the area where breakfast was served. The area was functional and bright but not luxurious. The receptionist was dressed in a dark skirt and a white shirt. She found my reservation and gave me my room key. I made my way to my room with my bags. My room was clean and pleasant. There was a bed, a built-in hanging and shelf area and bedside tables. There was a television and a telephone. I decided to write a note to a friend but couldn't find any paper.

The bathroom was a 'pod'. I mean it was pre-fabricated and built in one unit with a toilet and shower built in. There was a little bar of soap and shampoo/shower gel in a dispenser on the wall of the shower. There were two clean but smallish towels. The shower was lovely and hot and I washed my hair. There was no hairdryer but I phoned reception and one was brought to my room. I also needed more pillows and these were brought.

I went downstairs for a drink. The receptionist came to serve me at the bar. I noticed that breakfast was available here for less than £4. Also snacks and light meals were available. When I asked for directions the manager was called and advised me in a very helpful way.

What we see from Tamara's accounts is that good service can be offered even in a less luxurious environment and that a basic hotel can be sufficient for the customer's needs, depending on the occasion and budget.

Assessment practice

Draw up a comparison of how the Ibis, the Mercure and the Sofitel meet the expectations of different types of customers through the provision of different products and services. Write up your findings as a chart with detailed explanatory notes and discuss your work with your tutor. **M1**

Make sure you are not merely describing the products and services but are analysing the differences and similarities. Go to the Accor website for more information on the hotels.

Taking it further
Recommend improvements to the products and services provided by these hotels. **D1**

Theory into practice

Try this simple activity as an introduction to customer types and their expectations. Match up the customers in the table below to the most suitable form of hospitality and give the reason you think it is suitable.

Customer	Type of hospitality	Reason for choice
Jemima is a stockbroker – she is treating her boyfriend to a birthday dinner	A hotel belonging to a large chain situated at the edge of a city by a major road junction	
Joe is taking his twin 11-year-old boys away for a weekend for a summer treat	The Oxo restaurant, a smart expensive restaurant inLondon	
A property company wishing to put on a weekend exhibition about Spanish second homes	A city centre youth hostel	
A group of 200 doctors attending a conference about the latest research into airline passenger health	A university campus in the Easter period	
A group of students visiting Manchester for educational reasons	McDonald's	
A group of four young mothers who are taking a week away from their families for a rest and pampering	Splash Landings Hotel at Alton Towers	
Panday is six years old – her parents are taking her and six young friends out for tea	A spa resort in Majorca	

Classification

Classification systems help customers assess the level of service and quality to be expected from a hospitality provider.

National government tourism strategy

Policies for the hospitality industry are governed by the Department for Culture, Media and Sport (DCMS). In 2003, a new initiative known as Fitness for Purpose was introduced by the DCMS. The aim was to create a framework which provided customers with reassurance about the fitness for trading of hotels in England. It was part of the drive for better quality in tourism. A pilot scheme took place in 2003 and is now being implemented nationally.

Fitness for Purpose is an initiative promoting better inspection and regulation of tourist accommodation as a way of tackling poor safety and trading standards and ensuring that minimum legal requirements are met. It is targeted at hotels, guest houses and bed and breakfasts which are failing to meet minimum legal requirements on health and safety, food hygiene, trading standards and fire safety, in order to help them improve. It aims to give those businesses the support they need to raise standards in those areas, whilst also taking a lighter regulatory enforcement touch to well-run businesses that are already complying with the necessary regulations.

(Source: http://www.culture.gov.uk)

Common standards for grading were introduced and agreed to in 2006 by all the UK's main accreditation bodies – the AA, RAC, VisitBritain, VisitScotland and VisitWales. They replace any systems of accommodation accreditation previously used by these bodies.

The standards determine the level of the accommodation to be graded as well as its star rating. Accommodation levels range from hotels and guest houses to hostels.

Star ratings

Hotels are given a rating from one to five stars: the more stars, the higher the quality and the greater the range of facilities and level of service provided.

Self-catering accommodation is also star-rated from one to five. The more stars awarded to an establishment, the higher the level of quality. Establishments at higher rating levels also have to meet some additional requirement for facilities.

Holiday parks and campsites are also assessed using stars. One star denotes acceptable quality. Five stars denotes exceptional quality.

Ratings in other countries

The aim of the grading system is to make it easier for tourists to compare the quality of visitor accommodation offered around the country.

When you travel abroad, you will find that there is no standard system. The star grading system is more or less accepted in Europe but cannot wholly be relied on. Tour operators tend to use their own grading standards so that they can indicate a level of quality to their customers. An example is the 'T' system adopted by Thomson.

Restaurant ratings

There are different schemes for rating restaurants. The *Michelin Guide* is probably the best reputed. Inspectors from the Guide visit restaurants, often on the recommendation of satisfied customers. The rated restaurants are mentioned in the *Michelin Guide* for each country and it is quite an achievement just to be mentioned. If stars are awarded, this means the restaurant is of a high quality.

The following are the ratings as described by *Michelin*:

3 Stars: Exceptional cuisine, worth a special journey. One always eats here extremely well, sometimes superbly. Fine wines, faultless service, elegant surroundings. One will pay accordingly!

2 Stars: Excellent cooking, worth a detour. Specialities and wines of first class quality. This will be reflected in the price.

1 Star: A very good restaurant in this category. The star indicates a good place to stop on your journey. But beware of comparing the star given to an expensive 'de luxe' establishment with that of a simple restaurant where you can appreciate fine cooking at a reasonable price.

(Source: *Michelin Guide*)

Plan

Part of your assessment includes planning hospitality provision. You will probably choose something quite small and manageable to design. Here we will illustrate the stages in design by examining the planning of Heathrow Airport Terminal 5 and the catering provision within. The new terminal is due to open in March 2008, by which time the catering provision will have been in planning for 5 years.

Theme

The theme of the new terminal is that of open space and natural light. The building has been designed by the Richard Rogers Partnership and has a distinctive waveform roof. There are extensive views from the concourse to Wembley Stadium, Windsor Castle and the Gherkin. The new terminal will have the capacity to take about 30 million passengers per year. Glazed sky bridges will connect the terminal with bus, coach and taxi facilities. Food and drink facilites are important to the operation of the new terminal and the British Airways Authority (BAA) has allocated more space to food and drink outlets than usual.

'We're using Terminal 5 and the opportunity it has given us to rethink the whole passenger experience, as a trailblazer for all our planned development projects across all of our airports', says BAA Retail managing director Colin Hargreave.

The aim is to make the food and drink offering so compelling that passengers want to go through security and get in early to the area.

Extra space has allowed the provision of peaceful spaces within the outlets contributing to a stress free environment.

Level of service

The aim is to give the traveller what they want, original freshly prepared food and some of their favourite High Street brands. Because healthy eating is such an important trend BAA has picked catering brands who use freshly prepared menus and not pre-prepared fast food.

Research has shown that that 92 per cent of customers will be ABC1 – these are the most discerning of customers. Also 70–75 per cent will be travelling alone and must be made to feel comfortable.

Another important factor in terms of service is the dawn to late night trading that is necessary to cater for travellers. 50 per cent of trade is done between 5am and 10am.

Range of products and services

Trendy London-based High Street names including Giraffe, Amato, Itsu and Apostrophe have been signed up. Lovejuice, the juice bar and Prunier Seafood Bar will also be represented.

Giraffe will have 510 square metres and will feature a breakfast bar and a café style area to relax in and a dining area.

Location and customer flow

The location of the bars and restaurants has been carefully planned. Planes will pull up on both sides of the terminal so that passengers do not have to walk too far to gates. Many outlets will be sited with views of planes taking off and landing. The idea is to have a coffee or a meal and then stroll on board.

The average time passengers spend in the retail and food and drink area before boarding is one hour and twenty minutes.

(Source: Adapted from Airport Catering: Heathrow Terminal 5, 15 March 2007; http://www.caterersearch.com)

Once the bar and restaurant areas have been allocated to different businesses, those businesses will determine the design of their own area.

■ Theme

Each bar or restaurant may follow a corporate design or brand – it will probably have the same colours and features so that customers can easily recogise the brand and they will probably have seen it many times in high streets.

■ Furnishing

Furnishing forms part of the design and may relate to current trends, for example many bars now provide comfortable leather seating to encourage customers to linger – and buy more products. In restaurants, the furnishings will be more formal to allow people to eat in comfort at the tables. Bars and bar stools will be needed in a more traditional pub environment or in a juice bar.

■ Level of service

This will range from self-service for passengers in a hurry to full waitered dining service for those with more time … and money.

■ Location and size

This will depend on budget and negotiation with the aiport owners.

■ Name

Most bars and restaurants coming into Terminal 5 are chains so their names are already known and recognisable.

■ Layout and customer flow

These are related as the layout determines the customer flow. Remember that layout covers both front of house – that is, the areas the customer can see and use – and back of house – this means for restaurants the kitchen and preparation areas.

■ Products and services

These will vary according to the type of bar or restaurant. Coffee bars offer a range of good-quality fresh coffees and pastries and sandwiches. Restaurants may offer a fixed menu (table d'hôte) and an à la carte menu.

Consider this

Find out what the difference is between an à la carte menu and a fixed menu. Why are these terms often in French? Why do airport restaurants often offer an all-day breakfast menu?

Find out more about the new Terminal 5 at www.heathrowairport.com.

Assessment practice

Imagine that you are opening a small coffee and juice bar in the new Terminal 5. Produce a plan for your bar considering all the factors outlined in the text. Decide on its name too. Draw your plan on graph paper. It does not need to be to scale. Discuss the features of the plan. **P3**

Explain how your plan meets the needs of passengers at the airport. **M2**

The success of a hospitality provider is affected by several issues both internal and external. These can be assessed by means of SWOT and PEST analysis, terms which you may recall from other areas of your course, particularly marketing.

Key terms

SWOT – analysis of the strengths, weaknesses, opportunities and threats of an organisation. Strengths and weaknesses are internal, threats and opportunities may be internal or external depending on their nature.

PEST – analysis of the political, economic, social and technological factors affecting an organisation.

Internal factors

Products and services offered

The range of products and services is determined by management and, as we have seen, varies to meet the expectations of particular customers. The range is subject to change as customer needs are not static and change according to fashion and current trends. These, in turn, are part of the external environment of the organisation.

Competition

This can be an internal factor as large groups have many different brands and may be in competition with each other. For example, in the case study of Accor, we saw that the Ibis, the Mercure and the Sofitel hotels targeted different types of customers. However, a customer travelling to London has all these brands open to them so they are in competition to an extent.

Pricng strategies

Again, prices are pitched at the needs and expectations of different customers. However, all hotels measure their success by an average room rate achieved.

	Occupancy rate (%)	Average room rate (£)
2001	71.8	70.05
2002	72.2	68.38
2003	71.7	67.86
2004	73.1	73.63
2005	72.5	76.45
2006	73.2	79.50

(Source: TRI Hospitality Consulting Mintel UK Hotels 2006)

Table 19.5 UK hotel market statistics, 2001–6

The occupancy rate is also measured but this is less important than the average room rate achieved. Last-minute deals are always offered in hotels as an empty room does not make any money. Always ask 'Is that your best price?' when you make a late booking for a hotel. The rate will often be reduced.

Promotional strategies

You have studied promotion on your BTEC course and so you are aware of the complexity of planning strategy. This will be undertaken by head office in the case of a group but local promotions might be undertaken by local management with a set budget. Smaller establishments such as independent restaurants or guest houses undertake their own activities and they are likely to consist of fairly simple things such as promotion through the local tourist office or placing local advertising. Many establishments choose to have their own websites and they may update and host these themselves or employ web managers, depending on their expertise.

Location

The location affects hospitality operations as a convenient location should mean good customer flow and high occupancy rates. Restaurants must either be of such high repute that customers travel specifically to them or else must be in convenient town-centre locations.

Popularity and appeal of travel and tourism organisations

Customers choose a hospitality provider on the basis of its reputation. A brand is built up over a period of time by having high levels of service and good quality products. For restaurants, popularity is affected by reviews. Once it is established bookings flow and the restaurant is able to command high prices and be discerning about who is allowed in.

Case study:
Gordon Ramsay at Claridge's

Gordon Ramsay at Claridge's opened in October 2001. Huge popularity and critical acclaim followed, including the Tatler 2002 Best Restaurant Award.

Restored to its former Art Deco glory by designer and architect Thierry Despont, this unique venue exudes 1930s sophistication.

The restaurant is open for lunch and dinner and seats 65 guests. For those who want to be in the heart of the action, The Chef's Table in the kitchen seats four to six guests.

The restaurant also offers private dining for a whole range of occasions.

Awards
1 Michelin Star
5 AA Rosettes
Tatler 2002 Best Restaurant Award

Find out about the popularity of restaurants local to you. Look at local papers for reviews and find out how easy it is to book the popular ones. Discuss your findings with your group.

Sometimes, several of these internal factors are combined to attract customers and increase profitability. Hilton is one of the world's most famous hotel chains. It offers a range of different packages. However, sometimes these packages need to be adapted to appeal to local customers. An example is the provision of dinner murder mystery breaks at its hotel in Dartford Bridge, this includes a three-course dinner along with the entertainment.

External factors

Legislation

In some companies the Human Resources department is responsible for ensuring legislation is complied with. It should be aware of the latest legislation, as new legislation might make it necessary to set up special training to ensure staff comply or changes to legislation might affect recruitment. Examples of such legislation include the Disability Discrimination Act, which makes it unlawful for providers of goods, facilities or services to discriminate against members of the public on the grounds of disability. This also relates to employment.

■ Licensing Bill 2003

New licensing laws were proposed in 2003. These are fairly detailed but one of the major changes is permitting bars and pubs to extend their opening hours. The government maintains that fixed and early closing times result in rapid binge drinking just before closing time and that disorder and disturbance occur on the streets when everyone has to leave a pub at the same time. Everyone then needs to find public transport or a taxi at the same time or goes to fast-food outlets whose services are also put under pressure. A slower dispersal of people from pubs has resulted in less disorder. Hotels are affected where they have bars which allow non-residents.

Consider this

What is your opinion about the new licensing laws? Are people encouraged to drink more or less?

The chef must ensure that all staff in the kitchen are aware of and adhere to relevant legislation. In the kitchen this includes the Food Safety Act and the Control of Substances Hazardous to Health (COSHH).

The Food Safety Act 1990 makes it an offence to:

- render food injurious to health
- sell food which fails to comply with food safety requirements
  - if it has been rendered injurious to health
  - if it is unfit for human consumption
  - if it is so contaminated that it would not be reasonable to expect it to be used for human consumption in that state
- sell any food which is not of the nature or substance or quality demanded by the purchaser
- display food for sale with a label which falsely describes the food, or is likely to mislead as to the nature or substance or quality of the food.

Economy

The UK hotel industry turns over about £27 billion per year but is affected by economic issues including exchange rates which impact on tourist arrivals. When the pound is strong against the dollar and the euro, tourists are less likely to visit the UK as they find it expensive. Fewer visitors results in rooms being let for lower rates and in lower room-occupancy levels.

In addition, the domestic economy affects bookings. People are less likely to take leisure breaks and eat out when their disposable income is reduced through factors such as higher interest rates or increased taxation.

Availability of skilled workforce

Much of hospitality work is part time, 42 per cent in hotels and 50 per cent in restaurants. This compares with only 25 per cent part-time work across all industries. This might be a good thing in terms of flexibility for employees but the work is also low paid and often seasonal. Employers are allowed to top up wages with tips so that the minimum wage is met, in spite of strong criticism from trade unions. The employers argue that food and accommodation are often provided for workers and that this should be taken into account when setting wages.

These factors cause recruitment difficulties and jobs are often taken by those who have difficulty finding work in other sectors, such as refugees and people with few basic skills or those for whom English is a second language. Having workers who have problems communicating in English or lack other basic skills impacts on customer service and hotels and restaurants often have to keep people lacking such skills away from customer-facing activities, giving them, for example, kitchen work. Even there a lack of English may cause other problems as instructions on catering and kitchen products cannot easily be read.

A market assessment carried out by People 1st, the sector skills council for hospitality, found that there was generally a lack of training in management skills, information technology, basic skills, customer service skills and specifically in areas like food handling. From this we can conclude that more training is needed across the sector. It is the role of People 1st to encourage and influence employers to provide this training.

As there is a high turnover of staff in this sector there is a need for constant training to cover existing and replacement staff. However, if good quality training were available it would be expected that staff retention would improve. Some businesses have understood this and managed to reduce staff turnover and recruitment costs.

Key term

People 1st – the Sector Skills Council (SSC) for the Hospitality, Leisure, Travel and Tourism sector. It aims to represent the industry on skills matters, to optimise skills funding for the industry and to identify and endorse suitable training provision.

Other organisations encourage training, for example the British Institute of Innkeeping has developed a qualification for pub tenants which will eventually become a requirement for new pub tenants.

Many organisations offer on-the-job training leading to NVQs. Relevant NVQs in hospitality include the NVQ in Hospitality and Catering levels 1–3. Chefs are often offered college day-release to complete their NVQs but according to a recent Employers' Skills Survey there is a shortage of chefs, which has led to a tendency to deskill restaurant staff and provide a simple, standard menu which can be prepared by unskilled personnel.

The kind of training most often undertaken is that which enables organisations to meet their legislative requirements such as food safety training, health and safety and first-aid training.

The best quality training is usually available in the large companies, such as hotel groups where investment has been made in training and in policies to retain staff.

Competition

New businesses open and close all the time. Organisations merge or dispose of assets. These factors affect hospitality providers as they can mean more or less business for them.

Current trends

Customers' expectations change according to current trends. These may be imposed, such as the smoking ban in the case study below, or be related to health or fashion, for example the desire to eat more healthily. Hospitality providers must be aware of trends and provide products and services in anticipation of them.

Accessibility

If a hospitality provider is not accessible then it will not attract business. Therefore a restaurant that is off the beaten track has to be excellent to warrant a difficult journey. Accessibility does not just relate to location. Some restaurants are deliberately exclusive, for example The Ivy in London. This means that, as they are expensive and often booked far in advance, they are not generally accessible.

Proximity to markets

This is closely linked to accessibility. A coffee bar needs to be in a central location to be near to passing trade. Such bars are often located in bookshops so that people can read and relax over a coffee. Hotels are often next to motorways, near airports or exhibition centres to attract business people.

Case study: 5000 pubs under threat, warns report

(12 April 2007 16:30)

As many as 5,000 pubs and bars in the UK could cease trading by 2011 through a combination of the smoking ban, a clampdown on drinks promotions and declining beer sales, experts have warned.

A new report from consultancy Pricewaterhouse-Coopers (PwC) predicts that 8.6% of the 58,000 pubs, bars and nightclubs in the UK could disappear in the next five years, with drinks-only venues the hardest hit.

Stephen Broome, licensed sector industry specialist at PwC and author of the *From Beer to Eternity?* report, said: 'The experience from Scotland indicates that the overall impact of the [smoking ban] legislation should not be overestimated, but some premises will feel the impact more than others.

Drinks-only venues, and those without external spaces for smoking, are likely to be most vulnerable.'

The report followed earlier research from the Campaign for Real Ale (Camra), which found that 56 pubs a month were closing permanently, 80% of them in urban locations. Camra believes 1,300 pubs nationwide are currently under threat of closure.

To head off problems, Broome recommends a short-term approach of cash generation rather than profitability for pubs, that could include promotions and price cuts where possible.

(Source: http://www.caterersearch.com/Articles/
Article.aspx?liArticleID=312838&PrinterFriendly=true)

Hold a group discussion or even a debate about the introduction of the smoking ban. Base your discussion on the following key points:

- **Should there be a ban?**
- **Will it affect pubs in the long term?**
- **What has been the experience in Ireland?**

Assessment practice

Joshua Kintuck runs a pub in a small village in Suffolk. His partner is Spanish and a superb chef. She specialises in Catalan dishes, particularly fish dishes. Over the last ten years she has built up a reputation and people flock from far and wide to eat in the pub. On Friday and Saturday nights it is impossible to get a reservation without booking weeks ahead. Although the business is successful, it is not an easy life as the Kintucks take only one day off a week. Besides running the business and ordering and preparing the food, they have to hire and train staff. Their two children are grown up but have not chosen to work in the family business and work away from home. Because of the ties of the pub it is difficult for the Kintucks to find time to visit their children. To attract staff, Mrs Kintuck advertises in a London listing magazine. She has had some excellent young people whom she has trained as much as she has time for and she has been pleased with their performance. They are often young people who have come to the UK to learn English. Unfortunately, they do not always stay very long as there is a limit to the attractions of the countryside. This leads to a further round of recruitment and basic training. At the very least the new recruits need food safety training. Some of the staff she recruits are from outside Europe and Mrs Kintuck has found it difficult to understand all the regulations regarding the employment of non-Europeans.

Another problem facing the Kintucks is the change in licensing laws. They close promptly at 11pm at present and do not wish to open longer. Although the new laws do not mean they are forced to open longer, they are concerned that they may be under pressure from customers to do so. They do not know how they would manage to work any more hours.

1 Explain how the issues facing the pub/restaurant business in general affect their operations. **P4**

2 Assess how pubs and restaurants have responded to internal and external factors affecting their operations. **M3**

3 Analyse how the issues facing the Kintucks may affect the success of their business. Make recommendations for them. **D2**

Knowledge check

1 Give three examples of hospitality provision as a main business.

2 Which government department determines policies which concern the hospitality sector?

3 How do airlines provide hospitality?

4 Which is the largest hotel group in the UK?

5 How is hygiene maintained in a hotel?

6 Discuss three issues currently impacting on hospitality businesses.

7 Why is room service important?

8 What is a budget hotel?

9 Give three examples of the needs of a family in a hotel.

10 Outline the Food Safety Act.

11 How does location affect a restaurant's operations?

12 What are the issues about skilled workforce in hospitality?

13 Name the sector skills council for hospitality.

14 How will a smoking ban affect pubs?

Preparation for assessment

When you left college with a BTEC National qualification you found a job at a hotel in London belonging to a major chain. You were accepted onto their management trainee programme and have so far worked in two of their hotels. You are currently working in the marketing department where it has been decided to produce a monthly newsletter to be distributed to hotel staff throughout the group. The aim is to improve communication between management and staff and use the newsletter to inform staff of company policy and educate them about industry issues. The newsletter has to be of interest to staff at all levels from cleaning and waiting staff to managers.

The first edition will introduce some issues relating to the hospitality business.

You are to produce three articles for the first edition of the newsletter. You should consider the layout of the articles and how they might be illustrated.

1   The first article will describe the products and services involved within different types of hospitality provision. Explain how providers meet the needs of different types of customers.   **P1** **P2**

Grading tip

You must describe at least one provider where hospitality is the main role and at least one where it is secondary. Make sure you include a wide range of products and services for each organisation. For P2 you must consider at least three different types of customers.   **P2**

Your second article is a comparison on how two selected hospitality providers meet the expectations of different types of customers through the provision of products and services.   **M1**

Choose one of the providers you have researched and make recommendations on improvements to their products and services. You could write this as a critical review.   **D1**

2   You must also write a news column explaining how internal and external factors affect hospitality operations in travel and tourism organisations.   **P4**

Grading tip

Include at least three internal factors and at least three external factors.

Assess how hospitality operations in travel and tourism have responded to internal and external factors.   **M3**

3   In this section of the newsletter you are to introduce your design for a new spa and pool in your hotel. Show the location of the pool and spa facilities, the reception area and customer facilities in a diagram accomanied by an explanation.   **P3**

Give an explanation of your plan, stating how it meets the needs of the hotel's customers.   **M2**

Analyse how internal and external factors may affect the success of your pool and spa.   **D2**

Grading criteria

To achieve a pass grade the evidence must show that the learner is able to:	To achieve a merit grade the evidence must show that, in addition to the pass criteria, the learner is able to:	To achieve a distinction grade the evidence must show that, in addition to the pass and merit criteria, the learner is able to:
P1 describe the products and services involved within different types of hospitality provision **Case study page 172**	**M1** compare how two selected hospitality providers meet the expectations of different types of customers through the provision of products and services **Assessment practice page 181**	**D1** recommend improvements to the products and services provided by a selected hospitality provider **Taking it further page 181**
P2 explain how hospitality providers meet the expectations of different types of customers **Theory into practice page 177**	**M2** explain how the plan for hospitality provision meets the needs of the travel and tourism organisation's objectives and its customers **Assessment practice page 185**	**D2** analyse how internal and external factors may affect the success of planned hospitality provision in a travel and tourism organisation **Assessment practice page 190**
P3 plan hospitality provision for a travel and tourism organisation **Assessment practice page 185**	**M3** assess how hospitality operations in travel and tourism organisations have responded to internal and external factors **Assessment practice page 190**	
P4 explain how three internal and three external factors affect hospitality operations in travel and tourism organisations **Assessment practice page 190**		

Handling air passengers

Introduction

Air transport is a fast-growing sector of travel and tourism. The advent of low-cost airlines and competitive fares has led to an increase in the numbers of passengers flying and to further development and improvements in UK airports, particularly in the regions.

In this unit you will learn about the options available to passengers when arranging a journey, including the flight they book, and the route they plan to and from the airport. We will also look at the facilities available around the airport perimeter for overnight stays and car parking.

We will look at the complete process that passengers go through from arriving at the departure airport to leaving the arrival airport. You will learn about the regulations surrounding passports and visas for visitors arriving from destinations around the world.

Health, safety and security procedures are very important to air travel and you will consider the procedures used at airports and on airlines to mitigate health, safety and security risks. In particular, you will learn about the cabin crew's role in health and safety.

During your studies for this unit you should visit at least one airport so that you have first-hand experience of what is provided for passengers.

After completing this unit you should be able to achieve the following outcomes:

1 Know the options available to customers when travelling to and from airports
2 Understand the process of embarkation and the roles of airport and airline staff
3 Know the facilities and services available to passengers during the flight
4 Know the airport and airline services and facilities during the disembarkation process

Thinking points

Nearly half of UK residents fly at least once a year. You have probably flown already this year on holiday or to visit family. Many flights are taken for business reasons. In 2005, according to Civil Aviation Authority figures, more than 229 million passengers went through UK airports. These passengers are not all British. The UK's major airports act as hubs where passengers fly in and fly out again using the airport for transit only.

Since so much flying is done, naturally a whole industry is needed to service it. In this unit we will be exploring what happens in relation to the handling of passengers within the industry.

Transport

Research has shown that the following factors are important to customers in choosing an airline for a flight. Here they are in order of priority:

- Price
- Location of airport
- Destination
- Online booking
- Being on time
- Ease of check-in
- Previous experience
- Good customer service
- On-board seat comfort
- Friendly, helpful staff.

Theory into practice

Participate in a group discussion. Do you agree with the order of these factors? What would your group prioritise when choosing an airline for a flight? Why isn't customer service more important? Should destination be more important than departure airport?

Pull out key points from the group discussion and write them on a flipchart.

Having chosen an airline and decided to fly from a particular airport, passengers have to decide how to get to that airport. You will have noted that the location of the airport is particularly important to passengers. No one wants to travel a long way to reach an airport. If possible, a passenger looks for an airport near to home that serves their desired destination. However, London airports still offer the biggest choice of flights so many people travel to London airports to fly.

Major road and rail networks

All our main airports are close to motorways. In London, Luton is close to the M1, Heathrow to the M25 and M4, Gatwick to the M25 and Stansted to the M11. Manchester, Birmigham and Glasgow airports are all situated near major motorway links.

However, in spite of proximity to major routes, it is not desirable to encourage passengers to arrive by road. Any new airport development includes extensive plans for access by public transport in an effort to reduce the number of private cars arriving at the airport. Recently a new exit was built from the M11 in Essex to provide improved access to Stansted Airport. Passengers arriving by road add to congestion around the airport and massive amounts of land are needed for parking.

Rail is another option for arriving at the airport. London airports are particularly well served by rail. Regular trains are provided for passengers, for example the Gatwick Express. Three million passengers a year use this service, which runs between Gatwick and Victoria Station in central London. Heathrow is accessible by tube as well as by the high-speed rail link with Paddington Station.

Coach operators

Coach operators may be occasional visitors to an airport, arriving to collect a group of travellers. They can expect to be subject to strict procedures. Coaches cannot just pull up and wait for the aircraft to land; they have to park in a controlled holding area. Here they will be given a permit to go to the terminal but they can only go there once it is confirmed that the baggage for the flight they are meeting is in the claim area. These measures prevent congestion.

In addition, there will be scheduled coach services operating at an airport. The airport authorites will provide facilities for coaches to park and encourage people to travel by coach rather than by car.

Key term

Scheduled services – this means that the services run to a timetable that is set for the whole season.

Taxi and private hire

Within the airport complex there must be provision for bus stations, taxi ranks and rail stations. These are an integral part of the development of an airport, particularly as passengers are encouraged to come to an airport by public transport so that access roads are not congested and land is not overused for car parking.

Car parking

On airport parking

Car parks are located as near to the airport as possible to allow passengers quick access. Those nearest to the terminal are deemed short term and people are deterred by the price from parking there for long periods. Long-stay car parks are further away and passengers are transported to the airport by shuttle bus. Some airports now have 'mid-term' car parks. This simply means that the car park and the price are midway between the long term and the short term.

Case study: Glasgow airport transport options

Glasgow Airport Directions
The M8 Motorway via Junction 28 gives easy access to and from the airport. The airport is about 20 minutes' drive from Glasgow City Centre and about two minutes from Paisley, the nearest town. You can drop off passengers outside the terminal building, but if you want to see them off please use one of the car parks.

Trains
– Paisley's Gilmour Street railway station is the nearest to the airport. Just two miles from the terminal, it can be reached by taxi or by regular bus services.

– There are direct rail services from Paisley Gilmour Street to Glasgow Central, Ayr and Clyde Coast destinations. There are eight trains per hour (Monday–Saturday) and five per hour (Sunday) from Gilmour Street to Glasgow Central. If you need to transfer from Central station to either Queen Street station or Buchanan bus station, you can use bus service 398 which runs every 10 minutes between 07:00 and 22:00 Monday to Saturday and 10:00 and 22:00 Sunday. This service is free on production of a valid rail ticket, or 50p to other users.

By Bus
– All public buses depart from the front of the terminal building. Charter coaches pick up and drop off passengers at the short stay coach park on Bute Road, adjacent to international arrivals.

– There are frequent services to Glasgow city centre operated by Citylink and Fairline as a combined service 905. All services have drop off points at various locations in the city including close to Glasgow Central and Queen Street railway stations and at Buchanan bus station.

By Taxi
Airport taxis are available 24 hours a day to any destination and any distance. Taxi drivers are obliged to meter the entire journey and publish their scale of charges. Longer distance journey prices may be negotiated with the driver. The taxi fare from Glasgow Airport to Glasgow city centre is approximately £16.50.

Airport Car Hire
Alamo, Avis, Europcar, Hertz and National have desks in the Airport.

(Source: http://www.directglasgow.co.uk/glasgow-airport/travel-to-airport.asp)

Summarise the advantages and disadvantages of each of the methods of getting to Glasgow Airport from other areas of Scotland.

The car parks are not usually run by the airport but by specialist companies like NCP or Pink Elephant. They are able to charge large sums for passengers to have the privilege of parking at the airport. These companies are private car park operators. The airport in turn charges the car-parking company for use of their land. In some small regional airports it is still possible to park for next to nothing. The car-park companies also run a courtesy bus service (this is included in the price of parking).

Off-airport parking

Other private car park operators have benefited from car parking by finding pieces of land near to airports and marketing their car parks to passengers. All that is needed is the land and a courtesy bus service to get passengers to the airport. Passengers find these car parks less convenient as there is a greater distance to be transferred, however it is likely to be much cheaper than on airport parking. VIP car parking is available at some airports. This means that, for a fee, the passenger arrives at the airport and hands over their keys to a parking valet who parks the car for them and brings it back for their return.

Interterminal transport

This is the means of travelling from one terminal to another at an airport. Passengers might have to do this if they are in transit or to reach the correct gate.

Monorails

Stansted has a monorail system that transfers passengers very efficiently to their gates. The train is driverless and only has two stops, so it is easy for people of many different origins and languages to use as there is nowhere to get lost.

Light rail systems

The Docklands light railway serves London City Airport. Other cities will also have light rail services developed in the future. A rapid-transit light rail system for Belfast is being considered by the government. This would link Belfast City Airport with the city centre. The system will compare with bus services in terms of cost and flexibility.

Walkways

Covered walkways are usually provided from the short-term car park to the terminal and are an added benefit of being closer – which the passenger pays for. Moving walkways within the concourse allow customers to move quite lengthy distances without having to carry their luggage.

Car hire

On airport

Many people expect to collect their car immediately they disembark. It makes sense for car-hire companies to be located at airports. This provides better service for the customer, the car-hire company gets more business and the airport authority can charge the car-hire company for office space and for the large amounts of car park it requires.

Off airport

Sometimes car-hire companies are located off airport as it is cheaper and there is simply not enough land on the airport to accommodate extra cars. Passengers then have to be shuttled by bus from the airport to the car-hire depots and this is time consuming and not so convenient.

Private transfers and limousines

Some airlines provide luxury transport to the airport for their first-class passengers – all included in the price. Virgin even offers a bike service:

> *At first glance, making a Heathrow airport transfer to a business meeting, appointment or home on a motorcycle doesn't sound very practical. But our fleet of fully-customised Yamahas means we can take you and your luggage anywhere in London, stylishly and avoiding major traffic jams.*
>
> *When you meet your rider for a London airport transfer, he or she will provide you with all the protective gear you need. You can even keep in contact with business colleagues, friends and loved ones while on the move, with a built-in mobile phone, which can be used by passengers hands free.*
>
> (Source: http://www.virgin.com)

Figure 24.1 Motorcycle transport provided by Virgin allows passengers to be transferred quickly from the airport to their destinations

Consider this

How do you think you would enjoy travelling to the airport on a limo bike? What would you do with your bags?

Accommodation

Motels and hotels

Many motels and hotels have been built on or near airports to service the needs of departing and arriving passengers. They are often more expensive as they have a captive market. They offer features of particular interest to passengers, probably the most useful of which is the provision of screens displaying departures and arrivals of flights.

■ Car park inclusive packages

If a passenger intends to stay in a hotel the night before they fly they will probably save money by opting for a hotel that also offers parking. Many enterprising hotel chains and smaller independent establishments have entered this market. All the hotel has to do is provide a shuttle service to the airport and have enough space for parking several cars. This service is certain to attract people to the hotel. The following is an example near Manchester airport.

Manchester Cresta Court is the ideal place to get a good night's sleep before or after you fly. And if you're wondering where you are going to park your car while you're on holiday, we have some fantastic deals for you:

Room only from £49
Room with 8 days on-site parking from £59
Room with 15 days on-site parking from £69

The hotel is newly-refurbished and all rooms are en-suite with a colour TV, telephone, radio, hairdryer, iron, trouser press and tea/coffee-making facilities. There is also a restaurant, so you can dine before you fly and enjoy a relaxing drink in the bar.

Parking is either on-site at the hotel, or at a secured car park close by. Free transfers run to the hotel 24 hours a day and are bookable on arrival, perfect for an early fllight.

(Source: http://www.airparks.co.uk/news/hotels/cresta-court.html)

■ Transit accommodation

On-airport hotels are ideal for passengers in transit. They can get an overnight stay without leaving the airport and the hotels have screens with departure information so that passengers can stay in the hotel until the last possible minute. Some hotels even offer check-in facilities.

Assessment practice

You want to go to Corsica for a holiday. Flights are very busy as you are travelling in school holidays. The only flight you can find on the right date goes from Manchester Airport and takes you via Paris, Charles de Gaulle and then onwards to Ajaccio in Corsica.

Now you have to:

- decide how to get to Manchester Airport
- find a hotel to stay in the night before you fly
- find out which terminals at Charles de Gaulle you will be using and how to get from one to the other.

Produce a comparative table or visual display which shows all the possible ways of reaching the airport, with times and costs. Add details of possible accommodation at Manchester. Expalin how you will travel between terminals at Charles de Gaulle. State which options you will choose and why. **P1**

Departure airport facilities

Airline facilities

Airport owners and management determine what facilities should be offered at airports. Some are essential, for example washrooms must be provided and there needs to be some kind of information system to allow passengers to reach the right aircraft on time. Many are, however, discretionary and also surprising in terms of service offered to passengers. Some facilities are landside and therefore available to all visitors to an airport. Others are airside and only available to passengers.

The Civil Aviation Authority imposes Service Level Agreements (SLAs) at some airports. If the level of service is not met the airport incurs a financial penalty.

The SLAs cover all types of service but the following is one example.

People movers at Heathrow

5. As an example of how these SLAs are operated, we consider the SLAs for the serviceability of people movers at Heathrow in more detail. These SLAs cover passenger lifts, goods lifts, escalators and passenger conveyors. Serviceability targets have been set for each type of equipment at each terminal. All these targets are currently set at 99 per cent, excluding agreed and notified planned maintenance. At each terminal, BAA has appointed an 'interface manager' to act as the 'owner' of performance against the SLA targets.

(Source: http://www.caa.co.uk/docs/5/ergdocs/ccreportbaa/app6(5).pdf)

Key term

Landside and airside – landside areas of the airport are those which are accessible to the general public. Airside areas are those which are only accessible to passengers with valid boarding cards or personnel with airport ID.

Here are some travellers' views on various airports.

'I was very disappointed with Newark airport in New York. There was a coffee cart, a newsagent shop with a few souvenirs on sale and a duty free shop which was closed. Apparently, the manager hadn't turned in that day.'

'We had to spend five hours at El Prat airport in Barcelona. There were loads of reasonably priced places to eat and a lot of fashion shops including high street brands, not just the expensive designer names. There was a bookshop with lots of magazines and papers in English too. I wanted to buy some tissues and paracetamol as I had a cold but these couldn't be found. Nothing like Boots! Also it would have been good to have internet access as I was bored with the delay.'

'Tobago airport was amazing – we had to queue three times before we got to departures: at check-in, to pay departure tax and ages for security (only one x-ray machine). In the departure lounge there was a little bar and a few basic shops. There were toilets and far too few seats for two large plane loads of passengers waiting.'

'I had a delay at Carcassonne airport in France. There is one duty free shop in departures. Landside, there is a fairly good restaurant and some toilets and tourist information. Luckily it was a hot sunny day so I just sat outside on the grass and enjoyed the sun.'

What we can learn from these experiences is that it is the larger, more sophisticated airports which offer most facilities. Those airports in developing areas offer fewer. There are good reasons for this – experienced airport owners like the British Airports Authority (BAA) realise that offering facilities to passengers alongside airline customers gives an excellent source of revenue. BAA makes a great deal of money as a landlord offering space to rent to retailers and other companies in its airports. We will look at some of the facilities available.

Figure 24.2 Departure lounge at Heathrow

Ground handling facilities

Ground handling agencies provide services which support airlines at the airport, and airlines pay for those services. Some airlines prefer to employ all their own staff. An example of a ground handling agency is Servisair/Globeground. It offers many support services to airlines as well as passenger services, as the following extract from its website shows.

Servisair offers their Customers an integrated range of high quality passenger, ramp and technical services at over 140 locations around the world. We anticipate and respond to the specific and diverse needs of each of our Airline and Airport Customers, and the travelling passengers. Our dedicated employees deliver a wide range of services including but not limited to:

Passenger Services
Passenger checking
Ticketing
Lost and found
Irregularity handling (hotel accommodation, meal vouchers)
Security screening
Special services

Ramp / Technical Services
Baggage loading
Pushback, towing and repositioning
Aircraft cleaning, toilet/water
Aircraft de-icing
Load control, communications, flight operations, dispatch
Line maintenance
GSE maintenance
Supervision

Committed to making our service quality even more outstanding, we seek to work in partnership with each of our Customers, to design, develop and deliver outstanding and flexible service solutions. Along with our experience and commitment to continuous improvement, we design solutions that optimise the total cost of our Customer's ground operations.

(Source: http://www.servisair.com/CentralTwoCol.aspx?PageID–2699)

Off-airport check-in

This is a relatively new service and can be offered online or sometimes in resort. For example, Virgin Atlantic offers a check-in service at various hotels in the holiday destinations it serves. Passengers prepare their luggage, go to a pre-arranged point at their hotel to meet a Virgin representative and complete the check-in. They are then free to enjoy the rest of their time in resort until they go to the airport. Their luggage will already have been taken for them.

Retail outlets

BAA is one of the UK's most successful retail landlords. The shopping is so good at some airports, like Gatwick, that people who are not even travelling go to shop there. Shops are located both landside and airside. Airside shops are only available to travellers. When there are delays, these shops have a captive audience with little else to do but go shopping. Also, as people are often travelling because they are beginning their holiday, they are in holiday-spending mode which is a recipe for success for retailers and for the airport. Some airports have negotiated a deal with retailers where they take a percentage of takings rather than rent. Once through into the international departures area passengers have the opportunity to shop in the duty-free shops. Some airports have major shopping areas, like Gatwick or Heathrow. At these airports it would be quite easy to spend a whole day shopping. At Heathrow, there are numerous designer shops as well as gift and chocolate shops. Most airports have at least one shop where passengers can buy duty-free goods. These shops stock perfumes, cosmetics, all kinds of alcohol and tobacco.

■ Tax free and non tax free

A two-tier price system is in place for alcohol and tobacco and that is because the duty-free allowances only apply to passengers travelling outside the EU. Passengers travelling within Europe can buy alcohol and tobacco but they will have to pay the duty. Passengers travelling into the UK from outside Europe must be careful that they do not exceed their duty-free allowances. Customs issue leaflets with these on and they are displayed in the shops.

Information services

There are many sources of information at airports. There is usually an information desk where questions can be asked about facilities or services for those with special needs. There is often tourist and accommodation information, either at a staffed desk or in the form of leaflets. Leaflets around the airport provide information on services, security and regulations. Signage is very important to indicate services and where gates and check-in are located. Information screens give departure and arrival information. Airlines may give out information prior to travel. Virgin Atlantic issues several leaflets. One comes with the ticket and covers issues such as baggage, dangerous goods in baggage, denied boarding compensation and conditions of contract. Another concerns in-flight health.

Financial services

Passengers expect to find cash-point machines and also facilities to change currency. All UK airports have these facilities but they are not always available globally.

Baggage trolleys

Customers expect to find baggage trolleys available for their use. Some airports charge for these with the necessary insertion of a pound coin or a euro. This is irritating to passengers if they have no change. Less sophisticated airports still rely on porters rather than trolleys. Porters should always be tipped.

Private lounges

Private lounges are provided by airlines to give extra services to first- or business-class passengers. Economy-class passengers are allowed to go in for a fee of around £20. Business services will be on offer, for example internet access, faxing and telephone.

Airport chapel

Some airports provide a chapel or prayer room for the benefit of passengers, airport personnel and crew. These rooms are multi-faith so they are suitable for everyone whatever their beliefs. This is a service that does not make much money.

Other areas

Some airports provide a children's play area in the departure lounge and most airports will provide an aviation-viewing area for plane-spotting enthusiasts. Although all airports are no-smoking, there will usually be a specific smoking area where smoking is permitted.

Activity

The map in Figure 24.3 shows an overview of Manchester Airport. Study the map and comment on or explain the following:

- road access
- maintenance area
- location of aviation-viewing park
- location of the station
- location of car parks
- location of freight terminal.

If you want more information, go to the Manchester Airport website (www.manchesterairport.co.uk). Discuss your comments with your group.

▼ Figure 24.3 Map of Manchester Airport

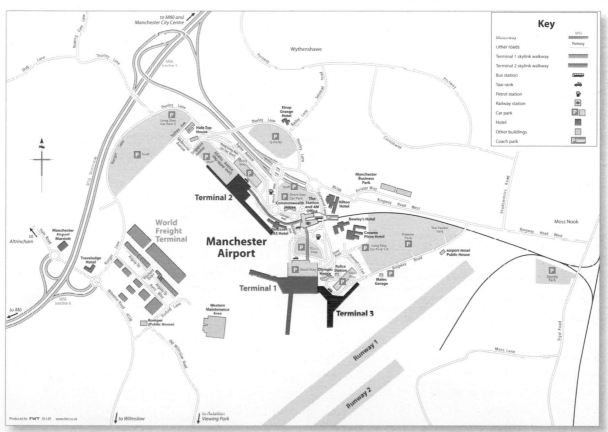

(Source: MADL (Manchester Airport))

Theory into practice

Put these areas of an airport into the relevant landside and airside areas:

- departure lounge
- customs and excise
- check-in area
- car park
- arrivals meeting hall
- runway
- baggage reclaim
- airbridge
- gate
- transport to satellite.

It is important to recognise that airports vary enormously in size. They will all have the infrastructure described but large airports may have it repeated for different terminals. At Heathrow, for example, there are four large terminals serving 63 million passengers a year.

The map in Figure 24.4 shows the arrivals floor of Terminal 4 at Heathrow. An arriving passenger first goes through immigration, claims their bag and then goes through customs.

Theory into practice

Go to http://www.heathrowairport.com/ terminalmaps/index_flash.htm?airport=Heathrow. Here you will find interactive maps of Heathrow Airport that you can study in detail. Have a look at the new Terminal 5 also.

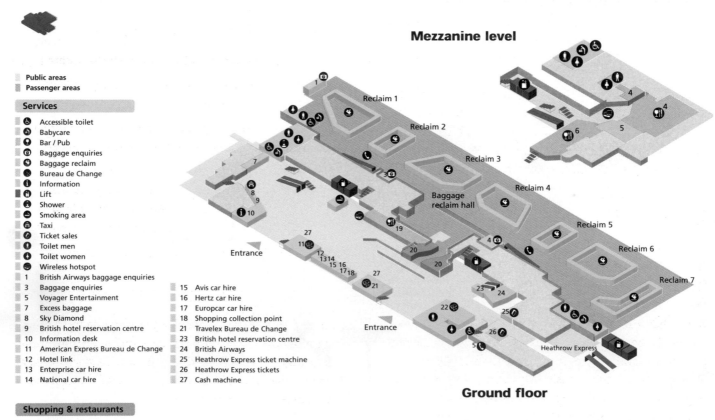

Public areas
Passenger areas

Services

	Accessible toilet
	Babycare
	Bar / Pub
	Baggage enquiries
	Baggage reclaim
	Bureau de Change
	Information
	Lift
	Shower
	Smoking area
	Taxi
	Ticket sales
	Toilet men
	Toilet women
	Wireless hotspot

1	British Airways baggage enquiries
3	Baggage enquiries
5	Voyager Entertainment
7	Excess baggage
8	Sky Diamond
9	British hotel reservation centre
10	Information desk
11	American Express Bureau de Change
12	Hotel link
13	Enterprise car hire
14	National car hire

15	Avis car hire
16	Hertz car hire
17	Europcar car hire
18	Shopping collection point
21	Travelex Bureau de Change
23	British hotel reservation centre
24	British Airways
25	Heathrow Express ticket machine
26	Heathrow Express tickets
27	Cash machine

Shopping & restaurants

4	Café Italia
6	Wetherspoon
19	Starbucks

20	Arrivals shop
22	WHSmith

▲ **Figure 24.4 Map of arrivals at Terminal 4, Heathrow Aiport**

(Source: http://www.heathrowairport.com/assets/B2CPortal/ Wrapped%20Static%20Files/Heathrow_Terminal4_Map_10-2006.pdf)

Facilities for specific needs

Unaccompanied minors process

An unaccompanied minor is a child travelling alone. Some airlines accept young people (aged 12–15) travelling alone. They may be given assistance. Airline policy on taking them differs.

Theory into practice

Find out the policy on unaccompanied minors and young people from three different airlines. Include any extra costs or procedures. You will be able to research this on the internet. Draw up a comparative chart on the policies. Make comments on your findings.

Facilities for children and infants

Apart from children's play areas, there are few facilities for children at airports. Restaurants cater for them in terms of menu and high chairs as they would anywhere. Baby-changing facilities are available. When boarding, families with small children are invited to board first.

Mobility assistance

Airports allocate parking spaces with easy access to bus stops for those with mobility problems. Help points to summon aid are usually provided in the bus shelters for those who require it.

Buses that tranfer passengers from car parks to the terminals are wheelchair accessible. Once in the airport, help points and phones are provided where people with special needs can easily request assistance. Airport buggies can transfer passengers to gates. Once the passenger has been assisted to check-in, the airline takes over responsibility for helping the passenger.

Communication assistance

The following extract explains the communication facilities available at Stansted.

Facilities for the hard of hearing

Induction loops are fitted in many areas of the terminal and satellites and are identified by the sympathetic ear sign.

- *All telephones throughout the airport are fitted with induction couplers.*
- *Public text phones are situated in the internal arrivals area and in the satellite two departure lounge.*
- *The main airport call centre for general enquiries has a minicom number 01279 663725.*
- *A number of airport staff are proficient in BSL stage one and the majority have been trained in deaf awareness.*
- *Many of the staff are able to finger spell.*

Facilities for the blind and partially sighted

Guide and hearing dogs are the only dogs allowed in the terminal buildings.

- *The airport directional signage is black on yellow to provide optimum contrast to assist all users.*
- *Reserved seating areas aim to provide low-level flight information screens, but if you have difficulty seeing the monitors generally, please advise your airline or handling agent at check-in.*
- *Your airline will provide you with assistance on request.*

(Source: http://www.stanstedairport.com/)

Many airport workers are able to offer languages other than English – they even get pay supplements for these skills and so are delighted to help non-English speakers when called upon. Leaflets are often available in other languages and even in Braille.

▲ Figure 24.5 Check-in desk at Heathrow

Routine processing functions

Check-in procedures

Those of you who are seasoned travellers will find checking in a simple process but for new travellers the process can be quite daunting. Getting to the airport on time can be stressful and then the passenger has to find the right place to check in and often has to queue.

Check-in desks open two or three hours before the flight is due to depart but the passenger must be aware of the latest time they can check in. This varies between airlines and can be as little as 30 minutes for a short haul flight or as much as two hours for a long haul flight. The airline informs passengers of the check-in time when they book. Passengers arriving after the check-in has closed miss the flight even if it is delayed. Airlines are very strict about this and if they were not then passengers would be less careful about arriving in time but this issue does give rise to many passenger complaints.

When the passenger enters the airport they will find screens advising them of the numbers of the check-in desks assigned to their flight. They then make their way to the check-in desk. Some airlines assign a separate desk for each destination, others have one queue for all passengers checking in. The latter system is more stressful for passengers as they may be in a long queue with people ahead of them who are taking later flights. Airline personnel are supposed to comb the queue and pull out those people who need to check in for flights leaving soon.

There are different types of check-in.

■ Online check-in

This is done off-airport at home or work using a computer. The passenger enters their details including passport information and a boarding card is printed. At the moment low-cost airlines offer this service to those who have hand baggage only. Once at the airport, passengers can proceed directly to security. With the major scheduled airlines a baggage drop-off is provided. Some passengers complain, however, that they spend as long queuing to drop off bags as they would have to check in.

■ Automated check-in

Otherwise known as self check-in. This is similar to online check-in except it happens via a dedicated machine at the airport. It is supposed to reduce queues at check-in but queues sometimes form at the machines as well.

▲ Figure 24.6 Security screening at Stansted

■ Manual check-in desks

Manual check-in desks staffed by airline representatives are the type we are most used to. At check-in the passenger must produce their ticket or e-reference number and their passport if travelling on an international flight. Photo ID is also required by most airlines for domestic flights. It is best for passengers travelling on domestic flights to carry a passport if they have one, as there can be disagreements about what constitutes a photo ID. For example, Ryanair only accepts a driving licence with a photo or a National Identity Card. An elderly person with a photo bus pass would not be allowed to travel.

The check-in person must ask the passenger questions about their baggage:

- 'Did you pack your bags yourself?'
- 'Could anyone have interfered with your baggage at any time?'
- 'Do you have any of these items in your luggage?' (A list of the items will be on the desk.)

A passenger giving an incorrect response to any of these questions will invite further investigation from security. With automated check-in these questions cannot be asked properly.

Security

After check-in passengers proceed to security screening. In the UK the procedures are very thorough and may take some time. The passenger puts all their hand baggage and coat onto a conveyor belt which passes through an x-ray. In the UK, passengers must sometimes remove their shoes. The baggage is examined on screen by a member of security staff. If anything untoward is noted, for example a knife in a bag, the bag is searched. Passengers are also screened. If anything metal is detected an alarm sounds and the passenger is searched. Random searches also take place.

This whole process must be taken very seriously; passengers who have made foolish jokes about bombs etc. have been arrested and imprisoned.

Hold baggage also goes through a screening process. Sophisticated baggage identification systems are used at some airports, for example Stansted. Baggage has a bar code attached at check-in which allows it to be identified at any stage of the process to arriving at the aircraft. The baggage is x-rayed as it is goes along the conveyor system and if it needs to be searched, the passenger is alerted and the bag is searched in front of the passenger.

■ Aviation Security Act 1982 and Aviation and Maritime Security Act 1990

These Acts cover safety and security at airports and on aircraft. It is an offence to endanger safety at airports or on an aircraft. It is also an offence for an unauthorised person to enter the restricted zone of an airport or an aircraft and to remain there after being asked to leave. The Anti-Terrorism, Crime and Security Bill of 2001 extends the Aviation Security Act and gives the power of removal of unauthorised persons.

If a passenger gives a false statement when asked questions, for example about their baggage, they can be prosecuted under the Aviation and Maritime Security Act.

Immigration (to destination country)

Travel agents will give passport and visa information to customers and tour operators will mention what is required in their brochures. Airlines include information on their websites. However, in all cases the onus is on the passenger to ensure they travel with the correct documentation. If they arrive at the airport without it they will not be allowed to travel. They must also ensure that they meet the requirements of immigration at their destination.

If the flight is international the passenger will show their passport and boarding card before being allowed through to departures. This is straightforward on exit although sometimes passport control are looking out for wanted people who may be trying to leave the country.

Consider this

The UK Passport Office website (www.passport.gov.uk) tells you how to apply for a passport. Forms are available from the Post Office. To find out about specific country requirements you have to ask the Embassy or Consulate of that country. Details can be found on websites. It is always a good idea to check because there are sometimes surprising requirements. For example, if you are British and visit the island of Grenada you should make sure your passport is valid for at least 6 months from the date of departure, and if you go to Australia you need a visa.

Theory into practice

Find out the requirements for:

- an EU resident travelling to Nepal
- an EU resident visiting Australia.

Check-in staff are very careful about checking documents, as any passengers who arrive in a European country without the proper documentation can be refused entry. The airline is responsible for ensuring passengers board with the correct passport/visa. Authorities fine airlines who make mistakes and the airline also has the problem of removing the passenger from the country.

Key term

National Identity Card – these are issued to residents of some countries and are valid for international travel. In the UK we do not have identity cards so a passport is required for international travel.

Boarding cards

The boarding card is given to the passenger at check-in, either automated or by the check-in person. This card gives details of seat number, if applicable, gate number and time of boarding. This is a vital document as the passenger cannot go through to departures or board the flight without it. It will also be required if the passenger wants to purchase anything in the duty-free shops.

▲ Figure 24.7 Example of a boarding card

Departure information

Passengers enter the departure lounge once they have passed through passport control and they are then airside. In a large airport this area can be interesting as it has many shops and eating places. Toilets are provided as well as screens giving departure information.

From the departure lounge passengers go to gates. The gates are the point where the passenger actually boards the aircraft by airbridge or steps. The gates may be located in a satellite, which is an extra building like a small terminal, built to accommodate more passengers and planes. In a small airport not many facilities are provided in the departure lounge, which is disappointing if there is a delay.

Changes to itinerary

Changes to itineraries are usually made because planes are delayed or cancelled. If delays occur because of conditions outside the airline's control, for example the weather, no compensation is due from the airline. However, travel insurance may cover this. If an airline decides to cancel a flight for reasons of convenience to schedules or because it is not full, then compensation has to be paid to passengers under 'Denied Boarding Regulations'.

The full booking conditions are usually found on an airline's website. However airline websites contain so much information that it would be surprising if a passenger read it all. Passengers should be able to find what they need to know quickly and the essential pieces of information should be with their tickets. Tour operators publish their booking conditions in their brochures so these are easily accessible to the customer. Travel agents are usually taking bookings on behalf of a principal such as an airline so they pass on the booking conditions to the customer.

Theory into practice

Look up the regulations on denied boarding and find out what you are entitled to if a flight is cancellled.

Standby passengers

Standby passengers are those who are hoping to get on a flight that is full. They register with the airline information desk and then get a seat if one becomes available.

Luggage procedures

Dangerous and restricted goods

There are regulations about dangerous and restrictive goods which are regularly updated. The latest amendments were made in January 2005. Certain items are not allowed in hand baggage:

- toy or replica guns
- tradesmen's tools
- catapults
- darts
- household cutlery
- sporting bats
- knives
- razor blades
- paper knives
- hypodermic syringes.

There are also items which cannot be taken in any baggage as they are regarded as dangerous:

- compressed gases
- corrosives
- flammable liquids
- radioactive materials
- weapons
- oxidising materials
- poisons and alarm devices
- infectious substances.

Consider this

Why do you think the regulations need to be regularly updated? What would happen if you were carrying a knife in your hand baggage?

Guides are issued by HM Revenue and Customs explaining what can and cannot be brought into the UK. Similar information is provided by other countries and before you leave the UK you need to check the destination country's regulations. If you travel to the USA, for example, you will be required to complete a declaration stating that you are not bringing in any restricted goods.

Strict controls are in place so that diseases in plants or meats are not transferred to one country from another and to give protection from the import/export of firearms, drugs and harmful goods.

Figure 24.8 shows an example of a UK leaflet.

IF IN DOUBT, LEAVE IT OUT!

DON'T BRING PROHIBITED MEAT AND FOOD INTO THE UK. MANY ITEMS ARE ILLEGAL AS THEY MAY CARRY DISEASES. CHECK THE RULES OR YOU COULD FACE SEVERE DELAYS, PROSECUTION AND FINES.

WORKING TOGETHER TO KEEP PESTS AND ANIMAL DISEASES OUT OF THE EU.

HM Revenue & Customs   defra

◀ Figure 24.8
Leaflet warning about importing foodstuffs

WHY ARE THERE STRICT CONTROLS?

Meat, food and plants can carry animal/plant pests and diseases, which can devastate our environment and our agricultural and horticultural industries. The 2001 Foot and Mouth (FMD) outbreak demonstrated the costly impact of animal and plant disease on rural communities, businesses and the economy.

This leaflet gives you a summary of the rules. It is not fully comprehensive. Pest and disease outbreaks can occur at any time and these rules are subject to amendment without notice.

WHERE YOU SEE THIS SYMBOL YOU MUST CHECK IF YOU ARE PERMITTED TO BRING IN THE FOOD ITEM FROM THE COUNTRY YOU ARE TRAVELLING FROM.

MAX 1KG

If you are in doubt, please check the rules at www.defra.gov.uk or call the helplines on page 6. Remember, what you can bring into the UK depends on where you are travelling from, not where the item has been produced or packaged.

FOOD MUST BE FOR PERSONAL CONSUMPTION AND FREE FROM DISEASES. THE STATED LIMITS ARE PER PERSON. IF YOU EXCEED THESE, THE WHOLE AMOUNT WILL BE SEIZED.

All travellers may bring in a limited quantity of powdered infant milk, infant food and special foods required for medical reasons in personal baggage. Items must not require refrigeration before opening and must be in commercially branded packaging, unopened unless in current use.

-2-

TRAVELLING FROM

From another European may bring in or send b free from diseases an

Austria, Belgium, Czec France, Germany, Gre Latvia, Lithuania, Luxe Poland, Portugal (inclu whole of Cyprus is part of th effective control of the Repu Slovakia, Slovenia, Spain, swoden

For these purposes European Union countries also include: Andorra, the Canary Islands, the Channel Islands, the Isle of Man, Norway and San Marino. Although Gibraltar is part of the EU, it is outside the Community for these purposes.

TRAVELLING FROM THE FAROE ISLANDS, GREENLAND, ICELAND, LIECHTENSTEIN OR SWITZERLAND

You may bring in or send by post to the UK the following items:

A COMBINED WEIGHT OF NOT MORE THAN 5KG PER PERSON OF THE FOLLOWING: Meat, meat products, milk and dairy products obtained from those countries.

5KG

1KG EACH OF OTHER ANIMAL PRODUCTS PER PERSON (eg Fish, shellfish, honey, eggs) IS PERMITTED FROM CERTAIN COUNTRIES.*

?1KG

*The rules vary by product and by country. Please check using the contacts on page 6.

-3-

ALL OTHER NON-EU COUNTRIES

to bring in or send by post to the

AND MEAT PRODUCTS as fresh, cooked or l meat, for example curries, ham, biltong, noodles which contain es of meat, meatballs, t pickles, cured or ked sausage, pâté and t paste.

×

K AND DAIRY PRODUCTS such as dried milk, concentrated milk, cream, butter, ghee, mithai, cheese and products made from or containing fresh cream.

×

For other products the rules vary by country. From some countries you may bring in or send by post to the UK up to 1KG of certain products. From other countries you may not be able to bring or send any of these products in. Please check using the contacts on page 6.

FISH AND FISH PRODUCTS such as fresh, dried, cooked, cured or smoked fish and fish products, for example oyster sauce, canned tuna and fish sauces.

MAX 1KG

SHELLFISH such as prawns, shrimp, oysters and scallops.

MAX 1KG

EGGS AND EGG PRODUCTS such as omelette, egg noodles and dried egg.

MAX 1KG

HONEY

MAX 1KG

-4-

(Source: HM Revenue & Customs)

Items not accepted in the cabin

Passengers are allowed to take bags into the cabin according to allowances as described in the next section. However, following a national security alert in August 2006, very stringent restrictions were placed on what could be taken into the cabin. One aspect related to the number of cabin bags:

UK Department for Transport restrictions relating to size and number of cabin bags

Restrictions relating to the size and number of bags allowed through security search remain in place for all air travellers departing a UK airport.

Passengers must comply with UK Department for Transport restrictions, which are:

ONE cabin bag, no bigger than 56 cm x 45 cm x 25 cm (approximately 22 inches x 17.5 inches x 9.85 inches).

In addition, customers may now carry musical instruments (guitar size or smaller) through security search provided they can be x-ray screened.

(Source: http://www.britishairways.com/travel/bagcabin/public/en_us)

Another aspect related to the carrying of liquids:

Passengers may carry small quantities of liquids, but only within separate containers each of which with a capacity not greater than 100ml.

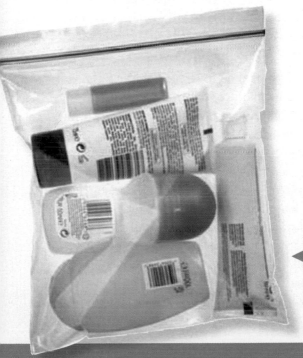

◀ Figure 24.9 Example of acceptable way to carry liquids

*These containers must be brought to the airport contained in a **single, transparent, re-sealable plastic bag**, which itself must not exceed 1 litre in capacity (approximately 20cm × 20cm). **The contents of the plastic bag must fit comfortably and the bag must be sealed**. Each passenger may carry only one such bag of liquids.*

The bag must be presented for examination at the airport security point.

(Source: http://www.dft.gov.uk/transportforyou/airtravel/airportsecurity)

Theory into practice

When you read this, it is very likely that the regulations for hand luggage have changed. Find out what the current regulations are by visiting the Department for Transport website at www.dft.gov.uk. Then choose two airlines and compare their luggage advice and allowances with the official advice.

Luggage allowances

Allowances are given for hold and cabin baggage. These differ between airlines and between classes of travel, thus a first-class traveller gets a bigger allowance than an economy-class passenger. The lowest allowance for hold baggage is 15kg on a low-cost flight and yet in first class on some Virgin routes passengers can take three pieces of up to 32kg each. The 32kg limit per piece is set for the health and safety of baggage handlers. Some airlines set restrictions by number of pieces rather than weight.

Restrictions on cabin baggage depend on how much space is available in the aircraft. Generally, passengers are allowed one piece of cabin baggage which must be within certain dimensions. A measuring device is provided at check-in.

Excess baggage charges

These also vary from airline to airline. They are a very useful source of extra revenue for airlines. For example, Flybe charges £5.50 per kilo excess, although the initial allowance is 25kg which is quite generous. British Airways charges £60 for an extra bag on European routes.

If you are travelling with a lot of luggage it is important to check allowances and work out costs alongside the fare.

Consider this

Some airlines now charge to carry any bag in the hold, not just excess baggage. Ryanair charges £5 to check a bag and Flybe charges £3.

Outsize luggage

Luggage may be outsize in dimension but still has to be within the 32kg weight limit to protect the health and safety of baggage handlers.

Outsize luggage is sometimes charged for – it depends on the policy of the airline. British Airways allow one piece of sporting equipment free as long as it fits certain dimensions. Sporting equipment is classed as outsize luggage as it cannot go along the normal luggage conveyor system as it would get damaged. Of course, like any luggage it sometimes gets lost as the following extract shows.

Budget airline easyJet has been forced to apologise to newly crowned snooker champ John Higgins after it temporarily lost his precious cue and trophy.

The Scottish potting machine was flying back from Luton to Glasgow yesterday afternoon after beating Ronnie O'Sullivan 10–9 in the final of the Masters.

But the 'Wizard of Wishaw's' delight turned to anguish as he was told his snooker paraphernalia and crystal trophy had gone missing.

The articles were located in the evening and an easyJet spokesman apologised to the snooker star for any inconvenience.

'It seems that they went through outsize baggage but for some reason they were taken off that conveyer belt and didn't get on the flight,' said the spokesman.

The cue would never have been lost, however, if it wasn't for a recent change in security policy that prevented Higgins from taking it on the plane.

© Adfero Ltd

January 24, 2006

(Source: http://news.cheapflights.co.uk/flights/2006/01/easyjet_loses_s.html; © Adfero Ltd)

Personnel and staff roles

Airports are major employers in the regions they serve. There are many departments in an airport and passengers will be unaware of most of them. They will, however, meet some personnel on their journey through the airport. All these personnel are part of one team at the airport and must work together in order to make sure that the passengers are processed efficiently throughout the airport and their journey.

The following are some examples of personnel found at airports and their job roles.

Airline staff

Airlines choose whether to employ their own check-in staff and despatchers or contract these services out to a ground handling company.

Ground handlers

The services provided by ground handlers were discussed earlier. If you wanted to work in ground handling you would apply directly to the ground handling agent, for example Servisair.

Personnel working for a ground handler in passenger services could be in one of these areas:

- check-in – working at the check-in desk ensuring passengers are checked in according to the airline's procedures
- customer service – deals with any specific problems that occur, looks after VIP departures and arrivals
- baggage handling – very physical work, loading and unloading baggage onto and from aircraft
- security screening – checking passenger baggage on x-ray and randomly searching bags or people
- special services – looking after passengers with special needs on behalf of the airline and guiding them through the airport.

Customer service agents

Customer service agents may work for a ground handler as described above or they may be employed in a customer service role directly by the airport.

Baggage handling agents

Again, these personnel are usually employed by the ground handling company.

Security staff

The role of security staff is of increasing importance due to terrorist alerts in major cities and at airports. Their recruitment and training are taken very seriously by airports and ground handling companies. You will see them at departures making security checks on passengers but they also work behind the scenes screening hold luggage.

Immigration officers

These people look after passport control but their most important role is checking on incoming passengers, as we will see later.

HM Revenue and Customs and Excise Officers

Passengers will also meet Customs and Excise Officers. These people work at the airport but are employed by the government and could be working at any port of entry including sea ports. Their role is to make sure that entering passengers comply with customs regulations and they try to apprehend smugglers. People with forbidden goods may be fined or arrested.

Retail staff

There are many retail jobs available in our airports as retailing provides such an important source of revenue. Working in the airport is much the same as working in any shop. Assistants must offer advice and generate sales for their company. Staff who work airside must be cleared for security.

Assessment practice

A group of schoolchildren aged 13 and 14 years old are taking a trip from your regional airport to Paris. Although they will be accompanied by teaching staff, the group leader wants to make sure they are aware of the procedures they will go through at the airport to reach their flight. Recognising your knowledge of these procedures, she has asked you to provide information for the children.

Prepare a step-by-step instruction sheet for the children, describing the procedures they will go though at the airport. Use illustrations if you wish.

You should include:

- the options available for the children to reach your regional airport **P1**
- the processes for embarkation and the role that airport and airline staff have during embarkation of customers **P2**
- the boarding process. **P3**

Grading tip

To meet the requirements for M1 you should carry out this activity for two airports and compare the facilities for travelling and embarkation. **M1**

Boarding

Passengers make their way through departures to the gate for boarding. Once passengers reach the gate they will wait in a seated area until their flight is called.

Key term

Despatcher – the despatcher is a member of ground crew and has particular responsibility for making sure that all passengers are on board and paperwork completed so that the aircraft can depart on time.

The air crew at this time are preparing the aircraft and doing their pre-flight safety checks.

Security checks

Passports have been checked at check-in but are checked again at the gate and against the boarding card so that the boarding card cannot be handed to another person after check-in. Staff also check the destination on the card to ensure the passenger is getting on the right flight.

Announcements are made to find late passengers and get them to the gate. If there are still people missing their bags are offloaded and they miss the flight. For security reasons the bags do not usually go without their owners.

Preferential seating

Wheelchair passengers and people with small children are always asked to board first and then the crew will call other passengers forward in turn according to seat numbers. On some flights seats are not pre-allocated and this leads to anxiety amongst passengers who want to sit with their friends and families.

Some low-cost airlines now offer a priority boarding service. This means for an extra fee of about £3 you can buy the right to get on first – another source of extra income for the airlines. If you travel first class you will wait in the first class lounge in comfort until you board and go straight to your seat.

Provision of air bridges or steps

Air bridges are a more comfortable way to board, as they protect passengers from the elements and are easier for those with reduced mobility or with children to negotiate. However, the airline pays more for this facility so low-cost airlines do not often provide them.

Passengers with specific needs

Passengers who may require help in boarding include those with reduced mobility and those with children.

The International Air Transport Association (IATA) provides definitions of wheelchair passengers:

- WCHR – cannot walk long distances, can manage stairs
- WCHS – cannot walk upstairs, cannot manage to board without a jetbridge or wheelchair from gate
- WCHC – immobile: relies on others for mobility.

Theory into practice

Find out what assistance British Airports Authority (BAA) airports and Ryanair offer to special-needs passengers to help them board. You will find this information on their websites.

Suspicious passengers and those under the influence of alcohol

At the gate staff will once again be on the alert for suspicious behaviour and are able to bar passengers from boarding the flight if necessary. Drunken passengers or those who threaten the safety of others will not be allowed to board. This is covered by the Air Navigation Order of 1995. The Order also covers smoking on board an aircraft.

Consider this

It is not only the passengers who must be sober! In 2007, a pilot was due to fly passengers from London Heathrow to New York. He was arrested minutes before take-off and breathalysed. Police have had the power to breathalyse crew since March 2004 if there is a suspicion that they may be drunk. Passengers had to wait for an hour until a replacement pilot was found.

Nervous flyers

Cabin crew are alert to nervous flyers. They are trained to greet them in a reassuring manner and will attend to them in flight as necessary.

Cabin baggage

Once on board, passengers must stow their hand baggage. Overhead lockers are provided for this purpose. If these are full, passengers can put bags under their seats but exits and aisles must be kept clear in case of emergency.

Onboard facilities

The level of service offered on board a flight varies according to the type of airline, the type of aircraft and factors such as length of flight, time of day and costs of providing services. In this section we will take a closer look at what passengers can expect on board a flight.

Classes on scheduled flights

Traditional or full service scheduled airlines usually offer different classes of service. A small aircraft such as a Boeing 737 operating intercity in Europe may have an economy service and business class service. The aircraft is not sufficiently large to offer business and first class. Even on a short flight, passengers are offered a meal appropriate for the time of day and a free bar in business class. In economy, passengers will be offered drinks but may have to pay for them on some airlines. British Airways, however, still includes food and drink

in its economy service. In business class, the food will be better and served on crockery instead of plastic and there will be more leg room. Providing this level of service can be difficult for cabin crew on a short flight. A flight from London to Amsterdam, for example, is only 40 minutes and yet the cabin crew may have to attend to over 140 passengers.

Figure 24.11 shows the configuration of a British Airways 737. Club Europe is the name given to business class travel.

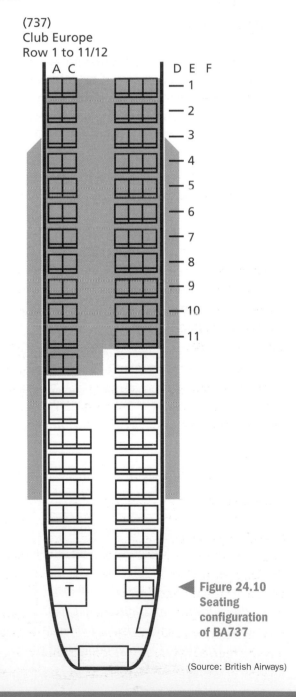

(737)
Club Europe
Row 1 to 11/12

◄ Figure 24.10 Seating configuration of BA737

(Source: British Airways)

Long haul flights have to provide catering over a longer period and these flights are on larger aircraft so there is capacity for more than two classes of traveller. Virgin Atlantic offers:

- Economy
- Premium Economy
- Upper Class.

On a typical flight to New York from London the service in economy would be as follows.

Departure at 2pm – passengers board and find pillows and toiletry bags on seats. These include a notepad and pen, tissues, eye shades and toothbrush.

Shortly after departure free drinks are served. After this lunch is served with a choice of two dishes. Throughout the flight passengers can request drinks and orange juice and water are brought round. Ice cream is also served and afternoon tea is provided about an hour before arrival.

Variations of this type of service are provided according to time of day and length of flight. Similar service can be expected from other airlines on long haul but Virgin Atlantic has an award-winning entertainment system with individual seat-back screens where passengers can choose which movie or television programme to watch or even play computer games.

Premium economy is the next class of service and is similar to economy but with more leg room.

Upper-class passengers travel in luxury with seats that convert to beds. A bar area is provided and there is a massage and beauty area so that passengers can have treatments if they wish.

The extract below shows what to expect when travelling in upper class.

- *Sleep – And stretch. At the touch of a button the seat flips over to become the biggest fully flat bed in business. Every seat has aisle access so there's no stepping over your neighbour.*
- *Work – Every suite is fitted with laptop power access and a large table with plenty of room to spread out or have an informal meeting.*
- *Play – With a multi-directional 10.4" TV screen, you're in your own private cinema. With a huge choice of films, TV programmes and games.*

- *Dine – Order what you want when you want from our Freedom menu, or why not invite a friend to join you for a drink or a snack.*
- *Relax – Put your feet up. Your soft leather seat reclines even for take off and your ottoman also acts as a seat for a guest or for beauty therapy treatments.*

(Source: http://www.virginatlantic.com)

Theory into practice

Money is no object! You are taking a long haul flight with one of the world's most reputable airlines – Emirates. You will, of course, be travelling first class. Investigate the services and facilities you will enjoy in-flight by researching Emirates' website. Imagine you are on the flight and write a letter to a friend telling them about the service.

Facilities on charter airlines

Charter flights used to try and emulate the service levels offered by traditional scheduled airlines but in economy class only. However, in recent years the charter airlines have changed the services they offer. Many now offer a premium service particularly on long haul flights, in response to customer demand. You would not expect this service to offer the luxury of Emirates or Virgin Atlantic but passengers do get more leg room and slightly better food than previously.

On short haul flights the trend has been to decrease the services offered and charge passengers for extras. For example, passengers can have a meal but will pre-order it and pay £10. Emergency exit seats with more leg room may carry an extra charge. Passengers who want to make sure they can sit together will pay extra to pre-allocate their seats. All these charges bring extra revenue to the charter airline or holiday company renting the aircraft.

Consider this

What would you do: pay £10 for an airline meal or take your own sandwiches?

Excel Airways is a good example of a charter airline as it operates both long haul and short haul flights. The long haul service operates to some of the Caribbean islands, for example Tobago and Grenada.

Excel Airways operates with two classes on the long haul routes. These are Long Haul Economy and Long Haul Excel One. The extract below gives details of some of the services on board Excel flights.

Services on board Excel flights

ONE PROMISE

From the moment of arrival at our dedicated airport check-in to the joys of shorter queues and extra baggage allowance, we will make sure you feel like a valued guest rather than just one of the crowd.

As you board your own dedicated, well trained and experienced cabin crew will take your coat and offer you a glass of champagne, bucks fizz or water.

Once on board, passengers can relax at the front in an exclusive 'away from the crowd' separate cabin; a maximum of seven rows of luxurious reclining leather armchairs, all with a 45" pitch. Blankets and pillows are supplied for added comfort.

ONE BETTER

Enjoy a choice of 3, three course menus with dessert, cheese and crackers accompanied by warmed rolls, fine wines, port, liqueurs and chocolates before settling back to watch a selection of the latest shows and movies on an individual hand held entertainment centre. Wake up to a continental breakfast / light meal served with tea, coffee and warmed sweet and savoury pastries.

ONE AIM

Your cabin crew are always on hand to attend to your needs and to serve a range of complimentary drinks and meals, a selection of newspapers and magazines, your own personal 'pampering kit' together with hot towels throughout the flight.

And the service doesn't end on touch down. Priority disembarkation and baggage collection before our other passengers means you can get on with the business at hand; relaxation and your holiday.

ONE SPACE

Go one better and transform your flight into a truly memorable experience. XLOne is about individuality, making you feel truly special in your own space in the sky.

(Source: http://www.xl.com/Customer_Info/Additional_One.asp)

Facilities on low-cost airlines

The whole premise of low-cost airlines is to cut costs as much as possible so that low prices can be charged. If costs are cut then services are either cut or paid for as extras. Sometimes flights are free apart from taxes to promote custom and the airline makes its profits from all its add-on sales. Low-cost airlines sell food and drinks on board. They charge a lot for excess baggage. In addition, their baggage allowances are lower (Ryanair has 15kg). In common with other airlines they sell gifts and perfumes on board. They also make revenue through commission on selling insurance, hotel accommodation and car hire through their websites.

These are the services that passengers on low-cost airlines can expect to be *excluded* from their fare:

- allocated seats
- food and drink
- headrest covers
- blankets
- entertainment.

■ Extra leg room

As we have seen, one of the main benefits of travelling in first or upper class is extra leg room. The least leg room is offered on low-cost flights but if it is a short flight and the price is low then passengers will be happy enough. First Choice Airways has made a marketing point of offering more leg room to passengers. Emergency row seats have more space so smart passengers can request those but some even smarter airlines have begun charging extra for these seats!

■ In-flight entertainment

The range is from nothing at all to the individual seat-back system provided by Virgin. Virgin has won awards for its system and this has a lot to offer, with a wide variety of films, television programmes, radio, games and destination information.

■ Food and beverages

We have noted that some airlines include food and drink and some charge extra for it. Once again, first-class passengers get more choice and anything they would like to drink including champagne.

■ Tax-free goods

This service is only available on flights out of the EU. Passengers choose from alcohol, cigarettes, perfumes and gifts at prices which are less than high street prices in the UK. They are not allowed to consume the goods on board and must stay within the customs allowances of the country they are entering – or pay duty.

■ Telephones and internet

These are relatively new facilities on board aircraft and not available on all flights. They are also very expensive to use.

■ Destination information

Passengers enjoy finding out about their destination and most airlines provide a magazine which will have at least basic information on how to get around, what to see and do. This information is provided before departure on their websites and some airlines, like Virgin, show documentaries about the destination.

■ Immigration documentation

If a landing card is required it will be given out and completed during the flight so that time is saved at immigration.

■ Medical assistance

The aircraft will carry a first-aid kit and possibly a defibrillator. Passengers cannot expect professional medical assistance on board unless another passenger happens to be a doctor. It is more likely that the pilot will divert to the nearest airport in the case of an emergency.

Facilities for passengers with special needs

Seating arrangements

Most airlines will offer passengers with special requirements the ability to pre-book their seat allocation as well as any special dietary requests.

When check-in staff allocate seats, they have to make sure that able-bodied people are seated at the emergency exits. They remember who should not sit in the exit row by the mnemonic CODPIE: Children, obese, disabled, pregnant, infants, elderly.

There are very few facilities for special-needs passengers actually on board aircraft. Some airlines may provide the following:

- disabled toilet facilities
- communication assistance
  - crew who speak more than one language
  - safety instructions in Braille
  - safety videos with subtitles
  - induction loops
- special meals
- extra oxygen.

Key term

Landing card – this is a document often required for non-citizens arriving in a country. It allows immigration to track who is arriving and that they have later departed.

Consider this

Why do you think extra oxygen is carried on a flight? Is it for the passengers or the crew?

Facilities for children

Infant seat belts are provided for children of up to 2 years old. After this age they must occupy their own seats.

Key term

Infant – a child under two years old. Infants travel free but have to sit on an adult's lap with a special seat belt.

Sky cots are also provided but when the seat-belt signs are on babies have to be taken out of the cot and held by an adult with an infant seatbelt securing them.

Airlines want to make provision for families and so welcome children by providing activity packs and children's channels on entertainment systems. Children's meals are available and toilets have nappy-changing facilities. Crew will warm up bottles for babies.

Some airlines accept unaccompanied minors as passengers but each airline has a different policy on this. At best, children as young as five are accepted for travel and a member of crew is designated to supervise them. There is a charge for the service. Many airlines do not accept unaccompanied minors as the cost is too great.

Theory into practice

Imagine you are taking a long flight (seven hours) with an infant and a small child. Make a list of all the facilities you might need to make life easier or safer. Go to the British Airways website which gives a lot of information on facilities on board for children, including special meals, entertainment and seating. Have a look at what is on offer and compare it with your wish list. BA is particularly good at catering for children. Are there facilities they provide you hadn't thought of? Make notes on your findings.

Roles and responsibilities of personnel in flight

The personnel on the plane are air cabin crew and flight crew. The passenger meets the cabin crew as they board the plane. They probably will not meet the flight crew but they might hear them say a few words on the flight. The role of both sets of crew is to look after the safety of the passengers and deliver them to their destination.

Giving information

The most important information given is about safety. When all passengers are on board and seated the crew present them with a safety demonstration. This usually takes place as the plane is taxiing before the crew have to take their seats for take-off. The safety demonstration varies according to the airline and type of aircraft but always covers:

- seat belts
- emergency exits
- emergency floor lighting
- oxygen masks
- life jackets
- safety information cards.

Cabin crew are given a script to read – a tape is often played with the same information in different languages. It is important that all passengers can understand the information. A typical safety briefing is given below.

Ladies and Gentlemen

Please pay attention to our safety demonstration. This is important even if you are a frequent flyer.

Your seat belt fastens and adjusts like this (demonstrate) and unfastens like this.

Infant seat belts are provided. Whenever the 'Fasten Seat Belt' sign is illuminated you must go back to your seat and fasten your seat belt securely. For your own comfort and safety we recommend that you keep your seat belt loosely fastened and visible at all times so that you are not disturbed during flight.

On this Boeing 737-400 there are emergency exits on both sides of the aircraft and these are being pointed out to you now. There are two at the rear of the cabin (point) two over wing exits on each side in the centre (point) and two at the front of the cabin (point).

Please take a moment to locate your nearest exit bearing in mind it may be behind you.

To help you find your way to the exits, additional lights will be provided in the aisle at floor level (point).

In the unlikely event of having to use the escape slide leave all hand baggage behind and remove high heeled shoes as they may impede your exit.

If the cabin air supply fails, oxygen will be provided. Masks like this (show) will be released from the panel above your head. Stay in your seat and pull the mask towards you. Place the mask over your nose and mouth like this and breathe normally. Do make sure your own mask is fitted before helping anyone else.

Your life jacket is underneath your seat. In the event of landing on water, remove the life jacket from its container and pull it over your head. Pass the tapes around your waist and tie them in a double bow (demonstrate). To inflate pull the red toggle. The air can be topped up using this mouthpiece. There is a whistle for attracting attention. Do not inflate your life jacket until you are outside the aircraft.

Please study the safety card provided in your seat pocket. It also has details of the brace position which you must adopt in an emergency landing. Please ensure that mobile phones and any other electronic equipment is switched off.

Please make sure that your seat is in the upright position, your table is folded away, the armrest is down and your seat belt is fastened. Thank you for listening and we hope you enjoy your flight.

Figure 24.11 Safety on board airbus 340-300 ▶

Theory into practice

It is not as easy as it looks! Ask your tutor to provide the props so that you can give the safety demonstration to your colleagues. Ask them to criticise (constructively) your performance.

The safety card referred to is provided in each seat pocket so that passengers can look at the card and remind themselves of safety features. The information on the card differs for each aircraft. Figure 24.12 shows part of the safety on board requirements for an Airbus A340-300.

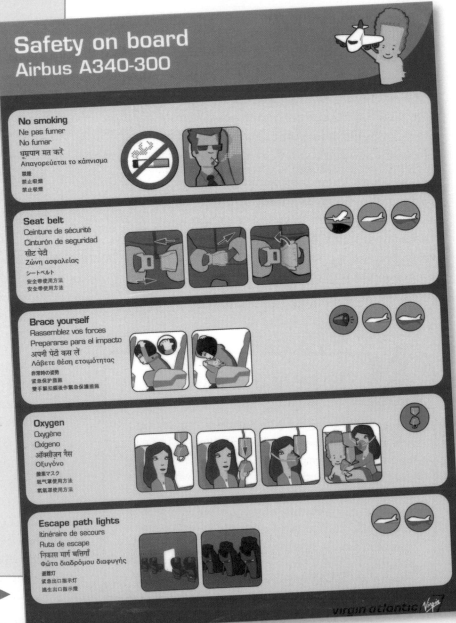

(Source: Virgin Airlines)

The crew must also inform passengers about smoking restrictions. Smoking is banned on aircraft and smoke detectors are fitted in the toilets in case anyone tries to smoke. Cabin crew have to tell passengers to keep emergency exits clear of baggage and to be careful when taking baggage out of overhead lockers. Passengers must switch off mobiles throughout flights and refrain from using other electronic equipment during take-off and landing. This is a lot of information for cabin crew to give and they also have to monitor passengers to make sure they comply with instructions.

In addition the crew must inform passengers about the food service, entertainment, if any, and about any other services on offer.

Health and safety

The cabin crew's most important role is to ensure the health and safety of passengers. If an incident occurs, for example a fire on board, the crew should know exactly what to do because of their training. Most people suffer no ill effects from air travel but there are health and safety issues of which air crew should be aware.

The Civil Aviation Authority has an Aviation Health Unit. Its responsibilities are to:

- provide informed advice about aviation health issues
- collate existing research on aviation health
- identify the need for future research
- manage and support future research activities.

Passenger complaints to the unit are concerned with:

- cabin air
- medical kits – or lack of them
- deep vein thrombosis (DVT)
- allergies
- cleanliness of aircraft.

Although these are passenger concerns they are not all proven issues, for example whether recycled air is more likely to transmit infection.

■ DVT

A serious concern is DVT or 'economy-class syndrome' as it is known. The condition is potentially life threatening and is thought to be caused by long hours of sitting in one cramped place.

Airlines are well aware of the DVT problem and offer advice on exercising in-flight to passengers. Air crew would be able to tell passengers about these exercises.

■ Jet lag

Another concern, although less serious, is jet lag.

Key term

Jet lag – the disruption of the body's circulation rhythms by travelling through time zones. The most common symptoms are extreme fatigue, irritability and sleep disruption. It can take a few days to recover from jet lag.

There are means of minimising jet lag. Passengers should get a good night's sleep before they travel and then try to adapt their body rhythm to the time zone of the country to which they are travelling. This is done by taking meals and sleeping at times appropriate to the new time zone.

■ Infectious diseases

The air on aircraft is recycled – the concern for passengers is the belief that airborne infections are easily transmitted between passengers. This could mean catching a cold, flu, measles, mumps or even tuberculosis. However, more research is required to see whether infections are transmitted on aircraft.

■ Hypoxia

This is the term used for oxygen deficiency. It occurs when there is a decrease in partial pressure of inspired oxygen. This happens in an aircraft when it flies at high altitudes such as 10,000 feet and above. The effects are usually mild but include reduced powers of judgement and self-criticism. People who drink a lot are more likely to suffer the effects of hypoxia and this in turn can lead to air rage.

Medical assistance

Cabin crew are trained in basic first aid but are unlikely to be able to deal with extreme medical emergencies. Some aircraft are fitted with defibrillators in case of heart attacks on board but if there is the likelihood of a fatality, usually pilots divert aircraft to the nearest airport. Emergency medical kits are usually carried on aircraft but the contents vary. There is only a requirement to have them if there are more than 250 passengers on board or the aircraft cannot reach an airport within 60 minutes.

Passenger welfare

It is the job of flight personnel to take care of passengers and attend to their needs. This ranges from reassurance if there is turbulence, for example, to providing drinks and ensuring comfort.

Managing passenger behaviour

Key term

Air rage – this can be described as disruptive behaviour by passengers on an airline. This could cover many situations but generally air rage is behaviour which jeopardises the safety of the aircraft or the passengers.

Air rage is due to a number of factors including:

- alcohol
- anxiety
- large numbers of people in a small space
- boredom
- no-smoking environment
- flight delays.

Unfortunately, incidences of air rage seem to be on the rise and cabin crew have to be trained to deal with them. This involves recognising the signs and knowing what to do. Most incidents occur in economy class and involve males in their twenties and thirties who have been drinking.

Crews are taught to pacify angry passengers where possible and keep them under control by talking. It is vital to try and defuse an angry situation. Physical restraint is the last resort but aircraft do carry handcuffs

and sometimes straitjackets. It must be stressed that the use of these devices is very rare.

Passengers are warned not to drink too much on board as the effects are aggravated at higher altitudes so drunkenness and dehydration occur more quickly. You will remember that such drunkenness is covered by the Air Navigation Order of 1995. Many successful prosecutions have been made. Ironically, airlines continue to serve alcohol throughout flights, and it is often free.

Sale of goods

Cabin crew are responsible for selling goods on board and earn commission on sales so are motivated to make sales. This is a good source of revenue for airlines and will be offered even on very short flights.

Food and beverage service

Again this is part of the job and is perhaps the least exciting part! Many passengers have to be served in a short time and some may be difficult to manage as they are eating in a cramped space and have to ask for anything they require as they cannot easily get out of their seats.

Assessment practice

Describe the role of staff and facilities offered by Excel Airways and Virgin Atlantic during a flight. Use the information above to help you. You will find more information on the airlines' websites. **P4**

Explain the importance of providing facilities to meet specific passenger needs both onboard and during the boarding process to Excel Airways. **M2**

Passport and visa requirements

General immigration procedures

Before retrieving their baggage, passengers go through immigration in order to formally enter the UK.

This is fairly rapid if you are a European travelling within Europe or a British citizen returning to the UK.

There are separate channels for EU residents and for others and non-EU passengers are subject to more stringent checks. Immigration officers are employed by the government and they check passports and visas to make sure that only those who have a right to enter the country do so.

Procedures for asylum seekers

Immigration officers shouls be aware of the rights of refugees under the 1951 Geneva Convention relating to the Status of Refugees, its 1967 Protocol and the European Convention on Human Rights. Asylum seekers arrive without papers and ask for asylum. They are questioned by immigration officers and then detained in detention centres until it is decided whether their case is valid and whether they should be allowed to stay in the UK.

Validity requirements for EU passport holders

Holders of EU passports are able to travel freely throughout Europe. Holders of other passports may require a visa to enter. The British Embassy is able to give information on who requires what.

Theory into practice

Find out what visa and passport requirements are needed for:

- a student from Australia who wants to work in the UK for a few months
- a student from the USA who wants to work in the UK for a few months
- a family visiting the UK from Japan
- a couple visiting the UK from Prague.

Customs

The following extract is taken from an HM Customs and Excise leaflet entitled *A Customs Guide for Travellers Entering the UK*.

For travellers arriving from outside the EU (including the Canary Islands, the Channel Islands and Gibraltar):

- *200 cigarettes or 50 cigars or 250gm of tobacco*
- *two litres of still table wine*
- *one litre of spirits or strong liqueurs over 22% volume; or two litres of fortified wine, sparkling wine or other liqueurs*
- *60cc/ml of perfume*
- *250cc/ml of toilet water*
- *£145 worth of other goods including gifts and souvenirs.*

In the UK there are three customs channels. These are:
- Red – for those with goods to declare
- Blue – for those entering from another EU country with nothing to declare
- Green – those entering from a non-EU country with nothing to declare.

Case study: customs checks

Using the information on the previous page, determine which channel each of the following passengers should use.

- Mr Rogers arrives in the UK from Rome, he has purchased 600 cigars and four litres of Italian wine.
- The Owens arrive in Manchester from Orlando, Florida. They have 400 cigarettes, two litres of gin and £667 of gifts between them.
- Mrs Edwards arrives from Cyprus into London. She has bought 50 cigars, one litre of wine and 50ml of perfume.

Mrs Nowaja arrives from Nairobi into Heathrow. She has an ornamental elephant with tusks. The customs officer confiscates it. Why?

Luggage reclaim

The belts for reclaiming baggage can take up a lot of space in a large airport. Also there is a large area devoted to moving baggage on a conveyor system underneath many large airports. The passenger doesn't see this, although they may sometimes wonder where their bag goes before it reaches the aircraft.

The baggage reclaim hall is situated after immigration in an airport. There are screens informing passengers which belt will deliver their luggage. There is little else in the hall apart from toilets and lost baggage desks, but most passengers will pass through quite quickly unless their baggage has been mislaid.

Passenger assistance

Assistance is usually only required if luggage has gone missing. In this case the passenger reports the problem and hopes it turns up later. Compensation is payable if baggage is lost.

Outsize luggage pick-up

Outsize luggage is delivered in a separate area and passengers must be alerted to this. Those passengers who struggle to carry their baggage may request assistance. However, there are few porters available in airports nowadays as most people use trolleys.

▼ **Figure 24.12 Passengers waiting for baggage reclaim**

Arrival facilities

Passengers arriving will easily find the following facilities at major airports:

- car hire
- currency exchange
- public transport.

A meeting place is always provided at arrivals so that relatives and friends can easily find people. Taxi drivers make signs with the names of the people they are waiting for. Flight arrivals information is given on screens throughout the airport so it is easy to see if a flight has landed. Airport websites in the UK give live arrivals information, so if you are going to meet someone you can check if their flight is delayed before you leave home.

Unaccompanied minors are handed over to the designated person meeting them by a member of the airline.

Short-stay parking is provided for people picking up arrivals. At Stansted a 15-minute free pick-up zone is available.

Transit passengers

Passengers who are transferring to another flight at an airport will wait in a transit lounge until their new flight is ready to board. Often baggage is checked right through and is supposed to arrive with the passenger at the end destination. Unfortunately, this is where much baggage gets lost when the transit process does not run smoothly. It is probably safer to collect baggage from the first flight and recheck it for the next leg.

Connections

If a passenger has booked a through ticket with an airline they will be advised of the best time flights to take in order to make a connection. However, if the first flight is delayed and they miss the connection the airline will put them on the next available flight. If the passenger has made their bookings with a low-cost airline, no through fares are available, each leg of the journey is sold as a separate fare and the airline bears no responsibility if a connection is missed.

Lost and damaged luggage procedures

Case study: missing luggage

Ann Lertora was taking a holiday. She travelled with Fledgling from New York to Tobago via Trinidad, the sister island of Tobago. When she checked in at JFK (Kennedy airport) her bag was labelled to Tobago, she was handed the receipts and she was told her bag would go right through to be collected on disembarkation in Tobago.

On arrival in Tobago there was no bag and handlers told her she should have collected it in Trinidad and rechecked it for Tobago. Ann reported her lost bag and completed a form. A clerk telephoned Trinidad baggage department but there was no reply. As the clerk was evidently busy, Ann suggested that she try and phone herself from their office. The staff were very friendly and welcomed her into the office but there was no information about her luggage. She asked the clerk if it was worth sending a fax but no one had time to do this. After three hours Ann gave up trying to contact Trinidad baggage handling or Fledgling and went to her hotel. For the next three days Ann, or a staff member from the hotel, tried to get in touch with Trinidad and failed. At Tobago airport each day they told Ann her bag 'might arrive today'.

The bag finally arrived two days before the end of the holiday. Ann took a taxi to the airport to collect it. She was told she was entitled to compensation but after an hour of waiting for staff to deal with her she once again gave up and returned to the hotel.

1 **Find out Ann's entitlement to compensation under the Montreal Convention.**

2 **Suggest improvements to customer service at Fledgling and the baggage-handling departments.**

3 **Ensure you know the location of New York, Trinidad and Tobago.**

Assessment practice

Your friend Mary Newbold is coming to the UK from Ireland for a short holiday. She will arrive at Manchester airport. Write her a letter explaining the disembarkation process at Manchester airport. Explain to her why the particular procedures they have are important. **P5** **M3**

Analyse the effectiveness of procedures at Manchester airport and recommend to Mary whether she should arrive there or at another airport. **D1** **D2**

Knowledge check

1 Why is it desirable for passengers to arrive at the airport by public transport?

2 What types of parking are usually available at airports?

3 Who is most likely to get a free limousine service to the airport?

4 What is a service level agreement?

5 What are the differences in security measures between landside and airside at an airport?

6 What are the benefits to the airport owner of shops at the airport?

7 What are the services offered by a ground handling agent?

8 Describe the procedure at the check-in desk.

9 What does a despatcher do?

10 How do low-cost airlines make money apart from the sale of airline seats?

11 Who does the Aviation Health Unit report to?

12 Explain what measures can be taken to prevent DVT.

13 How might you avoid jet lag?

14 Which Act covers drunkenness on board an aircraft?

Preparation for assessment

Lamborough City Council is considering investing in the development of Lamborough airport. The site and the small airport on it are owned by the City Council but the area is currently only used by light aircraft and one tour operator who use the airport for charter departures to holiday destinations. There would be extensive costs involved in development but the airport could be a source of considerable income to the Council if the development were successful. Before deciding on the extent of investment the Council wishes to take expert advice. You have been called in on secondment from your work in airport management to carry out research and produce a report which will help the City Council determine what development and facilities are needed at the airport.

Part 1

1 The Council wants to know what kinds of options are required by customers when travelling to and from the airport. Describe the options available to customers at major aiports and make recommendations to the Council on what to offer. **P1**

Part 2

2 You must advise the Council on the procedures to be adopted for embarkation and the type of personnel who will be needed. You need to visit or research two airports and find out about the procedures and facilities offered during embarkation. Include information on:
- the process for embarkation for all passengers
- the facilities provided during embarkation
- the roles and responsibilities of aiport and airline staff during embarkation
- the boarding process. **P2 P3**

3 Compare the facilites available at the two airports and the options for passengers travelling to and from the aiports and during the embarkation process. **M1**

Grading tip

If you are aiming for Merit level, write your descriptions and your comparison together. Explain what the similarities are between the two airports and what the differences are. Explain why differences occur. They may be because different types of customer are catered for or because different types of flight are operated.

Part 3

4 The City Council has received several requests from airlines who wish to operate from the airport. The Council is concerned that it only allows reputable airlines with a high level of service to use the airport. To give the Council an idea of service levels, you should research an example of each of the following categories of airline:
- traditional scheduled
- charter
- low cost

and describe the role of staff and the facilities available for customers during a flight. **P4**

5 You have been asked to give a presentation to Council members to explain why effective procedures are important at airports. Prepare notes for a presentation on:

- the importance of providing facilities to meet specific passenger needs both during the boarding process and onboard **M2**
- a description of disembarkation and transit processes at UK airports and why it will be important to have effective disembarkation processes at Lamborough airport **P5** **M3**

- the effectiveness of processes for handling passengers during embarkation and disembarkation at one of your researched airports, making justified recommendations for improvement that could be implemented by the Council. **D1** **D2**

Grading criteria

To achieve a pass grade the evidence must show that the learner is able to:	To achieve a merit grade the evidence must show that, in addition to the pass criteria, the learner is able to:	To achieve a distinction grade the evidence must show that, in addition to the pass and merit criteria, the learner is able to:
P1 describe the options available to customers when travelling to and from airports and between terminals **Assessment practice page 199**	**M1** compare the facilities available at two different airports for passengers travelling to and from the airports and during the embarkation process **Assessment practice page 213**	**D1** evaluate the effectiveness of processes for handling passengers during embarkation at a specific airport, making justified recommendations for improvement **Assessment practice page 226**
P2 describe the process for embarkation for all passengers and the role that airport and airline staff have during embarkation of customers **Assessment practice page 213**	**M2** explain the importance of providing facilities to meet specific passenger needs both onboard and during the boarding process **Assessment practice page 222**	**D2** analyse the effectiveness of disembarkation processes at a UK airport **Assessment practice page 226**
P3 describe the boarding process **Assessment practice page 213**	**M3** explain the importance of effective disembarkation processes at UK airports **Assessment practice page 226**	
P4 describe the role of staff and the facilities available for customers during a flight **Assessment practice page 222**		
P5 describe the disembarkation and transit processes at UK airports **Assessment practice page 226**		

Current issues in travel and tourism

Introduction

The travel and tourism industry is always affected by current events and issues that arise either within the industry or in the external environment. Travel and tourism companies continually have to react to changes and issues and it is vital that managers have a high level of awareness of issues impacting on the industry. In this unit you will have the opportunity to develop knowledge and understanding of an issue that is currently affecting travel and tourism. In so doing you will develop your research skills and gain an understanding of research methods. You should be able to make links with other units that you have covered on your programme. You will be introduced to useful information sources to help you with your research and you will be taken step by step through the planning and research process. This unit differs from other units in that it is assessed at Level 4 rather than Level 3.

After completing this unit you should be able to achieve the following outcomes:

1   Understand methods that can be used to research a current issue affecting the travel and tourism industry

2   Be able to conduct research into a current issue affecting the travel and tourism industry, using appropriate resources

3   Be able to communicate findings on a travel and tourism issue using appropriate media and conventions

4   Understand the impacts of a current issue on the travel and tourism industry.

Talking points

This unit is challenging as it encourages you to work at a higher level and to work independently on a research project. It gives you a chance to develop important research skills that will be invaluable to you in your working life. For those who choose to go on to university, you will find that you have a head start in knowing how and where to find information and how to use it. Learning how to do research properly is very important to you as not only does it help you find the information you need complete your project, but it gives you skills that you can apply in whatever career you choose in the future.

In this section we will discuss research methods, look at key terminology used in the field of research and consider appropriate methods for your own research. We will also begin to consider the types of issues in travel and tourism that would be suitable for you to research yourself.

Research methods

Key terms

Intervention – research that includes intervention will influence a respondent's behaviour or thoughts in response to the research. These methods are generally to be avoided as they affect the objectivity of the research. You may use intervention in terms of prompts when you need to help respondents remember key points in a discussion.

Non-intervention – these are research methods which are entirely objective observation, for example where there is no intention or possibility of influencing results. You should aim to use a non-interventionist approach.

Action research – this is an interventionist approach to research. It is based on investigating your own practice, usually with a small team of colleagues. It considers an area of working practice and seeks collaborative solutions to improve it. You might be able to use this approach if you have a work placement and a suitable issue to investigate in the workplace. It is unlikely that you will choose to use it for your research for this unit.

Research sources and data

Research sources can be primary or secondary and the data collected from those sources can be qualitative or quantitative.

Key terms

Primary research – research carried out for the first time by you. It includes any surveys or interviews you do.

Secondary research – research which someone else has done and which you are using to help you with your project.

Qualitative data – data about opinions and reasons for doing things. These are harder to interpret than quantitative data but can be very rich and informative.

Quantitative data – data that consist of facts and figures. These are easy to measure but do not always tell us why things happen.

We will look more closely at different research methods so that you will know how to use them and be able to choose appropriate ones when you are ready to start your own project.

Researching from secondary sources

You must:

- be clear about what you are to find out
- know where to search for information
- be able to assess the validity of the source
- be able to cross-reference information.

Be clear about what you want to find out

It is worth spending some time on this preparation stage: identifying the objective of the research. Research is time consuming and it is easy to get sidetracked, so make sure you know what you are looking for. If you have completed your research plan properly, you will know what you are looking for. You will also have had an opportunity to discuss your plan with your tutor. Ask questions and clarify anything you are unsure about.

Make a list of the different things you need to find out. Write down key words to help your search.

Know where to search for information

Decide which information sources to use. When searching on the internet, remember to choose a search engine such as Google. You can search for images, news stories, search their directory or search the web. The directory differs from the web in that it is human edited and sorted into categories. Be as specific as you can with your key words, in order to narrow your search. If you want to search for an exact phrase put it in inverted commas. You might notice some of your results are termed 'sponsored results'. This means those companies have paid to be listed and may come up first. Remember that search engines provide help if you get stuck. Look for the help link on the main page.

When you are collecting information, organise it as you collect it. If you are making notes from the internet or a book, group all the notes relating to a particular topic together. If you are photocopying or printing, highlight the relevant points immediately, and organise topics together.

A list of secondary sources of information for travel and tourism is given on pages 246–7.

Assessing the validity of a source

You need to make sure that your source of information is accurate, up to date and unbiased. It is important to do this with every source but it is more difficult to assess internet websites, as anyone can set up a website and they may not always represent objective information.

Use the following criteria for deciding whether your source is valid.

■ Who wrote it?

Are they qualified to write it? For example, you can be pretty sure that a textbook is written by a highly qualified person! A letter in a newspaper complaining about a package holiday may not be valid – it only represents one person's experience. Newspaper articles tend to be more trustworthy but again can reflect the paper's politics and opinions, so be careful.

■ What is the purpose of the information source?

If you are researching from holiday brochures or sales literature, remember the purpose is to sell, so they are biased in favour of certain products. They certainly will not tell you if there was an outbreak of food poisoning last season. A publication like *World Travel Guide* is considered more reliable than brochures as it is based on factual information as an aid to the travel trade and is not trying to sell.

■ Is the information up to date?

When was the information written? If it is a web page how often is it updated? If it is not up to date don't use it. Of course, if you are researching a topic that does not change, such as the development of tourism in the UK, then an older textbook will still be useful.

■ Does the author give sources of facts and figures?

You need to check this as you too need to quote sources. You may be able to go back to the quoted source and check for accuracy.

■ Does the author seem to be biased in their presentation of information?

You will recognise bias when you have experience of using different sources. Initially it is difficult to recognise but you can practise by reading several different newspaper accounts of the same event.

Case study: Ryanair passenger growth

Assess the validity of the following three pieces of information. Comment on the type of current research issue they would be useful for. Make notes on your findings and discuss them with your colleagues.

1 Fledgling publishes its monthly passenger traffic figures, including load factors, within the first five working days of the month.

	Passengers			Load factors		
	2006	2007	Rolling 12 months	2006	2007	Rolling 12 months
Jan	1,464,762	2,198,657	36,445,987	72%	70%	80%
Feb	1,538,425	2,233,091	36,998,023	76%	75%	80%
Mar	2,040,881	2,843,687	38,001,554	81%	70%	81%

Table 26.1 Passenger traffic 2006/2007

2 Figures from the International Passenger Survey show that during the first ten months of 2006 the number of inbound visitors to the UK stood at 26.9 million, 6 per cent up on the equivalent period of 2005, with spending 8 per cent up on the previous year. Over much of 2006 spend has, for the first time in quite some while, been growing slightly ahead of visits. VisitBritain expects that in 2007 both the volume and value of inbound tourism will increase by 3.7 per cent compared with 2006. If achieved this would mean that 32.5 million overseas residents will visit the UK next year, spending around £15.8 billion.

(Source: http://www.visitbritain.com/corporate/presscentre/presscentrebritain/pressreleasesoverseasmrkt/sep-dec2006/2007.aspx)

3 The following is an extract from a holiday brochure.

is this the parc for you?

Le Bois Dormant is the yin to Le Bois Masson's yang! For all the energy and fast-paced action of its sister parc, Le Bois Dormant provides equal levels of calm and relaxation.

And what makes this parc so great is that you get the best of both worlds – you can even use the brilliant facilities on Le Bois Masson!

your holiday at le bois dormant

You'll be able to tell from your first glimpse that Le Bois Dormant is completely different. A long winding path leads you to a beautiful central swimming pool area, with a terrace overlooking the water. The pool complex is split so sun seekers and fun seekers are equally happy.

Le Bois Dormant feels spacious and sophisticated, but still has a relaxed atmosphere. You get the feeling that nothing is too much trouble here. The parc feels like a home from home and is the perfect escape from the hectic pace of everyday life.

If you want to feel the wind in your hair, Le Bois Dormant is a superb start to many a stunning bike ride, and the Vendée is a flat region so all the family can relax in the saddle!

▲ **Figure 26.1 Life at a slower pace**

(Source: Siblu brochure 2007; © Siblu)

Be able to cross-reference information

Cross-referencing is a means of checking that the information is correct. It is more important if you are not absolutely certain that your original source is accurate. For example, you may have found some figures quoted on a tour operator's website and you may not be certain that they are up to date or accurate, so you look for a second source of the same information to check the figures. The second source could be official statistics or other tour operators' findings.

Case study: checking information

▲ Figure 26.2 Construction of P&O cruise ship *Ventura*

Ventura attracts record bookings

P&O Cruises' new ship *Ventura* attracted £27 million-worth of bookings in the first day of going on sale.

The line made 18,800 bookings in the first day of 2008 cruises on the ship going on sale – a record for a single day across the 13 brands in parent company Carnival Corporation.

A third of the 115,000-tonne ship's capacity for next year was sold in less than a week, with 35% of bookings new to P&O Cruises, revealed head of brand marketing Philip Price.

The launch-day bookings were more than triple the previous record of 5000 taken for the launch of *Oceana* in 2005.

The average age profile of those booking the new ship, which enters service next April, is 49 against the line's normal average age of 54.

(Source: http://www.travelmole.com/stories/1117388.php)

Think of three different ways you could check the information given in this extract.

Consider this

Keep details of your sources as you do your research.

Researching from primary sources

A research project should not rely entirely on secondary sources. You should carry out some original research of your own. You need to decide what type of primary research you want to do at the planning stage and incorporate it into your plan.

The most appropriate research methodologies for your project will be:

- interviews
- focus groups
- questionnaires.

Interviews

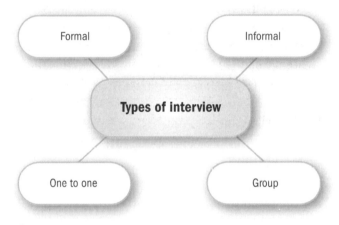

▲ Figure 26.3 Different types of interview

A formal interview is very structured, with a list of pre-prepared questions to be asked. It is similar to carrying out a questionnaire on a one-to-one basis or with a small group.

An informal interview allows more scope for the interviewee to develop the flow of the interview. You still need to prepare a list of topics that you want to cover in the interview but you can be flexible about what order they are covered in and if the interviewee suggests an issue that they consider particularly relevant you can include it in your discussion. Where this is done with a group it develops into a focus group.

In terms of your research project you are likely to find that an informal interview is more appropriate if you are speaking to an 'expert' such as a manager of a visitor attraction or a tour operator. The expert will bring points to the discussion that you may not have previously considered. This is most likely to be on a one-to-one basis.

On the other hand, if you are interviewing ordinary consumers you may want to use a formal approach if it is one to one, as the interviewees will depend on you to direct the interview. If you still prefer an informal structure consider carrying out a focus group.

Focus group

A focus group is very useful if you want to find out consumer attitudes or perceptions about a company or service. For example, you might hold a focus group to find out attitudes towards booking holidays with travel agents.

It is also a technique that you can practise and develop during the course of your project. This research method is used extensively in consumer marketing. How do you carry out a focus group?

- Decide what kind of people should be invited – for example, if your project is about attitudes to flying on low-cost airlines, you must invite people with experience of travelling on these airlines.
- Invite a group of people – between 6 and 12 – to a pre-arranged venue.
- Focus group participants are often paid. You are unlikely to pay them but you might offer refreshment as an incentive to attend.
- Prepare a list of discussion points but be prepared to be flexible – the discussion should flow from the interviewees. If it goes completely off track, you will have to pull it back. This is where experience helps.
- In a focus group an extrovert personality can easily dominate discussion. Try to bring in quieter members.
- Record the discussion – you cannot take notes and lead the session. You need a tape recorder or a scribe. Ask a friend or colleague to help you. You can reciprocate for them.

The following are some useful techniques that an interviewer can use in running a focus group.

- Playing devil's advocate – this means that the discussion leader deliberately takes an opposing point of view to a participant in order to stimulate a strong defence and further discussion.
- Sophisticated naiveté – the leader pretends not to understand a participant's point in order to get them to expand on it.
- Closed-book technique – participants in a focus group are aware they are taking part in research and may not choose to reveal too much of their real opinions. The closed-book technique is used to formally bring the focus group to an end. The leader thanks the participants and puts their papers away or turns off the tape recorder. The leader should be listening intently at this point as the participants will relax and may reveal some interesting attitudes to the leader or as asides to each other when they think they are no longer being recorded.

Consider this

Imagine you are researching into day trips taken by your colleagues. List some possible focus group topics arising from those research issues.

Questionnaires

Questionnaires are useful means of getting information from a large number of people. Remember you can use them in an informal interview if you choose. Refer to Unit 5 on Marketing, in *BTEC National Travel & Tourism Book 1* second edition, for guidelines on designing a questionnaire.

Theory into practice

Design a questionnaire that can be used to find out the frequency of using internet booking for flights among your friends and family. You need to find out:

- whether they book flights
- how they book flights
- how often they use the internet to book flights
- why they use the internet to book flights.

Pilot your questionnaire with your colleagues and then amend it in the light of their constructive criticism.

Taking it further

Carry out the questionnaire with at least 20 people and analyse the results. Prepare a short report on your findings. Include graphs and tables to illustrate your findings.

Travel and tourism industry

Now that you are more knowledgeable about research methods, you can begin to consider what kind of issues in travel and tourism you might want to research. Before you do that, Figure 26.4 provides a reminder of the sectors of travel and tourism.

Remember that your research issue must relate to the travel and tourism industry in general or to one of its sectors.

Types of current issue

We will look at some current examples of issues affecting the travel and tourism industry. Issues could relate to:

- changes in demand for products and services
- current affairs
- the environment
- health.

You may find one of these of particular interest to you and then decide to study it in greater depth. You can, of course, choose a completely different issue as long as it relates to travel and tourism.

It is important to spend some time considering possible issues for research as you must determine whether sufficient information is available in order to do your research properly.

The following example relates to changes in demand for products and services.

Are package holiday sales in decline?

This topic might have been brought to your attention by a news item or feature in one of your news sources. The extract overleaf comes from Holidaylettings.co.uk.

▲ Figure 26.4 The components of the travel and tourism industry

Package holidays declining at the expense of independent travel

Further evidence of the decline of the package holiday has come with the news that two of Britain's largest tour operators are to merge.

A rise in people booking their own holiday lets and flights has forced Thomson to take over First Choice.

At the same time German-owned Thomas Cook is in the process of merging with MyTravel.

A recent study by research firm Mintel estimates the package holiday market will shrink by one per cent over the next five years.

However, the market for independent holidays is forecast to grow a huge 45 per cent.

Expenditure on independent holidays is forecast to rise by a massive 78 per cent, to reach a value of just over £21 billion by 2009.

The Daily Mail reports that more than 20 million package holidays were being sold every year in the 1990s but this year it is likely to be less than 16 million.

A spokesman for the British Market Research Bureau told the paper: 'Online holiday booking has seen a dramatic increase and the ease of booking one's holiday online makes it a cheaper and quicker alternative than visiting a travel agent.

'With Britain embracing low cost airlines, it is now possible for people to visit alternative holiday destinations such as eastern Europe.'

(Source: http://www.holidaylettings.co.uk)

▲ **Figure 26.5 A package holiday destination**

Consider this

At this stage you have not chosen your topic – you are considering different topics as potential research issues. You still need to find out if more information about the chosen issue is accessible.

At first view this looks like a suitable topic for further research. Why? It gives a good overview of the topic including:

- information on a merger
- reasons for the decline
- statistics to interpret and analyse
- clues about where to look for further information.

What next? How will you find out what further information is available on this issue?

1 Look at other sources and see if any of them are reporting on this trend. Print out or save relevant articles for analysis. Remember to start your bibliography by noting all sources in detail.

2 Read the text and see what clues there are for further research possibilities. List them with notes. Figure 26.6 shows what your list might look like.

- Mintel – can I access their research data?
- Can I get other stats on how many package holidays are sold?
- Can I get stats on the rise of low-cost airlines?
- How many people use the internet to book holidays?
- What about the increase in tailor-made holidays?
- Lots of organisations are mentioned, e.g. British Market Research Bureau

▲ **Figure 26.6 Further research possibilities**

3 Armed with your list you are ready to appraise what information is available. Be prepared for this to take an hour or two even at this stage. You will find other information later. At the moment you just want to know if there is sufficient information available for you to do a good research job on the issue.

Consider this

Restrict your research to the internet and readily available sources at this stage. You do not have time to write to companies or do interviews with people before you select your research issue. If you don't know how to do internet research, turn to page 233.

Assuming you did this initial research, Figure 26.7 shows what you might find.

From this initial research we can see that the decline of package holidays is a suitable issue to research further. Each tranche of research leads to further possibilities and relevant statistics are available.

Consider this

Track your research – it is very easy to find a useful source and then lose it! Use the 'Favourites' listing on your PC or a hard copy notebook!

Theory into practice

In order to understand current affairs, you need to find out what is happening in the world and how it affects travel and tourism. For this activity you will need all of one day's newspapers. Sunday newspapers are ideal as they report on a whole week.

Work in small groups and go through one of the newspapers to find examples of natural incidents/ political change/interest rates rising, etc. Mark up each article with a few notes on how you think it impacts on travel and tourism.

When you are ready, present your articles and discuss them with your group. You may have found an issue that you would like to explore further.

- Can't access Mintel's data on the internet – may be able to access it through a library.
- Lots of other news articles are available on the increase in independent booking, e.g. on Travelmole.
- A quick Google search shows that there are several sites with information about numbers of package holidays sold. Bookmark these for revisiting later.
- Official statistics are available online at www.statistics.gov.uk.
- Last week, internet monitoring firm Hitwise reported that visits to UK travel sites were up 14 per cent in the first week of this month, compared with the same period last year. Travel websites, which are regularly among the most popular sites in the UK, accounted for one in every 20 visits to the web in the UK. This can be followed further.
- Found a BBC news item with figures on low-cost flights – will follow that too.

▲ **Figure 26.7 Research findings**

The case study below relates to current affairs and environmental concerns.

Case study: choice adds £1.50 levy

First Choice shops have turned green for a month, decking out windows with new displays and point of sale material, as the company launches a campaign to raise money for environmental charities.

The month-long campaign ushers in a permanent £1.50 charge to be added automatically for every adult booking, unless the customer opts out, and 75p for each child.

The money will go to the new First Choice World Care Fund, which donates it to Climate Care and the Travel Foundation.

In addition, First Choice will donate £1 per person to Climate Care for all bookings from winter 2007 onwards.

To draw attention to the fund, shops will have plants and foliage in the windows, while point of sale material, posters and plasma screens will highlight all the company's green efforts. First Choice Radio, which is broadcast across the retail network, will also feature information.

Rad Sofronijevic, operations director, said: 'All this will make customers feel better about going to their destination and they can find out where their money goes.'

For the past two and a half years, First Choice has added a 40p voluntary charge on every booking, raising £950,000 for the Travel Foundation. Retail trading director Cheryl Powell added that despite the hike to £1.50, the proportion of customers donating had remained constant.

'We are asking for a lot more, but it shows that staff are happy to talk about it,' she said.

Staff have received training on the initiative, and Sofronijevic said agents had given positive feedback. 'After our sponsorship of Red Nose Day they feel they work for a company that is making a difference to the environment and destinations,' she explained.

To focus staff efforts, a green mascot called Treesa Green will be unveiled at the managers and assistant managers' conferences from April 19. To encourage staff to get involved, First Choice has added a top green shop award to its annual company awards.

Nearly all First Choice shops have signed up to *TTG's* Scream If You're Green campaign.

(Source: *Travel Trade Gazette* 30 March 2007)

Imagine your research project is about the impact on travel and tourism of environmental pressure groups.

1 **Suggest a hypothesis for this project – you may want to consider the issue in relation to just one sector of travel and tourism to narrow your research.**

2 **List the further types of information that might be useful.**

3 **Suggest at least five sources for this information (use the list on page 246 to help you).**

4 **Carry out some initial research and decide whether this is a viable issue.**

The next example relates to another current affairs issue, that of liberalisation of the skies.

Assessment practice: open-skies deal may cut fares to USA

Business-class fares from Heathrow to the US could be slashed this winter following a long-awaited breakthrough in discussions to open up the transatlantic market.

Plans to allow any European or US airline to fly from the UK to the States could become reality by the autumn, potentially meaning many new services from Heathrow.

At present, only British Airways, Virgin Atlantic, American Airlines and United Airlines are allowed to serve the US from Heathrow, although Air India and Kuwait Airways also have limited access to New York. The new deal would allow any European or US airline to fly from Heathrow to the US.

This could mean airlines such as Lufthansa operating long-haul from Heathrow, although it is more likely that US carriers currently confined to Gatwick, such as Delta, would switch to the main London hub.

BMI would immediately offer the US from Heathrow if permitted.

But chief executive Nigel Turner added: 'We have been here before. Let's win the argument first, then we'll announce what we're doing.'

The new entrants would dent the most profitable parts of BA and Virgin Atlantic's businesses.

But the deal is unlikely to bring economy fares crashing down, as these are already very competitive, with many seats being sold at a loss.

BA condemned the deal as being 'designed to bolster US interests'.

The EU estimated that the number of transatlantic flights would rise from just under 50 million to 76 million in five years because of lower fares. It claimed passengers would save between £4.35 billion and £8 billion over the period.

EC transport ministers will vote on March 22 on whether to approve the measures, ahead of a summit in Washington on April 30.

The changes could be in place by October 28 as Germany chairs the European Council and is very keen for a deal. However, sticking points include US unwillingness to allow European airlines to invest more in US carriers and a refusal to allow European airlines access to the US domestic market.

(Source: *Travel Trade Gazette* 9 March 2007)

You may need to do some background reading to fully understand this issue. Look through newspaper archives on the internet to find out more.

Explain different methods that can be used to research this issue. **P1**

Grading tip

Ensure you include primary and secondary methods and consider both qualitative and quantitative data from several sources. Give your reasons why the chosen methods would be effective, highlighting the advantages and any disadvantages of each.

In this part of the unit you will learn how to produce a research plan.

Research plan

Once you have done your initial investigation and selected a current issue for research you are ready to write your research plan. This is completed before you start your project and provides a useful summary of what you are going to do. Your tutor will expect to see this to ensure that your chosen issue is suitable for research and that you are sufficiently prepared to begin your project.

Key term

Research plan – an overview of and rationale for the research project.

The research plan should contain the following elements:

- Title
- Setting of hypothesis
- Terms of reference
- Aims and objectives of the project
- Research methodology
- Sources of information
- Dates – for tasks, monitoring and review
- Contingencies
- Ethical issues
- Evaluation.

We will look at the research plan in more detail and consider an example.

Title – this sums up what your study is about.

Hypothesis – the statement that you are going to test or investigate.

Terms of reference – this gives some background to the project, explains the context, that is, a description of

events that led to this issue arising in travel and tourism and why the issue is important.

Aims and objectives – this section covers what you hope to achieve and the limitations of the project. Limitations ensure that you do not make your project so broad that your research does not address a specific issue.

Planned outcomes – this section explains what you expect the results of your research to be.

Research methodology – this section explains how you are going to conduct your research and the methods to be used to collect your data. The different methods that you might use for your research will be covered later in the unit. You might wish to refer to that section briefly now to help you write your research proposal.

Sources of information – when you did your initial research to test the suitability of your current issue, you bookmarked useful websites and you noted relevant sources of information that you wanted to revisit. List these now and include any others which have since occurred to you.

Contingencies – back-up plans: perhaps an alternative source of information if one fails or a different research method.

Task dates – these should be detailed in your plan so that you are not tempted to leave all your research until the last minute.

Review dates and monitor – the review dates will indicate both formal and informal reviews. You should review your progress yourself and adjust your plan accordingly. In addition, you should arrange tutorials to monitor your progress. This is important as it is easy to go off track and waste time researching irrelevant points.

Ethical issues – this relates to confidentiality, types of questions to be asked, how and when the research will be carried out. You must make sure that you adhere to the Data Protection Act 1998 when storing personal information.

Evaluation – Did your methods work? How will you know whether your research project has been successful?

What will you measure it against? Did you achieve your objectives? Did you use appropriate sources of information? What would you do differently next time?

Example of a research plan

Title: A study of the package holiday market and factors contributing to its decline

Hypothesis: Package holidays sales are in decline

Terms of reference: Several news reports in travel and tourism trade publications have indicated that sales of traditional package holidays are in decline. If this is so, the impact on the industry is of great importance as it would affect the core business of tour operators and travel agents. This research project will test whether the assertion is true by looking at available data and will assess the reasons for decline, if they can be found. It will also consider if and how tour operators are reacting to the issue of decline in package holidays.

Aim: To investigate the possible decline of traditional package holiday sales

Objectives

- To determine whether sales of traditional package holidays are in decline
- To determine if specific package holiday destinations are in decline
- To assess reasons for any decline
- To investigate the reactions of tour operators to any decline

The research will be limited to sales of outbound holidays from the UK. Domestic tourism is excluded from the research project.

Planned outcomes: Sales of package holidays are in decline because increased use of the internet means that travellers can easily book their own flights and accommodation. Research as described will prove or disprove this.

Research methodology: Secondary research will be carried out using the sources of information listed in this proposal. The research will include analysis of available statistics.

Primary research methods will include:

- A focus group with people who are intending to book holidays this year – discussion will centre on whether they will be booking a package holiday or other type of holiday.
- An interview with a tour operator to find out if its data suggest package holidays are in decline and to ask what its strategies are for addressing this. This will be an informal interview with unstructured questions.

The data will be analysed and a report produced on the findings. Interview records and notes and tapes from the focus group will be available with the report.

Sources of information

- Mintel – data given in *Travel Trade Gazette* article
- Statistics on package holidays taken from the Office for National Statistics
- Travelmole.com – archive search
- www.technology.guardian.co.uk
- Low-cost airline websites for information on increases in passenger numbers
- www.hitwise.com for information on booking of holidays
- Local tour operator to be approached for interview (name and address)

Contingencies

- Look for other sources of statistics in case Mintel is not available
- Find an alternative tour operator for interview
- Look at other news websites such as e-tid if Travelmole does not have sufficient information
- Allow plenty of time for research

Ethical issues

- Ensure that the tour operator is reassured about use of its name (i.e. the name will not be used)
- Agree ground rules with focus group participants

Evaluation

- Arrange tutorials at regular intervals to review progress
- Ask a colleague to read the work
- Evaluate regularly against objectives

Evaluation of the project

You should consider different ways of evaluating your work and reflecting on what you have achieved and how you achieved it so that you learn from the experience for future research projects.

Below are some aspects of the project that you can include in an evaluation.

- Did my plan help me? How?
- Did I stick to my planned deadlines?
- Did I choose suitable research methodologies? Why were they suitable or not?
- Did my sources of information produce sufficient, relevant information?
- What other sources could I have used?
- Were my findings presented in a logical way supported by relevant data?
- Was my referencing correct?
- Were my conclusions valid?
- Did I produce viable recommendations?
- To what extent did I work independently?
- What would I do differently next time?

Consider this

Once you have completed your research plan, you should have an opportunity to talk it through with your tutor on a one-to-one basis. Your tutor should give agreement to your research plan before you continue.

Adding timescales

Once you and your tutor have agreed your plan, you are ready to refine it and add timescales. Your plan will be a working document and undoubtedly will change. This is fine as long as you write changes on the plan and they do not mean that you end up trying to do all the research at the last minute. You will need to discuss why and how your plan changed in your evaluation at the end of the research project. You will be expected to say how

you dealt with problems that occurred in doing your research, so make sure you note them as you go along.

It is better to get your initial research plan agreed with your tutor before producing it in too much detail.

Your plan gives you a structure to work to, enabling you to make sure you have covered everything and that it is presented in a logical order.

When working out timescales allow time for writing up the project and for completing an evaluation. Include regular meetings where your tutor can check on your progress and discuss any problems that occur.

Timescales for research plan: Are package holiday sales in decline?

The following timescales have been assumed for this plan. The school/college is running a semester timetable so this unit is timetabled for half a year or 15 weeks. The first three weeks have been spent introducing the unit, deciding on a research issue, completing initial research and the research proposal for the chosen issue. Week 4 is spent on one-to-one tutorials to assess the research proposals and allow students to write their research plans. This leaves approximately ten weeks, allowing for contingencies and evaluation at the end.

Notes on the plan

- All the objectives must be covered in the plan.
- Each objective must link to the research methodology you are going to use to achieve that objective.
- The plan includes both primary and secondary research.
- Timescales are clear.
- There is scope to record changes to the plan.

Consider this

What kinds of changes are likely to be recorded in the last column of the plan? Why would these arise? Discuss this with your colleagues.

Week	Objectives	Research method	Sources of information	Changes to plan
1	Determine if sales are in decline (initial research suggests that this is the case)	Secondary research Analyse statistics and produce relevant graphs and notes	TTG and Travel Weekly searches of recent archives Mintel statistics as given in the TTG article. Search www.statistics online Research low-cost airline websites	
2	Determine which particular package holiday destinations are in decline	Secondary research Write up notes on findings – keep relevant articles/statistics for appendices	Trade mags archives as before	
3	Start to assess reasons for decline	Secondary research Categorise possible reasons and write up notes on supporting evidence	From trade sources including Travelmole and e-tid websites	
4	Assess reasons for decline	Add primary research plan focus group by inviting friends and family to participate – set a date for the focus group and arrange room and time. Borrow tape recorder to tape discussion	Focus group	
5	Assess reasons for decline	Carry out focus group Transcribe tape or make detailed notes from tape Analyse findings and write up	Focus group	
6	Assess reactions of tour operator	Telephone local operators to arrange interview Prepare questions (informal interview – primary research)	Tour operator	
7	Assess reasons for decline	Secondary research – find out about internet booking	Hitwise website	
8	Assess reactions of tour operator	Primary research – carry out interview and analyse findings	Tour operator	
9		Start writing up report Mop up research for any checks to be made		
10		Finish writing up report – check appendices and referencing, write bibliography		
11		Evaluate the report and the methodologies used		

Sources of information

There are hundreds of sources of information available to you. These include:

- Books
- Journals
- Newspapers
- Websites
- Television programmes
- Published research papers
- Official statistics
- Questionnaire results.

When you select an issue for a project you must be certain that sufficient data are available for you to research your topic in depth and reach an appropriate level of analysis. This means you have to do some initial research to check on sources and find out exactly what kinds of information are available.

To help you with this initial research and to get ideas on a range of topics you should use some or all of these resources. This particular list consists of resources which report on news and events related to travel and tourism.

■ Online news information

www.travelmole.com – a news and resource centre for the travel industry.

www.thisistravel.com – published by Associated New Media, the publishers of the *Mail* newspapers. It is aimed at consumers but is a useful source of news.

www.e-tid.com – e-tid.com is a business travel news digest covering all sectors of the travel industry, from aviation and tour operating to hotels and cruises.

www.travelwirenews.com – home of eTurboNews, whose aim is to present a fair and balanced coverage of the ongoing issues that concern the travel trade. This is an international newsletter and has subscribers in 230 countries.

You can subscribe to all of these news websites at no cost. Subscription means that you will be e-mailed regularly with travel and tourism news items. You will also be able to access the archives of information and past features on the websites.

■ Trade magazines

These are an excellent source of news. The magazines can be subscribed to in hard copy or you can access them online. Your library may have some of them. If you access them online you will have to register but registration is free.

Travel Trade Gazette (ttglive.com)

Travel Weekly (travelweekly.com)

Caterer & Hotelkeeper (catereronline.com)

Leisure Opportunities (leisureopportunities.co.uk)

Attractions Management (attractionsmanagement.com)

Leisure Management (leisuremanagement.co.uk)

■ Newspapers

Read a quality newspaper regularly. Although the travel sections are important, you should be reading all of a newspaper, as many international and national news events impact on travel and tourism, for example any incidences of terrorism in an area affect tourism.

All the Sunday newspapers have travel supplements. Newspapers can be accessed online but some of them charge if you want to search the archives. You do not have to pay to search recent editions. Guardian Unlimited is a particularly useful source of travel features and it is free to register.

Theory into practice

Choose three of the news sources listed above. Access each of them and find a breaking news story related to travel and tourism. Describe the story and then compare the reporting of the story from each source. Comment on similarities and differences. Discuss your conclusions with your group. Keep any useful stories for further research.

Once you have regular access to these news sources – and read the bulletins – you will find that your topical knowledge of travel and tourism improves immensely. You will find that some news stories develop over days and weeks and have even greater impact on the industry. You will find it easier to choose an issue for your research project with your increased knowledge.

It is a good idea to select two or three initial ideas for your project as it may be that further information, particularly statistical information is not easy to access. There is not room here to list all possible sources for all types of travel and tourism issues so we will examine some general sources of information and in the case studies later in the unit you will find some examples of sources of information for specific issues.

You will have come across many of these sources before and indeed you will have used many of them.

Information about tourism in the UK – a useful introduction	www.visitbritain.com
Information about tourism in the UK – a useful introduction including statistics	www.staruk.org.uk
Department for Culture, Media and Sport	www.culture.gov.uk
World Tourism Organisation	www.world-tourism.org
Customer comments about service on airlines and in airports	www.airlinequality.com
Columbus online world travel guide	www.wtg-online.com
Locations and addresses of tourist offices worldwide	www.tourist-offices.org.uk
Spanish Tourist Office	www.spaintour.com
French Government Tourist Office	www.franceguide.com
New about visitor attractions from the British Association of Leisure parks, Piers and Attractions (BALPPA)	www.balppaorg.uk
Tour operator – My Travel website	www.mytravel.com
Company website for the Thomas Cook group – also has a history section	www.thomascook.co.uk
Website for the First Choice group of tour operators	www.firstchoice.co.uk
Group website for TUI – parent company of Thomson – the tour operator	www.tui.com
Website for the organisation representing the Association of Independent Tour Operators	www.aito.co.uk
Website for the Association of British Travel Agents	www.abta.com
UK Foreign Office travel advice	www.fco.gov.uk
Information on technology in marketing travel and tourism	www.eyefortravcl.com
Information on GDS systems	www.galileo.com www.sabre.com www.datam.co.uk
International Civil Aviation Organisation (ICAO)	www.icao.int
Civil Aviation Authority (CAA)	www.caa.co.uk
Official site of Scotland's national tourist board	www.visitscotland.com
Official site of Northern Ireland's national tourist board	www.discovernorthernireland.com
Official site of Wales's national tourist board	www.visitwales.com
Cruise Information service	www.cruiseinformationservice.co.uk
British Airports Authority	www.baa.co.uk

Table 26.2 General travel and tourism sources on the internet

Theory into practice

The Virtual Training Suite on the internet has a package which introduces you to travel and tourism resources on the web. Visit www.vts.rdn/tutorial/travel to go through a teach-yourself tutorial which will allow you to practise your internet information skills. On your way round you will be able to collect sites of interest and keep them for future reference.

You might begin by brainstorming a whole list of possible research topics and then selecting two or three for further exploration. Some researchers find mind mapping is a useful starting point to determine whether a research topic has further potential. All you need is a piece of paper with your potential topic written in the middle. From this you write notes indicating all the possible approaches and sub-topics arising from this issue.

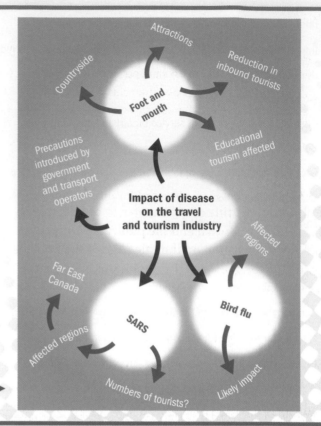

Figure 26.8 Mind map for disease ▶

Attractions
Countryside
Foot and mouth
Reduction in inbound tourists
Educational tourism affected
Precautions introduced by government and transport operators

Impact of disease on the travel and tourism industry

Affected regions
Far East Canada
SARS
Bird flu
Affected regions
Numbers of tourists?
Likely impact

Assessment practice

At this stage you should be ready to try and produce your own research plan. You could produce a research plan for one of the issues discussed in the first part of this unit or you could choose another issue that interests you. Make sure you produce the plan according to your own timescales rather than those given here in the example. **P2**

Explain how the proposed research plan enables exploration of the current issue. **M1**

Assessment practice

If you are ready to start carrying out your research go to page 256 and start the assessment for **P3**, **M2** and **D1**.

Referencing

References are a list of sources from which you have made direct quotes or extracted data. Everything you cite in your report should be listed once alphabetically by author in your reference list. The bibliography is a list of all sources that you have used to carry out your research not just those you have quoted. It should be written in the same way as the reference list.

The Harvard referencing system (also known as the name and date system) is the one that is conventionally used. In the text you should cite your source using the name of the organisation or individual who published the material you are quoting from or otherwise using, together with the name and date of the publication in which you found it. Quotes in text should be preceded by a colon and indented within the main text. Do not use quotation marks. The author, year and page number should follow the quote.

Example:

Company aims vary, particularly according to whether they are profit making or non profit making. A profit making company must make money to stay in business and to satisfy the shareholders, who, after all, have invested in order to make money.

(Dale, 2007, p.65)

In the reference list at the end of the text you should include the name(s) of the author(s), the date of publication, the title of the chapter or article, the title of the book or journal and the publisher. You will find this information on the title page of the book or document you are using. In a book this is inside the front cover.

Example:

Dale, G. (2007) BTEC *National Travel and Tourism Book 1*, 2nd edition, Heinemann.

You must include newspapers and websites as well as books and journals.

For sources from the internet you name the author or editor of the page, if known, followed by the year. The title follows in italics with online in brackets (online) Available from with the web address and the date you accessed it.

Example:

Guide to the Harvard System of Referencing 2007 (online), Anglia Ruskin University, available from: http://libweb.anglia.ac.uk/referencing/harvard.htm (accessed 3 May 2007).

There are many study skills books and websites which explain how referencing should be done.

26.3 Be able to communicate findings on a travel and tourism issue using appropriate media and conventions

You should start thinking about how to present your research project at the planning stage. Your tutor may have a preferred method of presentation such as a written report but most are flexible and if you have an innovative idea for presentation discuss it with your tutor. Here we look at some methods of communicating your findings and presenting your information.

Communicating findings

Points to consider:

- Presenting your own and others' arguments – you work must be objective, it must try to present all sides of an argument. In fact, you should not decide where you stand on a particular issue until you have finished doing your research and looked at all the arguments.

- Summarising data – when you do research you end up with a lot of data. You cannot present all these data to an audience, it would be too boring and too difficult to understand. It is your job to summarise the data and make them easy to understand for the audience. Present the summary in a visual way to aid comprehension.

- Drawing conclusions – once you have looked at the arguments and analysed your research findings what are the conclusions? Draw out key points from the findings. It will help you to remember that conclusions give meaning to the data. Look for links between sets of data.

Example:

Research shows that arrivals to Cape Verde (a Portuguese colony off the coast of West Africa) are increasing. There are two new charter flights servicing the islands from the UK. There is an obvious link between the introduction of the charters and the increase in visitors.

- Engaging your audience – you want your research findings to be read so consider how to present them. If you are going to present orally look at the tips in the next section. If you are going to present in a written format, consider layout, use of colour and language.

Appropriate media to communicate findings

You might choose to use one of the following:
- Extended document
- Group discussion
- Oral presentation
- Report.

■ Extended document

This should be of sufficient length to cover in detail all the elements of your plan. The information must be structured in a logical way and you must make sure that spelling, punctuation and grammar are accurate. Get someone else to proofread your work for an extra check once you have read it yourself.

■ Group discussion

This is a difficult medium to use unless you are very experienced. You have to be able to control the group discussion while still being able to put forward your arguments in a structured way. You could use it by carefully planning the discussion around your key points and being prepared to halt discussion and move on to your next point. It is a useful means of getting feedback on your research findings.

■ Oral presentation

You may decide to present your work orally. You will still have to do a lot of written work to keep track of your research, analyse findings and draw conclusions. However, you will not have to produce a full written report. Instead you can use your research findings to plan a presentation. From your notes you will plan a presentation which includes the following elements:
- Introduction – description of the research issue, the

aims and the methodology chosen. You will also tell your audience what is going to be covered in the presentation.

- Findings – divide this into sections and make sure that the different sections are flagged up to the audience by using bullet points on an overhead projector or PowerPoint slides, or by introducing each section verbally. You should use cue cards to remind you of the key points you want to make in each section. Practise your presentation so that you are not totally dependent on the cue cards and you are not tempted to read from them.

Consider this

Eye contact with the *whole* audience is very important when making a presentation. Do not direct the presentation at one person. You can smile too if you like!

- Visual aids – your presentation will be of greater interest if you support it with visual aids. You may choose to produce a PowerPoint presentation which can include charts and pictures; you may use a series of overheads or handouts. If you use handouts give them out at the beginning or the end but not when you want your audience to listen to you. They will get distracted by the handout and you will lose their attention.
- Conclusions – draw attention to the main conclusions from your findings.
- Recommendations – if these are appropriate, discuss these last.
- Questions – unlike a written report there is an opportunity with an oral presentation to invite your audience to seek clarification or expansion of points. You can limit the time for questions if you wish. If you get a question that you cannot answer, throw it open to your audience as in 'Thank you for that question, who would like to comment on that?'
- Thank your audience at the end.

■ Report

This written method is often easier than an extended document, as it has a very clear structure to help you.

How to write a report: structure

The following elements should be included in a report:
- Title page
- Contents page
- Introduction (Terms of reference in a formal report)
- Findings
- Conclusions
- Recommendations
- Appendices (if used)
- References/bibliography.

Reports can be informal or formal. An informal report is arranged under headings without numbering. A formal report has a system of numbering headings and then subheadings. The introduction is numbered '1'. The findings are numbered '2' and each sub-section 2.1, 2.2 etc. The conclusions are numbered '3'. Recommendations are not always required but if so they are numbered '4'.

■ Contents page

You can compile this at the end or as you go along. Ensure page numbers are given for each section. There is a system in Word to do it for you if you want to use this.

■ Introduction

This section explains the research issue and the aims of the report. You should also give an overview of the research methodology used. Remember that in a formal report this is headed 'Terms of reference' and will give more detail on the what, why and how.

■ Findings

This is the main part of the report and is where you summarise all the research findings from both your secondary and primary research. It is where you present the main results from your research and analyse all the data that you collected. You may include description, facts, tables, graphs and quotes as long as they are referenced.

■ Conclusions

Having presented all your findings you should draw some conclusions. This will be a series of important points resulting from your research.

■ Recommendations

These are not always required but if so should be presented as a series of points for action resulting from the conclusions.

■ Use of appendices

You can attach information, statistical data and pages from the internet in appendices. They should be labelled Appendix 1, 2 etc. and attached to the back of your work. They must be referred to in your work. For example, in your report you might state 'Statistics show that Paris is the most popular short-break destination – see Appendix 1'. Sometimes the reader needs to see the statistics or graphs and charts as they read the report as they are important to understanding a point. In this case, include them in the main body of the report and quote the source.

Appropriate conventions to communicate findings

Whatever method you choose to present your work you must consider the following points.

Use of vocabulary

- Use the correct terminology for travel and tourism, for example 'arrivals' and 'receipt'.
- Use terms and vocabulary that can be clearly understood by your audience.
- Use correct spellings.
- Vary your sentences and choice of words.

Grammatical expression

Reports are always written in the third person. This means you do not use 'I found that …', for example. You say 'It was found that …'.

Use correct grammar – if in doubt, look it up or ask.

Structure

- Have a clear purpose to the work.
- Clearly introduce your topic.
- Use report structure to help you if you find extended documents difficult.
- Have an introduction and a conclusion.

Logical sequence

- Each paragraph or section of a report should deal with one topic.
- Link one topic to the next.
- Do not jump around topics.

Plagiarism

Everything you write must be in your own words. It is unacceptable to copy from another source unless it is a direct quote. This must be acknowledged with details of the source and the date. If you do copy directly from a source without acknowledgement, this is called plagiarism and is very serious. In extreme cases it may result in legal action being taken against you.

Assessment practice

With a partner, prepare for a presentation on the increase of air passenger duty on flights. Use appropriate conventions to convey findings. **P4**

Use appropriate sources of information and use a standard referencing system such as Harvard. **P3**

Consider this

When carrying out research:

- Plan well – don't just browse at random
- Check the validity of your sources
- Never plagiarise
- Present your work in a logical way with appropriate headings
- Use appendices and always refer to them in the main body of your report
- Add a bibliography.

Grading tip

For a Merit, you must communicate clearly, concisely and coherently using specialist vocabulary, making connections and synthesising arguments. **M3**

26.4 Understand the impacts of a current issue on the travel and tourism industry

In this section we will consider some more examples of current issues affecting travel and tourism. This time you will look more closely at the impact of these issues. You should be ready to conduct your own research and may already have determined the issue you want to research.

Issues can impact on the industry, or a sector of it, in various ways.

- Loss of customers – because of a terrorism issue in a particular country or a long-term health scare.
- Development of new markets – due to new technology in travel allowing easier access or tourism development in a country.

- Loss of revenue – due to decline in customers as they choose different destinations or book by other means.
- Changing demands – due to environmental awareness. For example, many travellers are concerned about the impact of their travelling on destinations and wish to visit those which have sound environmental policies or travel with a responsible tour operator.

- Additional costs – due to fuel surcharges or increases in taxation.
- Changes to products and services – due to decline in popularity of existing resorts, for example mainland Spain.

Several of these impacts can result from only one issue. We will look at some examples.

Assessment practice

American passport rules

Operators demand an end to entry confusion

Operators are calling on US officials to mount an urgent campaign to end confusion over the country's entry requirements for visitors.

They are worried that consumers are shunning the destination because they think getting into the US is too troublesome.

This perception could be part of the reason why UK arrivals dropped by 4% in the first eight months of last year compared with the corresponding period in 2005.

Operators fear the decline in first-time visitors is even greater – which is worrying because repeat business is traditionally high in the US.

'The public perception is still that there is more hassle involved in visiting the US than there is in visiting other destinations,' said Travel 4 product manager Julian Lawman.

'This perception is not terribly accurate but there has not been an effective promotional campaign or counter-argument to address it.'

Premier Holidays product manager Heidi Blades criticised US authorities for poor communication.

'There is still a great deal of confusion as to what is required visa-wise,' she said. 'Information on this, although available to consumers, is often confusing as some of it is contradictory.

'Entry requirements seriously need to be addressed. They have certainly had a negative effect on travel to the US.'

Travel chiefs in the US have formed a lobbying group to encourage policy-makers in Washington to address the problem of the country's declining image overseas.

'As a nation, we must do a better job of welcoming international visitors,' said Stevan Porter, chairman of the new Discover America Partnership and president of InterContinental.

The partnership is due to unveil a plan of action to politicians on January 31.

(Source: *Travel Trade Gazette* 12 January 2007)

1 Identify the issue.
2 Explain the impacts on the travel and tourism industry. **P5**
3 Provide a comprehensive analysis of this issue, combining and recognising different points of view. **M4**
4 Use your findings to recommend actions for the travel and tourism industry. **D2**

Grading tip

If you wish to use this issue for your research, you should use it for all grading criteria so that you research in sufficient depth.

Assessment practice

The emirate that means business

Until a couple of years ago, Le Royal Meridien Abu Dhabi was on the beach.

But now a park, car park and six-lane highway separate the hotel and the water, and it's a 500-yard walk to the sea front.

Twenty-six floors up in the hotel's revolving restaurant looking down, I was thinking that this was the sort of thing that happens in Dubai.

But then I thought, no, if this was Dubai there would be three skyscrapers between here and the beach plus a shopping mall, indoor ski-mountain and a theme park (you get the idea).

Instead, there's a park which is green and well-manicured, with benches and pretty fountains. Admittedly, there is the road, but that, I found out later, is to keep the traffic away from the city centre. And then there is the Corniche.

This is a promenade which stretches the length of one side of Abu Dhabi island, about four miles in all, linking the port with the Emirates Palace and the Breakwater.

I decided to walk along the Corniche to get a feel for the place. It took me two hours in a pleasant temperature of 20°C to stroll from the hotel to the Breakwater.

During this stroll, I did not pass a single shop, bar, café or restaurant. And by the same token, I didn't see any litter, graffiti, teenage hoodies or anything that made me think this city is not as perfect as its tourism authority would like us to believe.

But even though I enjoyed the walk – the weather was perfect with a beautiful green and blue sea as well as views across to man-made Lulu Island – it just wasn't particularly stimulating.

Abu Dhabi is, and always has been, a place to do business, from pearl diving and gold, to being one of the biggest oil and gas centres in the Middle East. Leisure very much takes a back seat.

For tourists, shopping is one of the attractions. There are two main malls. Abu Dhabi Mall adjoins the Rotana Beach Hotel and has more than 200 shops and a multi-screen cinema. While on the Breakwater, the Marina Mall, with similar shops, cinema, cafes, an Ikea and a 100-metre viewing platform, offers the best views of the skyline in the city.

I wandered round this mall, comparing prices with the UK. With a healthy exchange rate to the pound there were some good bargains, particularly for electrical products.

Like Dubai, this emirate has transformed itself in an astonishingly short space of time – it's just done it at a far more measured pace.

Later that night I found myself at the hotel's Irish bar, PJ O'Reilly's, and I thought: this isn't a bad place to visit. Even if the DJ was singing *My Way* rather than playing it.

(Source: *Travel Trade Gazette* 26 January 2007)

1   Identify the issue.

2   Explain the impacts on the travel and tourism industry. **P5**

3   Provide a comprehensive analysis of this issue, combining and recognising different points of view. **M4**

4   Use your findings to recommend actions for the travel and tourism industry. **D2**

Grading tip

If you wish to use this issue for your research, you should use it for all grading criteria so that you research in sufficient depth.

Knowledge check

1 What is the difference between quantitative and qualitative data?

2 Give two sources of travel and tourism statistics.

3 How can you track your research?

4 What is 'action research'?

5 What should be included in a research plan?

6 Why do you need a research plan?

7 Give two examples of research methodologies

8 When would you use a focus group?

9 Why do you need to assess the validity of an information source?

10 Think of two ways to communicate your findings other than a written report or oral presentation.

11 What is the referencing system that is commonly used called?

12 What is plagiarism?

13 Why do you need to do an evaluation when you have completed your project?

Preparation for assessment

You work for a travel and tourism marketing organisation which conducts research for and on behalf of industry members. The company has been invited to contribute research findings to a series of workshops at the World Travel Fair. Although the company will not be paid for this work, it is a prestigious event and may result in new business.

Staff have been asked to carry out research on a variety of current issues affecting the industry. Each member of staff will present their findings orally at one of the workshops. You have been given several weeks to prepare for your presentation and you have also been asked to present a workshop on research methods.

1   Prepare for your first workshop: you are to explain different methods that can be used to research a current issue in travel and tourism. Present the advantages and disadvantages of each method. **P1**

Grading tip

You must cover at least two research methods and all different kinds of sources and data.

2   For your second workshop you must choose an issue that currently affects the travel and tourism industry. You may choose one of the examples in the unit if you like.

a) Produce a research plan which can be used to investigate your chosen issue. **P2**

b) Explain to your boss/tutor how the plan enables exploration of your chosen issue. This can be done orally or in a written document. **M1**

c) Carry out research into your chosen issue, using at least four different types of sources of information and using a standard referencing system. **P3**

d) Produce a sheet on the limitations of your sources, that is, what you could not find out from them. **M2**

Grading tip

'Different types' means websites, trade journals, books and official statistics, for example, *not* four different websites.

For a Merit you need to show that you have worked independently and you must have used primary and secondary sources, qualitative and quantitative data.

e) Present your research findings, explaining how the chosen issue impacts on the travel and tourism industry, remembering your audience of professionals at the World Travel Fair.

P4 P5 M3 M4

Grading tip

Make sure you use appropriate vocabulary and other conventions in your presentation.

For a Merit you need to provide a comprehensive analysis of the chosen issue which combines and recognises different points of view. You must communicate clearly, concisely and coherently using specialist vocabulary, making connections and synthesising arguments. **M3 M4**

f) Use findings from your research to recommend actions for the travel and tourism industry. **M3 M4 D2**

g) Carry out an evaluation of the research undertaken and recommend improvements to your own research skills for the future. **D1**

Grading criteria

To achieve a pass grade the evidence must show that the learner is able to:	To achieve a merit grade the evidence must show that, in addition to the pass criteria, the learner is able to:	To achieve a distinction grade the evidence must show that, in addition to the pass and merit criteria, the learner is able to:
P1 explain different methods that can be used to research a current issue affecting the travel and tourism industry **Assessment practice page 241**	**M1** explain how the proposed research plan enables exploration of a current issue **Assessment practice page 248**	**D1** evaluate the research undertaken and recommend improvements to own research skills in the future **Assessment practice page 248**
P2 propose a research plan to investigate a current issue affecting the travel and tourism industry **Assessment practice page 248**	**M2** conduct independent research into a current issue, using at least four different types of sources of information, showing awareness of limitations of sources **Assessment practice page 248**	**D2** use findings from research into the current issue to recommend actions for the travel and tourism industry **Assessment practice page 253**
P3 use appropriate sources of information to research a current issue using a standard referencing system **Assessment practice page 252**	**M3** communicate information about a current issue clearly, concisely and coherently using specialist vocabulary, making connections and synthesising arguments **Assessment practice page 252**	
P4 communicate a current issue affecting the travel and tourism industry, using appropriate conventions to convey findings **Assessment practice page 252**	**M4** provide a comprehensive analysis of the researched current issue, combining and recognising different points of view **Assessment practice page 253**	
P5 explain how a current issue impacts on the travel and tourism industry **Assessment practice page 253**		

Index

Page numbers in *italic* type refer to illustrations and tables, those in **bold** type refer to key terms.